THE NORMANS

THE NORMANS

R. ALLEN BROWN

THE BOYDELL PRESS

For Abigail

© 1984 R. Allen Brown

First published 1984 by
The Boydell Press
an imprint of Boydell & Brewer Ltd
PO Box 9, Woodbridge, Suffolk IP12 3DF

British Library Cataloguing in Publication Data

Brown, R. Allen
   The Normans.
   1. Normans – History   2. Normans –
   Near East – History
   I. Title
   940'.0441   D148

   ISBN 0-85115-199-X

Half-title page:

Norman knight of the mid-twelfth century: opening initial to text of Geoffrey of Monmouth's *Historia Regum Britannie*, possibly written at Bec
(Leiden, Bibliothek der Rijksuniversiteit, MS BPL 20 f.60r)

Designed by Paul Bowden
Photoset by Rowland Phototypesetting Ltd
Bury St Edmunds, Suffolk
Printed in Italy by Mondadori spa, Milan

Contents

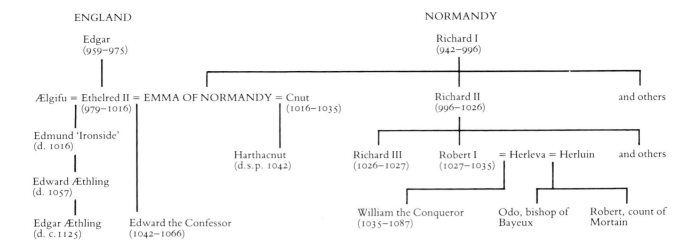

Table 1. The ruling houses of England and Normandy in the late
tenth and eleventh centuries with the dates of the reigns.

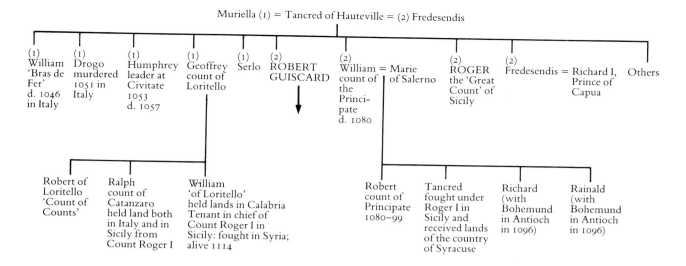

Muriella (1) = Tancred of Hauteville = (2) Fredesendis

(1) William 'Bras de Fer' d. 1046 in Italy

(1) Drogo murdered 1051 in Italy

(1) Humphrey leader at Civitate 1053 d. 1057

(1) Geoffrey count of Loritello

(1) Serlo

(2) ROBERT GUISCARD

(2) William count of the Principate d. 1080 = Marie of Salerno

(2) ROGER the 'Great Count' of Sicily

(2) Fredesendis = Richard I, Prince of Capua

Others

Robert of Loritello 'Count of Counts'

Ralph count of Catanzaro held land both in Italy and in Sicily from Count Roger I

William 'of Loritello' held lands in Calabria Tenant in chief of Count Roger I in Sicily: fought in Syria; alive 1114

Robert count of Principate 1080–99

Tancred fought under Roger I in Sicily and received lands of the country of Syracuse

Richard (with Bohemund in Antioch in 1096)

Rainald (with Bohemund in Antioch in 1096)

Table 2. The family of Tancred of Hauteville

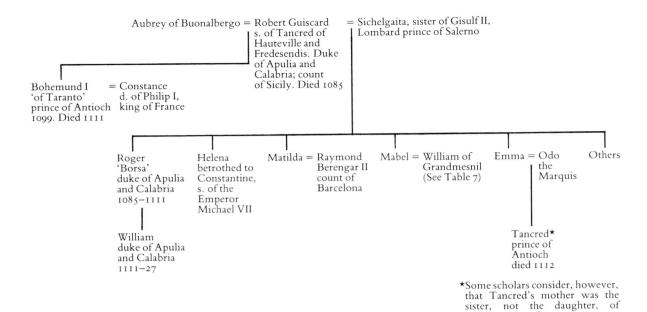

Aubrey of Buonalbergo = Robert Guiscard = Sichelgaita, sister of Gisulf II,
                                          s. of Tancred of   Lombard prince of Salerno
                                          Hauteville and
                                          Fredesendis. Duke
                                          of Apulia and
                                          Calabria; count
Bohemund I   = Constance   of Sicily. Died 1085
'of Taranto'   d. of Philip I,
prince of Antioch   king of France
1099. Died 1111

Roger   Helena   Matilda = Raymond   Mabel = William of   Emma = Odo   Others
'Borsa'   betrothed to   Berengar II   Grandmesnil   the
duke of Apulia   Constantine,   count of   (See Table 7)   Marquis
and Calabria   s. of the   Barcelona
1085–1111   Emperor
                Michael VII

William   Tancred★
duke of Apulia   prince of
and Calabria   Antioch
1111–27   died 1112

★Some scholars consider, however,
that Tancred's mother was the
sister, not the daughter, of
Robert Guiscard.

Table 3. The family of Robert Guiscard

Preface

1066 is said to be the most memorable date in English history. The whole history of the Normans, however, and their achievements amongst which the conquest of England is only one item, are, to say the least, not so well known. An account of all that, therefore, is the purpose of this book, in as much detail and with as many illustrations as space and cost will allow. There will also be found in it not only a necessary explanation and analysis but also a proper and no less necessary amount of narrative. For narrative has fallen so far out of favour among historians that it is all too possible to go through life increasingly knowledgeable about societies and institutions, movements and trends, without ever discovering what actually happened or who did what to whom.

The Normans are among the great matters of modern history and therefore deserve study even though it is now the fashion to pretend that only the most recent events are of relevance to the present. Further, anyone studying the Normans, like them cannot be confined to any one branch of activity, whether secular or ecclesiastical, military or political, intellectual or artistic. To appreciate them we must be as comprehensive in our interests as they were in their achievement. Such an approach, moreover, is a sovereign remedy against that over-specialization which has become the curse of history as now practiced, and threatens to make it inaccessible to the public. Specialization, a narrow concentration and focussing of interest, may be the best way at times to advance the frontiers of knowledge, here a little, there a little; but consolidation is no less essential for any understanding of the past.

Much water has flowed under the bridges since this book was begun three or four years ago, some of it murky. The most agreeable current was that on which I floated to southern Italy and Sicily, there to follow the Normans as I had long wanted to do, and to find, of course, the monuments and traces of their half-forgotten occupation as impressive and evocative as those nearer home in

2

Molfetta (Duomo Vecchio) in Apulia.

Britain and Normandy. There is no substitute for setting foot on historical territory, and merely to look across the sun-drenched Adriatic from Bari or Trani or Molfetta, or across the Straits of Messina towards Sicily from Reggio di Calabria, is to know why the Normans felt impelled ever to move onwards. Similar experiences of Antioch and Outremer, for me, alas! had to be retrospective, but were none the less vivid for that, whether they were memories of Jerusalem and Bethlehem and the Sea of Galilee, or Lattakieh and Damascus, or the huge profile of Margat along the skyline, seen from the turret of a patrolling armoured car.

More recent but murkier experience was to find, with some relief, the manuscript of the book rejected by the publisher—or perhaps one should say package-maker—who first commissioned it. I have therefore to express more than an author's usual and conventional gratitude to the present publishers, not least Dr Richard Barber who has seen the work through the press, and in so doing has allowed, amongst other things, sentences of more than half-a-dozen words and paragraphs of more than three inches. I owe much more than the usual conventional thanks also to my wife, who not only endured (though not without complaint) mountain tracks hazardous to motor-cars in Italy and Sicily, but also coped with the typing of this and two other books and all of them over Christmas. I am also very much obliged to many friends for help and counsel, in my Special Subject classes on Monday afternoons, in the 'Marquess of Anglesey' on Monday evenings when scholarship is discussed, and specifically to Dr Graham Loud of Leeds University for much advice and many off-prints (plus his thesis), and to the Rev. Dr H. E. J. Cowdrey of St Edmund Hall, Oxford, who most generously allowed me to read his book on abbot Desiderius in advance of its publication. Nevertheless, I have no doubt that mistakes, all of my own, still abound. If so, it may be pleaded that many at least result from the attempt to be comprehensive. This book, after all, is not entitled 'The Normans in Normandy'—or in England, or Wales, or Scotland, Italy, Sicily or Antioch—but, with grand simplicity, 'The Normans'. They themselves might have approved of one of my favourite quotations from Browning, that—

> '. . . a man's reach should exceed his grasp,
> Or what's a heaven for?'

Thelnetham, Suffolk   R.A.B.
30 December 1983

3

NORMANDY AND HER
NEIGHBOURS IN 1066

.... Boundaries of Norman Bishoprics

0   10   20   30   40 mls
0   20   40   60 kms

Pevensey   Hastings

FLANDERS
PONTHIEU
NORMANDY
BRITTANY
MAINE   BLOIS   ÎLE DE FRANCE
ANJOU TOURAINE
POITOU

Boulogne

St-Valery-sur-Somme
Abbeville

Valognes
St-Sauveur-le-Vicomte

Fécamp   Arques   St-Aubin-le-Cauf
                                Varenne

Lessay   Ryes   Graville-Ste-Honorine   Auffay   Mortemer
          Hauteville   Lillebonne   Clères
COUTANCES   BAYEUX   St-Wandrille
   Cérisy-la-Forêt   Dives-sur-Mer   Bonneville-sur-Touques
                  Briquessart   CAEN   Varaville   Jumièges   ROUEN
          Montbray   Troarn   Cormeilles   Montfort-sur-Risle
                                Val-ès Dunes   LISIEUX
Cherrueix   Le Plessis-   Le Grand Mesnil   Bec   Vexin
        Dol   AVRANCHES   Grimoult   St-Pierre-sur-Dives   Bernay   Brionne
Dinan   AVRANCHES   Falaise   Ste-Foy-de-   Beaumont-le-Roger
      St-James   Mortain   Montgomery   Meules   Tosny
                        St-Germain-de-Montgomery   La Croix-St-Leufroy   Vernon   St-Clair-sur-Epte
                                Exmes   St-Evroult   Conches   ÉVREUX
                        Domfront   Echauffour   ÉVREUX   Mantes
                                        SÉES   Breteuil
Rennes   Ambrières   Verneuil   Tillières   Ivry
                              Alençon   Nonancourt
          Mayenne

                        Bellême

      Ste-Suzanne

Chapter 1 Introduction

The Norman impact upon their world was decisive, and so far-flung that one book is scarcely enough to contain it, let alone explain it. A catalogue of their achievements, however difficult to compile and define, is the best way to begin by way of introduction. Of these the first and not the least was the creation of Normandy itself in the short century and a half between 911 (the traditional date of the first grant of territory in north-western France to the Viking Rollo and his Norsemen by King Charles the Simple) and, let us say, the 1060s. That creation was of a state, by contemporary standards the strongest of the feudal principalities into which France, the kingdom of the West Franks, was then divided, and also of an ebullient, integrated, confident and self-conscious society which in the later decades of the eleventh century seemed to make of the known world its oyster. In the autumn of 1066, having imposed their suzerainty or overlordship upon the neighbouring counties of Maine and Ponthieu, and wholly or partly upon those of Brittany and Boulogne, the Normans, as all the world knows, with their auxiliaries, with their knights and their horses, their archers and all the panoply of war, sailed to conquer the far larger and richer kingdom of England in one of the few decisive battles of western history, fought near Hastings on Saturday 14 October. From England they pressed on to begin the conquest of Wales which was completed by Edward I two hundred years later; they penetrated more or less peaceably into the lowlands of Scotland to alter society there scarcely less fundamentally than in England; and a century after Hastings they crossed into Ireland to begin the series of occupations of that land by the 'English'. But if every schoolboy and the man in the street still know something of the Norman Conquest of England, the concurrent conquest of southern Italy and Sicily is far less commonly remembered. Beginning about the year 1000, it was completed in 1091, and in some ways was even more impressive than the conquest of England. The latter, all due scholarly qualifications made to avoid anachronism, was a state or national enterprise, planned and led by Duke William, with all the resources he could command as a prince and feudal suzerain. Italy with Sicily, by contrast, was a piecemeal affair of purely private enterprise, in some sense even in the duke's despite, as individual knights and companies of knights, some of them political exiles from the duchy, won for themselves their fiefs, their principalities, and ultimately their kingdom in the sun, in one of the most romantic episodes that even the West's first fine careless rapture of the eleventh century can produce. Further, these marvellously irresponsible seizures of land and lordship were made at the expense of two of the Great Powers of the age, Byzantium and Islam—and were legitimized by the Papacy, no less. Yet neither we nor the Normans have so far finished even the list of political and military triumphs which were obviously altering the whole pattern of an emergent Europe in the second half of the eleventh century. Before that century was done the Normans were to break out of the confines of Western Europe altogether with two powerful contingents, one from Normandy itself (under the Conqueror's eldest son, Duke Robert 'Curthose') and the other from southern Italy, in the van of the First Crusade, launched by Pope Urban II at Clermont in 1095. It is entirely appropriate that amongst the first

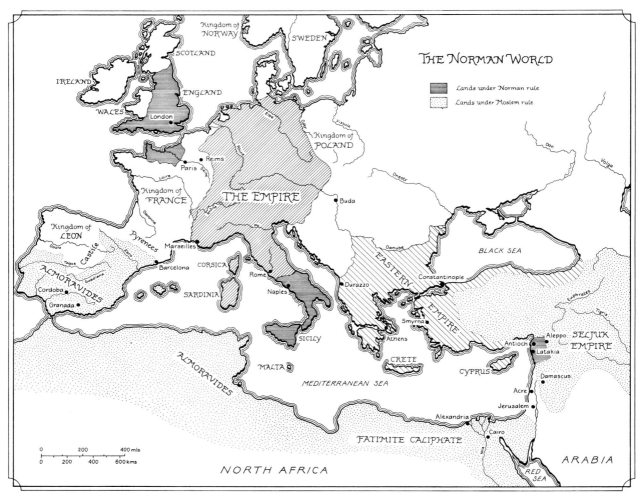

crusaders to fight their way on to the walls of Jerusalem when the city fell to Christendom on 15 July 1099, was the Norman Tancred of Hauteville from Italy, while along the hard-fought way, before Jerusalem was ever reached or gained, another Norman principality had been established, by Bohemond of Hauteville, Tancred's uncle, at Antioch in Outremer, *i.e.* the crusading states 'beyond the sea'.

> 'And thou shalt come from thy place out of the north parts, thou, and many people with thee, all of them riding upon horses, a great company, and a mighty army'.

Thus the prophet Ezekiel (38:15). By the year 1100 the Normans had established a kind of commonwealth, their direct territorial hegemony extending in a loose chain of states from the Marches of Wales beyond the Severn and the Dee, through Normandy and southern Italy and Sicily, to Antioch and the Orantes. In addition there had been individual Norman participation in the early stages of the reconquest of Spain and the Iberian peninsula from Islam— which, like so much else in European history, begins at this time—and even campaigns against Byzantium from Italy across the Adriatic.

The political achievements and military triumphs so far listed, however, are necessarily only the tip of the iceberg, or the merely physical impact upon the outside world of an integrated society which seems almost omnicompetently omnipotent. The Normans were not merely victorious on the battlefield and administratively efficient. Their achievements were no more limited to these spheres than they were to Normandy. They contributed generously to most of the profound developments of their age and in many they led the way. One must think not only of their knights, but also of the potent and lasting concept of chivalry. One must admire not only their castles and, say, the White Tower at London, but also their churches, which include Durham Cathedral. In approving, or (more possibly today) disapproving of their warfare, it is necessary to remember that all their major campaigns were undertaken with the blessing of the Papacy, of whom in Italy they became the formal allies, and that they more than any other people were responsible for the idea and ideal of Holy War, which produced the Crusades and was the characteristic contemporary solution to the age-old problem of the Just War. Indeed, the Normans excelled not only in warfare but also in religion, and the two things have never been incompatible, nor certainly were they then, as the Military Orders of the twelfth century, the Templars and Hospitallers, will start-ingly demonstrate. Nor was Norman Christianity exclusively of the muscular variety, nor their pre-eminence in ecclesiastical his-tory only a matter of their being often the allies of the Papacy or the champions of orthodox reform in one of the West's great ages of religious reformation. There was no lack of spirituality in Nor-mandy, difficult though that may be to measure. It is no coincidence that the great period of Norman expansion in the second half of the eleventh century coincided with the high-water mark of a com-prehensive Norman ecclesiastical revival. The Norman Church resulting was not merely an efficient province of well-ordered

dioceses, each with its synod, cathedral chapter and archdeacon, ruled by the archbishop of Rouen and under the close control of the duke. Revival and reform had come first to the monasteries, and Norman monasticism, derived from Cluny but with a difference, was pre-eminent in an age excelling in monasticism.

Further, to speak of the Church in contemporary Latin Christendom is to speak also of learning and culture, of art and architecture, and of the twelfth-century renaissance which begins in the eleventh. Not for nothing were scholars of the calibre of Lanfranc and Anselm attracted to Normandy, the land of opportunity for intellectuals no less than knights, and some of the Norman monastic schools especially—Fécamp, St Evroult, Bec above all—were outstanding in a period when standards were very high. The Norman ecclesiastical revival of the eleventh century, moreover, included a programme of church-building on a majestic—indeed, imperial[1]— scale, much of which still in our day remains to bear witness to this great age of Normandy. Such buildings surely show that the Normans were not merely the Romans of their world, but also the Greeks. And all this was for export as required, so that, for example, not only was almost every major church in England rebuilt in the Norman fashion soon after 1066, but their libraries were transformed also. The Normans may have possessed the gift of adaptation, which may in part explain their huge success; but everywhere they went they brought profound change with them, so that it is difficult to exaggerate their contribution to the history of the West.

The Normandy of the later eleventh century was rich and prosperous—for how else could those buildings have been raised, those campaigns waged, the clerics, monks and knights maintained? There was also an expanding population which, especially in the form of endless younger sons, helps fundamentally to account for its territorial expansion. But to speak of these things is at least to begin an explanation, which is not the function of an introduction. In the rest of this book the whole history of the Normans will be attempted and their achievements set down in detail. That also is the place for discussion of how and why these things came about, and their results; but two points may perhaps be made at once. The first is that the controversial matter of the Norman Conquest of England, inevitably of particular concern to English-speaking readers, only comes properly into focus when thus set in its proper context of the whole saga of Norman history. The second is that if, as may be said, the Normans were in the end to adapt themselves out of existence, they most certainly did not vanish as though they had never been, and the world we know and inhabit would be a very different place without them.

Cluny III. Only the south transept (begun 1088) remains standing.

Chapter 2 Origins

In view of the huge effects of the Norman impact upon Europe in the age of their greatness, it may well seem appropriate that they themselves are the direct result of a cataclysmic period of European history, namely the ninth and earlier tenth centuries. That period saw a triple onslaught upon the West by Moslem, by Magyar and by Viking, and, largely as a result, the disintegration of the precocious Carolingian unity imposed upon most of Latin Christendom by the Franks under their king and emperor Charlemagne (*i.e.* Charles the Great, Carolus Magnus) and his immediate successors. The Moslems, the forces of Islam, came from the south and, having been turned back from southern France (as we can see with hindsight) by Charles Martel's great victory at Poitiers in the previous century (732), now concentrated especially upon Italy. In particular, in the decades following 827 they overran Sicily, which was thus added to the Islamic world of the Middle East, the North African littoral and the Iberian Peninsular, and so remained for almost two centuries until the Normans reconquered it in the eleventh century. The Magyars came from the east and, from the close of the ninth century until their final defeat by Otto I at the Lechfeld in 955, devastated not only Germany but also deep into France (where they reached Orleans in 937) and into Italy from north to south. The Vikings came from the north but, because of their extreme mobility by ship and horse, by sea and river valley, seemed to come from all directions at once. Scarcely any part of Europe escaped their depradations, which nowadays are misleadingly played down, and while the whole saga of the Viking movement extends from the eighth century to the end of the eleventh, the first full fury of the Norsemen was concentrated in the ninth when they penetrated, by raid and trade and settlement, from Russia (of which they can claim to be the founders) to Iceland, via northern France and Britain especially.

Each of these three onslaughts is a part of a separate historical

Aachen. Interior of Charlemagne's Palatine Chapel (792–805)

movement all of which happen to coincide in the period of the ninth and earlier tenth centuries, and our particular concern is with the Vikings. Nevertheless, the three should be considered for a moment as a whole in terms of European history. Thus regarded, they become the second wave of assault upon the West,[1] not much less important in its results than the more famous first, the 'Barbarian Invasions' of the fifth and sixth centuries which, traditionally, spell the end of the western Roman Empire. There was indeed a world of difference between that Roman Empire and the Frankish 'Empire' of Charlemagne which eventually succeeded it (Charlemagne was crowned emperor by Pope Leo III in St Peter's at Rome on Christmas Day 800), but also there was continuity, not least in the hearts and minds of men. *Renovatio imperii Romani* is the legend engraved on a golden seal attributed to Charlemagne, and at his palace of Aachen one may still see and feel something of the reality of that revival (*renovatio*) as well as the impossible ideal. As for the second wave, the assaults upon the west in the ninth and early tenth centuries, they, more than anything else, destroyed the Carolingian polity and brought about a break in European history which is no less important for being no longer in favour with many historians. Politically, the mould of Carolingian unity was broken, and the pattern of the future emerged in the kingdom of the East Franks which will become Germany and the kingdom of the West Franks which will be France. In the latter, political fragmentation went further with the emergence of the feudal principalities which for centuries were to be the reality of the French kingdom and of which Normandy was one. Further, after the Vikings, the Magyars and the Moslems, there was revival, renaissance, and thereby change; a new world, some would argue, rising Phoenix-like from the ashes of the old. Amongst its salient features were a reformed and thus changed Church increasingly led by a reformed and thus changed Papacy, a reformed and changed monasticism, and a new type of society which we call feudal. And in this new world Normandy was completely new, for it had not existed before.

Amongst the Viking settlements which followed their raids and devastations, those which concern us directly are England and Normandy. We may take England first. There, having destroyed all the Old English kingdoms save only Alfred's Wessex and a part of Mercia with which it amalgamated, the Vikings—principally Danes but with a strong Norse element west of the Pennines—occupied all the rest of the country. This was the 'Danelaw', more than half England to the north and east beyond the Thames and Watling Street. There has been considerable debate about the actual density of Viking settlement,[2] but the answer—which on the analogy of Normandy is likely to have been the imposition of a new and alien ruling class—scarcely affects the outcome, namely that the Danelaw became predominantly Scandinavian, culturally and politically. Further, though Alfred and his immediate successors conquered the Danelaw, so that Wessex expanded to become the kingdom of all England, they did not absorb it; and England was to be subjected to a second Danish onslaught at the turn of the tenth

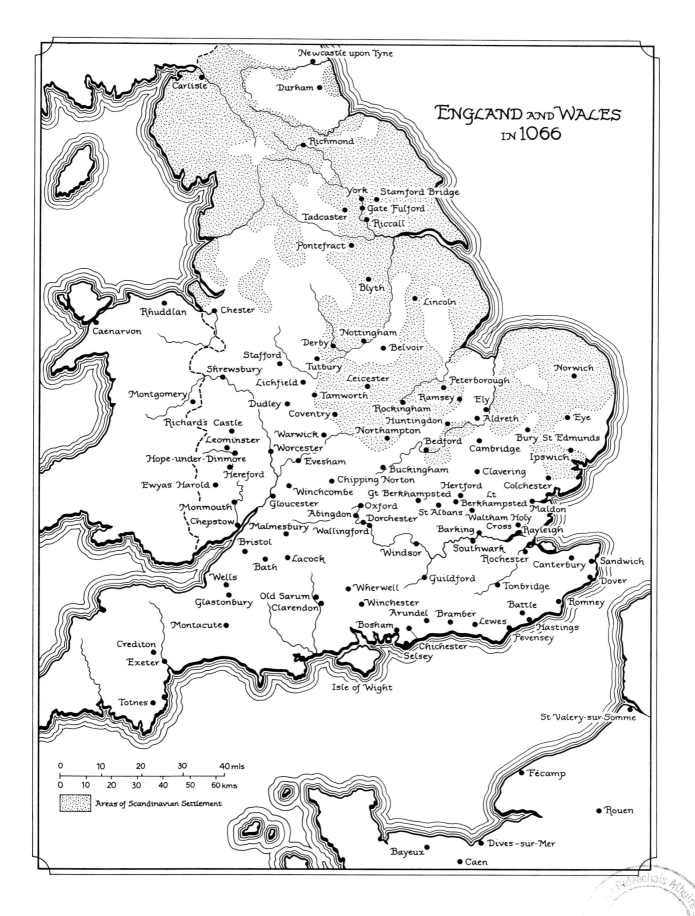

ENGLAND AND WALES IN 1066

Newcastle upon Tyne
Carlisle
Durham
Richmond
York · Stamford Bridge
Tadcaster · Gate Fulford
Riccall
Pontefract
Blyth
Lincoln
Rhuddlan · Chester
Caenarvon
Derby · Nottingham
Belvoir
Stafford
Shrewsbury · Tutbury
Lichfield · Leicester · Peterborough · Norwich
Montgomery · Tamworth · Rockingham · Ramsey · Ely
Dudley · Coventry · Huntingdon · Aldreth · Eye
Richard's Castle · Northampton · Bury St Edmunds
Leominster · Warwick · Bedford · Cambridge
Hope-under-Dinmore · Worcester · Buckingham · Clavering · Ipswich
Ewyas Harold · Hereford · Evesham · Chipping Norton · Hertford · Colchester
Monmouth · Winchcombe · Gt Berkhampsted · Lt · Berkhampsted · Maldon
Chepstow · Gloucester · Oxford · St Albans · Waltham Holy
Abingdon · Dorchester · Cross · Rayleigh
Malmesbury · Wallingford · Barking · Southwark
Bristol · Windsor · Rochester · Sandwich
Lacock · Guildford · Canterbury · Dover
Bath · Wherwell · Tonbridge
Wells · Old Sarum · Battle · Romney
Glastonbury · Clarendon · Winchester · Arundel · Bramber · Lewes · Hastings
Montacute · Bosham · Chichester · Pevensey
Crediton · Selsey
Exeter
Isle of Wight
Totnes
St Valery-sur-Somme
Fécamp
Rouen
Bayeux · Dives-sur-Mer
Caen

0   10   20   30   40 mls
0 10 20 30 40 50 60 kms

Areas of Scandinavian Settlement

13

and eleventh centuries in the reign of Ethelred II (979–1016). The result was the outright conquest of the new English kingdom, by Swein Forkbeard of Denmark and Cnut his son, just fifty years before the Norman Conquest. This time there is no question of any Danish folk-migration, but Cnut became king of England in 1016 and brought his retainers and his housecarls with him, and his two sons, Harold 'Harefoot' and Harthacnut, reigned after him until the accession of Edward the Confessor in 1042. During these years England became part of the Scandinavian world, and the aristocracy and ruling class (as Edward himself discovered) became increasingly Scandinavianized. The rest of society could not be unaffected, and so by 1042, as still in 1066, Anglo-Scandinavian rather than Anglo-Saxon may be thought the more appropriate description of the Old English kingdom.

The degree to which England had been Scandinavianized by 1066 requires more emphasis than it commonly receives; but, be that as it may, it is in the Viking descent upon, and eventual conquest of, England that we find the beginnings of the connection between the Old English kingdom and Normandy, itself a Viking colony, which culminates in 1066. True that by then Normandy was scarcely Scandinavian whatever may be the case with England, but at the turn of the tenth and eleventh centuries Viking fleets attacking England used Normandy as a base and an emporium for their English loot. The resulting enmity between Ethelred II and the Norman duke, Richard I, was such that it required a papal envoy to resolve it and to make a treaty between them in 991.[3] In 1002 Ethelred married Emma, daughter of the same duke Richard, presumably further to prevent Norman help to Viking raiders. That marriage was, of course, to be the root of William the Conqueror's claim to the English throne.[4] Although according to William of Jumièges Ethelred soon afterwards launched an inglorious attack against Normandy,[5] the marriage established a close relationship between the Wessex and Norman ruling houses which was also to lead to the events of 1066. As defeat at the hands of Swein Forkbeard approached, Ethelred sent his young sons by Emma, Edward and Alfred, to the Norman court for shelter and there they long remained. Cnut's own marriage to the Norman Emma after the death of Ethelred may have been partly intended to counter active support for the 'aethlings' or princes, and may have succeeded with duke Richard II (996–1026); but Robert the Magnificent, his successor, (1027–1035) evidently acted as their champion and patron and at one time prepared an invasion of England on their behalf which was rendered abortive only by the weather.[6] When therefore the elder and surviving aethling, Edward the Confessor, eventually succeeded his half-brother Harthacnut (son of Cnut and Emma) in 1042, he could certainly be regarded as the Norman candidate for the English throne, and with his Norman sympathies, his gratitude to Normandy, and his nomination of his cousin William as his heir, we approach very close indeed to the Norman Conquest, which is the business of a later chapter.[7]

The duchy of Normandy itself is the direct result of the Viking onslaught upon Western Europe and northern France especially. Its official beginning is the so-called treaty of St-Clair-sur-Epte, part legend and part fact, whereby, in the year 911, Charles the Simple, king of the West Franks, granted to a band of Vikings, long operating in and devastating the area of the Seine valley, under their leader Hrolf or Rollo, territory about the lower Seine and the city of Rouen. Normandy thus begins as a kind of French 'Danelaw', though its future was to be very different from its English counterpart. Two further grants of territory followed in 924 and 933 respectively, both by the next king, Rudolf, and the second to Rollo's successor, William Longsword. Until recently the established view has been that these three grants between them comprised the future Normandy: the first, in 911, consisting of Upper or eastern Normandy bounded by the rivers Bresle, Epte, Avre and Dives; the second and third, conceding Lower or western Normandy in two stages, namely the Bessin (about Bayeux) and the Hiémois (about Falaise) in 924, and the Cotentin and the Avranchin (the districts about Coutances and Avranches) in 933. Thus Normandy was created at a stroke (or three); not only its extent but also its frontiers were precisely defined from the beginning by the *pagi* or Carolingian administrative districts granted, and its dukes were thus immediately endowed with the powers of the Carolingian counts their predecessors.[8] Recently, however, the late Professor John Le Patourel convincingly questioned this thesis,[9] which may be thought inherently improbable and is, like much else about early Normandy, derived more from the known facts of the eleventh century than from the sparse evidence of the tenth. Certainly such sources as we have, chiefly the histories of Flodoard and Dudo of St Quentin, do not spell out the grants with any such certainty or precision and in what they do say are not even in agreement with the thesis.[10] It is therefore suggested that the Normandy which emerges into the clear light of the mid-eleventh century is, much more than has generally been supposed, a piecemeal composition—after 911, 924 and 933, from whatever territories were then granted—and much more the creation of its dukes and warrior Viking settlers, as aggressively expansionist in the beginning as they were to be thereafter. 'Norman expansion began as it went on; its origins were the origins of Normandy itself'.[11] Still more recently Professor Eleanor Searle, in a remarkable paper which at last justifies Dudo before the multitude of his detractors (he, after all, was officially commissioned by dukes Richard I and II to write the history of Normandy), interprets his story as that of the descendants of Rollo's Vikings more or less confined to Upper Normandy, and hard-pressed by the resurgent Franks, until reinforced by new and invited Norsemen from the west in the 960s. Those who would were subsequently converted to Christianity and settled by Richard I, who took to wife in a 'peace-weaving' marriage the daughter of one of their leaders, *i.e.* the duchess Gunnor. This whole affair becomes almost a second founding of the future duchy, and the date is 966.[12] In favour of these reinterpretations, it is known that fresh bands of Viking settlers, by no means necessarily dependent on the dukes initially, arrived in Normandy throughout the tenth century after 911;[13] that the Conqueror himself pushed forward the frontiers of his duchy by his acquisition of Alençon, Domfront and the Passais in 1051–2;[14] and that before his reign Lower Normandy was scarcely under effective ducal control nor substantially colonized by his monks and vassals.[15] Similarly the comital powers (i.e. those of the former Carolingian counts whom they displaced) which the future dukes of Normandy undoubtedly enjoyed, are less likely to have been taken over or conferred completely and directly in 911 than to have been recovered or revived piecemeal, here a little, there a little, over a long period.[16]

The first Viking settlers in Normandy, it is agreed, were predominantly Danish, though their leader, Rollo was of Norse extraction. It also seems clear that they were comparatively few, their settlement concentrated especially by the coast, in the lower Seine valley and to the north of it, and (eventually at least) in the northern Cotentin. The settlement is likely to have been for the most part the imposition of a warrior ruling class, displacing the former Frankish lords. And such, it may be added, the Normans would ever remain, their later conquests being, like their settlement of Normandy, aristocratic colonization and the imposition of lordship. The society of these originally Viking settlers long remained an open one, not only receiving Scandinavian newcomers throughout the tenth century as we have seen, but also liberally recruiting Frankish neighbours and other immigrants from further afield, and marrying Frankish ladies, if only because Viking women were in short supply. Immigration, indeed, becomes another lasting feature of Normandy and, no less than emigration, will be cause and proof alike of future Norman greatness. Meanwhile for these and other reasons which include the adoption of Christianity as one of the conditions of St-Clair-sur-Epte, and led in this as in so much else by their dukes, the Northmen of Normandy became increasingly Gallicized, increasingly Norman we may say, until by the mid-eleventh century they were more French than the French or, to speak correctly, more Frankish than the Franks. Within two generations of 911, it is said, duke William Longsword (927–43) found it necessary to send his young son, the future Richard I, to Bayeux to learn Danish which was thus presumably no longer spoken in and about Rouen.[17] As late as the close of the tenth century, it is true, Richer of Rheims could still call the same Richard I (943–96) dux pyratorum (duke or leader of pirates),[18] but he is a prejudiced witness. By then the Normans, their dukes in the lead, were definitely turning their backs upon Scandinavia and their faces, hearts and minds to Frankia.

In their extraordinary powers of assimilation and adaptation we meet, of course, another permanent feature of the Normans and their Normanitas which it will be the business of the next chapter to analyse and define. There, too, the Norman inheritance and adaptations from the Frankish Carolingian past will be particularly examined, but it is appropriate to stress here the lasting contribution of the original Viking spirit to the Norman future when almost all other links with the Scandinavian past were broken, compounded of that very facility of adaptation which obliterated so much else, but also of daring, adventure, land–hunger and wanderlust. To all this Lucien Musset adds a further component in what he calls, in splendid phrase, the 'endless availability' (*disponibilité illimitée*) of the Normans.[19] Perhaps we may gloss this by saying that they were Fortune's favourites in having the eleventh century as the epoch of their expansion, a period of ebullient development in every sphere, of open frontiers and great opportunity, when anything could happen and very often did. Certainly the Normans made and took every opportunity in the brave new world of feudal Europe. Bliss was it, doubtless, in that dawn to be alive, but to be Norman, we may say, must have been very heaven.

INCIPIT EP'A WILLELMI CENOBITE AD WILLE
MVM ORTODOXV ANGLORVM REGEM.
IN NORMAN HORVM DVCVM GESTIS.
O VICTORIOSO ATQ ORTO
DOXO. SVMI regis Hutu
anglor regi Wille mo.
Gemeticensis cenobita omniu
cenobitaru indignissimus
willelmi ad conterendos ho
stes samsonis forticudine et
ad discernendu iudiciu salomonis
abyssu Opus hoc prudentissime
Rex et serenissime in normannor
ducu gestis de diuersis excerptum
codicibus iuxta meæ exiguitatem
industrie contexui useqs dicans ideam
celstudini ob recolenda priscor patru int pcipuas laicarum
dignitatu administrationes piissimor actuu exempla
cronicor bibliotece delegandu decreui Quod n rethoru
uenusta excornatu qurtate n politi sermonis uenali lepore
seu nitore sed inelimato stilo tenui oratione p plana deduc
tu cuilibet lectori ad lucidu elaboraui Urq qd maiestatis
lacere ambiunt pelari uiri litteraru picia admodu erudia
q striccis gladiis aumati circueuntes eluminatis prauoru
insidiis lepuclu salomonis diuine legis puigili munimine
satagune tueri Subtilissimi qqs ingenii uigore celica dis
pensatoris prerogatiua uobis collati qlio in armor regi
mine sic in cunctis qbs intendere q ppende pponitis mira
ualere efficacia multi multimode pbaueu. Munusclm
q tantilli nostri laboris placida manu sumite nobilissima
gesta celebri memoria dignissima uestra et antiqua
phas paginas recolite Principiu naqs narrationis usqs
ad Ricardu scdm a dudonis pici uiri historia collegi q
qd posteris ppagandu karte comdauit. a Rodulfo comite
pphu Ricardi fre diligent excussiuit. Reliq u q parti relatu
plurimor ad corroboranda fide eque idoneor annis et rerum
expimos. certissimo indice pprio uisu didici priuati mea dono. Sane
genealogia Rollonis a paganis maioribus nati et multa etate sua
in paganismo acta tande ad scam infantia saluberrimo fonte
renati necu somniu ei cu pluribs id generis ab historica serie
descui animaduertens ea penit adulatoria nec specie honesti

Chapter 3 The Normans in Normandy

It is the business of this chapter to describe and analyse Norman society in the second half of the eleventh century, both on the eve of and during the great period of expansion, in the hope that by this means some explanation of that expansion, and of the whole Norman achievement, may be forthcoming, and the inimitable spirit of *Normanitas* defined. Something of the receptivity of that society, which made of Normandy the land of promise for immigrants both lay and clerical, has been said already,[1] and of its adaptability which made of it by the mid-eleventh century more Frankish than the Franks,[2] having taken and developed Frankish language, religion and feudalism, Frankish war and law and a Carolingian concept of the state, a new monasticism and a new architecture. Something, too, has been said already of the inheritance from the past, and here we may almost add that the Normans kept the best of both worlds. The original Viking spirit must be allowed to underlie their outrageous enterprise[3] and, no doubt, that part of their prosperity derived from trade and commerce.[4] The art and craft of ship-building was obviously not lost either. No one looking at the Bayeux Tapestry's depiction of the great sea-borne expedition of 1066[5] can fail to be reminded forcefully of the Viking world to which the Normans had originally belonged, even though the fact that the fleet required against England had to be built for the purpose shows how far they had moved into the Frankish feudal world where military capacity depended more upon war-horses than ships. (It is instructive in this respect to compare England, where in the eleventh century, down to and including 1066, fleets seem always to have been available to kings and great magnates alike). The Scandinavian right of banishment (*ullac*) was also retained to be a component of the powers of the eleventh-century Norman duke, as were also certain other judicial or quasi-judicial rights like jurisdiction in the plea of house-breaking.[6] Yet in the end the Frankish Carolingian inheritance was to be the more important,

William of Jumièges presenting his *Deeds of the Norman Dukes* to William the Conqueror (from Orderic Vitalis' autograph copy of his edition of the work: Rouen, Bibliothèque Municipale, MS.Y.14., f.116).

not least in the growing power of the duke and the creation of a powerful and unified state between 911 and 1066, and was of course increasingly so as the Normans became increasingly Gallicized towards the end of the tenth century.[7] If, therefore, it be asked at the outset, 'Who were the Normans?', the answer can only be, those who, whether by birth or adoption, saw themselves and were accepted as members of that society. In this the Normans were little different from present day English (or should it be British?) or Americans, even though, in any case, the mid-eleventh century was still a long way from any concept of the nation state.

In sharp distinction to the earlier period, the evidence for the history of the Normans and Normandy from the mid-eleventh century is abundant[8], which, in so far as it is written evidence, is itself the mark of literacy and thus civilization. The early Viking settlers of the Scandinavian phase left little behind them, even in the form of material artifacts, and for the tenth century we have little to go on save Dudo of St-Quentin, eked out by a few charters, and references to the Normans by writers outside who were often hostile. For the second half of the eleventh century the case is very different. There are two first-class contemporary historians, William of Jumièges and William of Poitiers, plus the unique record of the Bayeux Tapestry; there are the retrospective histories of writers slightly later but extremely well informed, such as the incomparable Orderic Vitalis or, *multum in parvo*, Gilbert Crispin's 'Life of Herluin'; there is an impressive and rapidly increasing number of charters of various types; and there is the overwhelmingly impressive evidence of Norman buildings and other artistic creations, to say nothing of histories and other evidence more specifically relating to the Normans in Italy and Antioch or on the First Crusade. Historians—or medieval historians at least—are never satisfied, but under this bright if generally sympathetic light[9] Normandy and its society in the middle and later eleventh century come quite sharply into focus, and a number of outstanding characteristics can be clearly seen.

In any discussion of these characteristics it is neither paradoxical nor perverse to begin with religion, for that is fundamental. Whatever we may do in our private lives, as historians we cannot do without it. Modern western civilization begins as Christendom, and for the Normans Christianity was not only one of the conditions of St-Clair-sur-Epte and a principal means whereby they were transformed into respectable members of Frankish society, but also thereafter in one way or another a motivation for all their endeavours. At every point the Norman Church was integrated with Norman society, which it formed and moulded. Christianity, increasingly Latin Christianity and, we may almost say, Norman Christianity, was of the essence of that *Normanitas* we seek. The Norman Church provided not only motivation but also unity, identity and inspiration. The battle-cry of the Normans at Hastings, after all, was *Deus aie!*, 'God help us!' The Normans invaded England with papal blessing, carved out their principalities in Italy and Sicily as allies of the Papacy, and stormed the cities of Antioch and Jerusalem as champions of the new concept of Holy

Here William gave arms to Harold. The knighting of Harold at the end of the Breton expedition. (1064).

Here William came to Bayeux. William the feudal prince, superbly armed and mounted, rides into his city of Bayeux, represented by its castle.

Where Harold made an oath to duke William. Harold's oath, upon the relics and (right) a portable altar (with the consecrated host?).

Here earl Harold

returns to the land of England.

And came to king Edward. In this remarkable scene, Harold, normally represented as noble and upright, is contorted, presumably with guilt at his secret intention of perjury.

Here the body of king Edward is borne to the church of St Peter the Apostle, i.e. the newly dedicated Westminster Abbey.

Here king Edward in bed addresses his faithful friends; and here he is dead. The death of Edward the Confessor.

Here they gave the king's crown to Harold.

Here sits Harold, king of the English, Stigand the archbishop. The coronation of Harold, clearly by Stigand.

St-Michael-in-Peril-of-the-Sea. The
abbey church of Mont-St-Michel
(1024–84). The east end was rebuilt
in the fifteenth century and the west
end demolished in the eighteenth.

The Conqueror's abbey church of St
Stephen at Caen, west facade
(dedicated 1077. The present spires
are later).

War which they themselves did much to form.[10] It is sometimes said that they exploited the religious sentiment of the age, but it seems fairer to assert that they effortlessly embodied it, and, once again,[11] one must insist that there was no lack of spirituality in Normandy, as witness Norman monasticism or the prayers of St Anselm. One surely approaches very close to the true spirit of eleventh-century Normandy in the great churches then raised throughout the duchy, and which made Raoul Glaber's 'white robe of churches'[12] almost a seamless web—Jumièges and Mont-St-Michel, St Stephen, Holy Trinity and St Nicholas all three at Caen, Cerisy-la-Forêt and Lessay.[13] What we may see in them is not only faith, and faith in good works, on the one hand, with wealth and technical skill on the other, but also confidence, lordship, magnificence and pride.

By 911 organized religion in the metropolitan province of Rouen had been destroyed, bishops evidently surviving in that city but nowhere else, monks fled with their precious relics, their buildings abandoned and ruined. Revival began almost at once and was led, significantly for the future, by the dukes. Rollo accepted baptism as one of the conditions of St-Clair-sur-Epte, and thereafter, according to Dudo, had all his companions baptized and instructed in the faith. His successor William Longsword, who is presented by Dudo as both a Christian prince and martyr, refounded Jumièges about 940 (which may or may not account for the remaining ancient fabric of the tenth-century church of St Pierre,[14] next to the great Romanesque church of St Mary) and ardently wished to become a monk there himself. Richard I between 961 and 963 restored the abbey of St Ouen at Rouen, St Wandrille (*alias* Fontanelles) in the Seine valley, and Mont-St-Michel. At the last named in its impregnable position—St Michael-in-Peril-of-the-Sea, who became a

Cerisy-la-Forêt from the east. The abbey was founded by duke Robert the Magnificent, but the present church dates from the late eleventh century.

St. Pierre at Jumièges. Interior, looking west, of the tenth-century church (left).

Mont-St-Michel. The subterranean chapel of Notre-Dame-sous-Terre.

particular cult of the Normans—some form of religious life may have continued throughout the Viking period, and some of duke Richard's work survives in the subterranean chapel of Notre-Dame-sous-Terre beneath the nave of the present church, making this unpretentious and much altered building, together with the western fragment of St Pierre at Jumièges, the earliest surviving Norman ecclesiastical architecture.

Paray-le-Monial in Burgundy from the north-west; a scaled-down version of Cluny III (c. 1110).

Duke Richard II as the benefactor of the abbey of Mont-St-Michel (from the twelfth-century cartulary of Mont-St-Michel (Bibliothèque de la Ville d'Avranches, MS 210).

Already comment is called for. Everything so far mentioned has been the refoundation by the Normans of an abbey destroyed by the Norsemen, and revival is coming first to the monasteries. By the mid-tenth century the Norman dukes at least had come to subscribe to the almost universal respect held by civilized contemporaries for monasticism as a vital social function and superior way of life. 'Seven times daily will I worship thee', and by their ceaseless round of prayer the monks fought the spiritual battles of society as the knights waged war against terrestrial foes. Not merely protection and patronage of the Church, therefore, but a liberal patronage of monks, was thus an essential part of lordship and the princely office. This is the beginning of the monastic age *par excellence* in the West to which the Normans now belonged, and of monastic revival and reform emanating from various centres, of which Cluny, in Burgundy, is the most famous and most important. The monasticism which duke Richard I restored to Mont-St-Michel, St Wandrille and St Ouen was derived from Ghent (whence St Dunstan of England also received much) through the agency of St Mainard, himself a pupil of the reformer Gerard de Broigne. What has been called 'the decisive moment in the history of Norman monasticism'[15] came only in 1001, when Richard II was able to persuade the Cluniac reformer William of Volpiano, then abbot of St Bénigne at Dijon, to come and bring monks to his father's church at Fécamp, at that time served only by canons. Richard I himself had

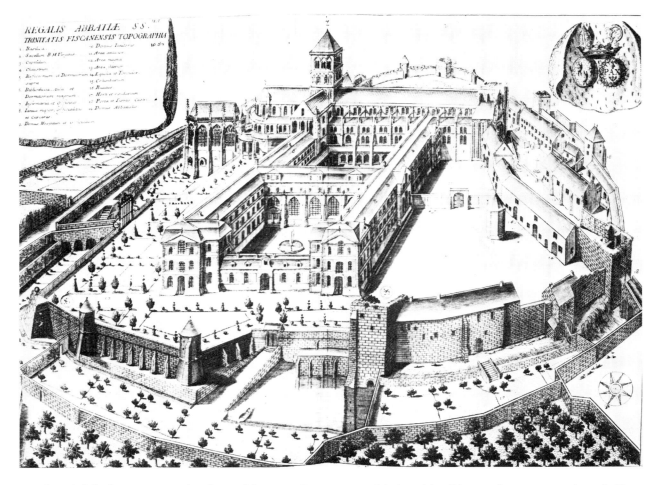

tried and failed to get monks from Cluny to Fécamp, and it is said that William of Volpiano at first demurred, objecting that he understood the Normans to be more apt to destroy than build the temples of the Lord.[16] But come he did, and from Fécamp, 'the Saint-Denis of the dukes of Normandy' in Prentout's striking phrase,[17] his influence spread to almost all the Norman monasteries, including almost all those yet to come. In this way—appropriately enough at the millennium—the Normans were connected to the most formative influence in this formative age, though even Cluniac monasticism they were to make something of their own, not least by the time and emphasis given to learning in their cloisters and monastic schools. From then on it was roses all the way. Of the ten religious houses already in existence at the accession of William the Conqueror in 1035 all were ducal foundations, but in his time the movement spread to the new Norman aristocracy who established at least a further eighteen monasteries before 1066. In a famous passage relating the foundation of St Stephen's and Holy Trinity at Caen, respectively by William himself and his duchess Mathilda (in penance for their marriage within the prohibited degrees), Orderic Vitalis had this to say:

> The barons of Normandy were inspired by the piety of their princes to do likewise, and encouraged each other to undertake similar enterprises for the salvation of their souls. They vied with

Fécamp, from an engraving of 1687. The abbey church and claustral buildings are central, the ducal lodgings or château to their right.

26

each other in the good work, and competed in giving alms generously as befitted their rank. Each magnate would have thought himself beneath contempt if he had not supported clerks and monks on his estates for the service of God.[18]

By 1066 no one, however prejudiced, would call the prince of Normandy and his magnates pirates,[19] and one substantial reason is the excellence as well as the number of the Norman monasteries, particularly distinguished even in an age distinguished by its monasticism. Like almost everything in Normandy they were new, and thus vibrant with a new-born spiritual endeavour. They were reformist in an age increasingly anxious for reform. Their new buildings, and especially their great churches rising on every side, could often rival anything to be found in Latin Christendom. They were, above all, up to date. They were also in many cases distinguished for their learning, their teaching, and their schools—at Fécamp, St Wandrille, Holy Trinity at Rouen, St Stephen's at Caen, Jumièges, St Evroul, Cormeilles and, above all, Bec. Occasionally we can penetrate within their walls, and Orderic Vitalis has left us an agreeable, and doubtless typical, picture of Abbot Thierry of St Evroul encouraging his monks to work harder,[20] as Gilbert Crispin tells us that Abbot Herluin did at Bec ('Of what use is a man who is ignorant of letters and of the commandments of God?').[21] John of Fécamp, who succeeded William of Volpiano as abbot there in 1028, has been called 'the greatest spiritual writer of the epoch before St Bernard'.[22] As for Bec, different from the rest in its comparatively humble foundation (in 1034 by Herluin, formerly a household knight of count Gilbert of Brionne), in the indepen-

Le Bec Hellouin. Of the medieval buildings, only the great fifteenth-century bell-tower (and a contemporary gateway) remain standing.

The tomb of Herluin in the present church (the former refectory) at Le Bec.

dence, the austerity and the humility of its beginnings, fate and virtue decreed that it was to rise in a few short years to be the most outstanding, the most influential and the most famous of all the Norman monasteries. Its pre-eminent distinction resulted from its learning and its schools, opened by Lanfranc, one of the foremost scholars of his age, and producing as one amongst its long list of *alumni*, Anselm, 'the most luminous and penetrating intellect between Augustine and Aquinas'.[23] Of Lanfranc's teaching at Bec Orderic wrote that 'the fame of his learning spread all over Europe, until many flocked from France, Gascony, Brittany, and Flanders to sit at his feet', and of the monks at Bec (first under Lanfranc and then Anselm) that they 'are so devoted to the study of letters, so eager to solve theological problems and compose edifying treatises, that almost all of them seem to be philosophers'.[24] By all means let us admit that Lanfranc and Anselm, like John of Fécamp and William of Volpiano, came from Italy; but this was the age of the wandering scholar, and in Normandy they found a receptive climate and a fertile soil.

A portrait of Lanfranc as archbishop from a manuscript of c. 1100 (Oxford, Bodleian 569).

In accordance with contemporary attitudes—monasticism first and the rest will follow—revival and, still more, reform came later to the secular church, about whose lower echelons we in any case know little, and as a centrally directed policy can scarcely be said to begin before the Conqueror's reign and the 1050s. Orderic Vitalis has a calumnious passage about the early Norman priests of Danish extraction, addicted to both arms and concubines, and of how, when reform came, they were more willing to give up the former than the latter.[25] Nevertheless, by 990 the diocesan framework of the province of Rouen had been reconstructed (the word is just) with its six suffragan bishoprics of Avranches, Coutances, Bayeux, Sées, Lisieux and Evreux, though in the far west the bishops of Coutances evidently could not reside in their cathedral city for some decades thereafter. In 1055 the young duke William, having first deposed with papal approval his own uncle, the unworthy Mauger, appointed the reforming Maurilius, a monk of Fécamp, to the archiepiscopal see, and after that a series of reforming councils brought things to order. The newly organized and reorganized Norman secular Church was, like the monasteries, up-to-date, functioning for the most part according to the tenets of the latest reformist thinking, though there were no high-Gregorian notions in Normandy yet about prelates detached from the responsibilities of government and administration, or a Church free from the ultimate control of the prince. There were separate ecclesiastical councils or synods at provincial and diocesan level, separate courts for the operation of a distinct ecclesiastical jurisdiction, a due study and practice of canon law, properly organized dioceses with cathedral chapters and archdeacons as the link-men between the bishops and the parish clergy. The bishops upon whom so much turned were intensely aristocratic—'cette galerie de seigneurs-évêques, issus de la haute aristocratie normande'[26]—but not necessarily the worse for that. Before 1052 two members of the ducal family, Robert (987–1037) and Mauger (1037–55), were successively archbishops of Rouen. In the Conqueror's day, even William of

Poitiers seems a little embarrassed in insisting that the appointment of Odo, bishop of Bayeux (1049–99), John, bishop of Avranches (1060–67, thereafter archbishop of Rouen 1067–87), and Hugh, bishop of Lisieux (1049–77), was due to their merits and not their close relationship with the duke.[27] Geoffrey, bishop of Coutances (1049–93) was a Mowbray, and Yves, bishop of Séez (1035–70), was the head of the great family of Bellême. The Norman bishops even of the middle and later eleventh century have not always received a good press, but we do not have the evidence to make accusations of lack of spirituality, and we do know that they were energetic and efficient. They served God and the duke in church and state: they were amongst the makers of Normandy.[28] Some, perhaps most, were lavish patrons of art and learning, including Odo of Bayeux, and almost all were great and ambitious builders. Side by side with the monastic churches, new cathedrals rose

Odo bishop of Bayeux, on the left, and Robert count of Mortain on the right, in council with duke William, from the Bayeux Tapestry.

Bayeux Cathedral from the south-west. Though the cathedral was much rebuilt in the twelfth century and later, the western towers are largely from Odo's church, dedicated 1077.

throughout eleventh-century Normandy. Time, in the form of later rebuilding, has treated them more harshly than the *abbatiales*, and little beyond the crypt of Rouen and the crypt and (altered) west front of Odo's Bayeux (dedicated 1077) now survives to show their scale and majesty.

The second element in mid-eleventh-century Normandy which contributed to its greatness was a new and virile aristocracy. A substantial number of this aristocracy we have, indeed, already met, for they provided many of the bishops and abbots, they were the founders and patrons of many of the religious houses, and they furnished many of the inmates also, for Norman monasticism (like monasticism elsewhere) was as aristocratic as the Church of which it formed a part. It is always a mistake to make a sharp distinction between the Church and the world, and never more so than in the closely integrated society of Normandy in this period. The Norman aristocracy, however, unlike the Church, cannot be traced back far into the tenth century, for its most outstanding feature, after its forceful energy, was its newness. The great names and feudal houses of the future, Montgomery and Montfort, Beaumont and Ferrers, Mortimer and Mowbray, Tosny and Warenne, scarcely appear before the year 1000. Some were doubtless in some phase of establishment before, but they are not recorded. Not all were Norman in origin, Tosny being a case in point and immigration being no less a feature of Norman history than emigration. Since in that age the most prominent aristocrats in any generation in any principality tended to be hand-picked by the prince, and since in any case Norman aristocratic colonization of the future duchy scarcely began before 911, there is no cause to impose upon Normandy the latest sociological and demographic theories of the continuity of a late Carolingian aristocracy into the early feudal period. Whatever may have been the case in contemporay France, eleventh-century Normandy was ruled by new men with no personal or blood relationship with Carolingian lordship save what may have been grasped by marriage.[29] Only the duke or prince, it seems, could trace his lineage back in unbroken male succession even to the date of St-Clair-sur-Epte, a fact which must have added greatly to his great prestige. He too, alone was 'count' (*comes*)[30] until that title was sparingly conferred on others only in the eleventh century, and even so only upon members of the ducal house.

The prestige, evidently steadily increasing, of the ducal house from the beginning, is, indeed, one of the features of Norman history, and is not put in question by the 'anarchy' of William the Conqueror's minority (1035–47) which was much more about succession to the ducal office than of opposition to it by recalcitrant nobles or the alleged centrifugal tendencies of feudalism. Like so many of those features, it reaches a culmination in the reign of the mature William, and is relevant here because of the reverse of the coin, which is (to use the inappropriate terms customary in discussing the matter) the close control of his secular aristocracy exercised by the Norman duke. Such seemingly effortless control was compounded of other elements than prestige of office: we must add personality and, above all, the huge powers of patronage accruing to the feudal prince and suzerain in a state where all the greatest magnates are his vassals and his tenants, and tenure is conditional on loyalty. In consequence, and with his own vast landed resources to dispose of at will, the prince was able to make and break, to lift up and cast down—as in a famous passage Orderic Vitalis described how the Conqueror's son, Henry I, put down the mighty from their seats and raised up others 'so to say, from the dust'.[31] Though the hereditary sentiment and desire was as strong then as later, in a period of personal rule and personal lordship much depended on personal relations, and there was always room at the top because the pole of politics was so greasy. Certainly in the time of duke William's ascendancy the aristocracy which shared the honours of his duchy with him, and followed him to England to be made far greater than they were before, were almost a hand-picked group, purged of those who had lost the duke's trust; while of those enjoying his favour the most favoured of all were his two half-brothers, Robert of Mortain and Odo of Bayeux, and his closest friends, Roger of Montgomery and William fitz Osbern ('whom of all his intimates he had loved the most since their childhood together' says William of Poitiers of the latter),[32] both of whom were also his kinsmen like so many others of the Norman magnates.[33] Aristocracy, especially militant, is now sadly out of fashion, but without these men there would have been little Norman achievement, and it is to be remembered that they too, like the duke, were the patrons of monks and churches, and thereby of architecture, art and learning.

William the Conqueror, from the Bayeux Tapestry.

31

All the Norman lay nobles of the mid-eleventh century were, of course, warriors, for in this age (and long after) *noblesse oblige* meant that almost above all else, and the higher you were in the social hierarchy, the harder if possible you fought. They were mounted warriors also; in short, they were knights themselves as well as the lords of many other and less elevated knights. We therefore pass from the small group at the top to the large and fluid class (the word is even less appropriate than usual) of knights which extends all the way from great magnates to relatively poor landless knights. The latter, it must be stressed, emulated their betters, shared much the same attitudes and motives, and honed their ambitions no doubt to the even sharper cutting edge of young men on the make. Chivalry and religion, now beginning to blend, not least in the concept of Holy War, provided a code for all, even if honoured in the breach as well as the observance like most codes, and the burning desire for lands and lordships governed actions. A common military training, the sharing of almost a common way of life in the lord's household, and the common accolade of knighthood, gave coherence to the class, however broad, and marked off knights from lesser men. Too much can be and is made of the gap between great magnates and mere knights, as of that between landed and stipendiary knights.[34] The contemporary concept of the 'three orders' of men, those who prayed, those who fought and those who laboured, had more reality than a modern and anachronistic obsession with economic categories. Of course not all knights were great men, but all great men were knights, which meant that knighthood brought social elevation as well as membership of a military élite. The young duke William himself was knighted in his early youth—*arma militaria sumit*—whereupon his biographer, William of Poitiers, adds characteristically that a tremor ran through all France.[35] Later as king of

Duke William on the morning of Hastings, from the Bayeux Tapestry.

32

Seal of Henry II (1154–89), King of England, duke of Normandy and Aquitaine, count of Anjou, 'equestrian' side showing the king armed and mounted as a knight.

England (as doubtless he had done before as duke of Normandy) he was to depict himself upon his seal armed and mounted, that is as a knight, and in this he was followed not only by all his royal successors but also by all his lords and vassals on their equestrian seals. Orderic Vitalis could refer to such eminent magnates as Ralph de Tosny, Hugh de Grandmesnil and Arnold d'Echauffour simply as *milites*.[36] The word *miles*, in fact, is used as a title of distinction (and therefore must mean knight and not ordinary soldier) in surviving Norman charters as from 965.[37] It is clear from the pages of Orderic and elsewhere that knighthood by the mid-eleventh century was a rank, status and honour only conferred upon a young man (*tiro*) after a long and arduous apprenticeship to arms, to horsemanship and to all contemporary courtesy.[38] The conferment was by a ceremony usually described as the bestowal of arms, and is thus shown in a well-known scene on the Bayeux Tapestry which surely represents the knighting of earl Harold by duke William in 1064.[39] For those less elevated, and for young men on the make, knighthood was the essential precondition of advancement in the career of arms—and there was no other career for anyone with any pretensions to gentility save the Church. The way to the top was by service to a lord in his military household, thus to obtain with luck one's fief or one's heiress; by these means those who were not lords could hope to be so. Poverty is often a relative term, and though the poor knight not infrequently appears in history books, it is doubtful if in reality he ever existed, especially in an age when, literally, money was not everything. Certainly he cannot have existed in the eyes and minds of peasants as the gentlemen rode by.

In short, the military élite of knights who now dominated Frankish warfare, not least in Normandy,[40] had become a social élite also. Nor could it have been otherwise, because of the expense. The warhorse alone, the *destrier*, specially bred and trained, and preferably led (by the right hand, hence the name?) not ridden to the place of battle, was enormously expensive, and more than one was needed for a good engagement. The hauberk, the long coat of mail which marked out the knight in action and acquired an almost mystical significance,[41] was expensive too, and so were good swords and all the other necessary gear. Not only this, but knighthood required the total dedication of a life-time from youth up in horsemanship and arms, divorced from and elevated above all other and less honourable pursuits. One may perhaps think of the dedication of modern show-jumpers and 'eventers', but for the knight life as well as honour and prizes were at stake. 'You can make a horseman of a lad at puberty; later than that, never', and again, 'He who has stayed at school till the age of twelve and never ridden a horse is fit only to be a priest'.[42] Such training and such skills, which also must include the ability to ride and fight in combination, could best or only be obtained in the households of lords, who also had patronage to dispense. Like the Battle of Britain in 1940, this was a type of warfare in which only gentlemen could engage; and, as then, not only courage and hard-won technical proficiency, but also excellent and elaborate equipment were required. Those superbly mounted and accoutred knights who dominate the Bayeux Tap-

A sixteenth-century suit of mail similar to an eleventh-century hauberk of which no example survives (from the collection of Ian Peirce).

Replica (made by Ian Peirce) of an eleventh-century sword (from the collection of G. P. A. Brown).

estry do so not only because they were chiefly responsible for a famous victory, but also because they were the dominant members of a victorious society who wished to see their deeds recorded, for themselves and for posterity. With Norman knights, in fact, we are dealing with a ruling class, actual and potential; and we are coming very close to the ethos of society and the spirit of *Normanitas* we seek. Finally, though we are surely right to mark off our knights sharply from the peasantry, and the bourgeoisie in towns, we must not do so too sharply from the Church. Knighthood did not have to wait for St Bernard in the early twelfth century to make it respect-

Norman knights before Hastings, from the Bayeux Tapestry.

able even in the eyes of clerics, and Norman knights were as closely integrated with the Norman Church as was the Norman aristocracy at the head of both. Individual knights, some of whom were lettered like Robert of Grandmesnil,[43] might later turn to the cloister and the Church, as Orderic Vitalis quite frequently and casually relates. Robert of Grandmesnil himself became an abbot (of St Evroul), as did Herluin, the founder of Bec. William of Poitiers, the Conqueror's biographer, went to the schools at Poitiers, became the duke's chaplain having previously been his knight, and ended his career as archdeacon of Lisieux.[44] Norman society in its upper reaches was an integrated society, which is not the least of reasons for its manifold achievements.

In dealing with the overlapping classes of aristocrats and knights we are dealing also with warfare of a particular type and with feudalism, two of the most important borrowings (which they then developed) of the Normans from the Franks along with Latin Christianity, and all three very close to the heart of *Normanitas*. We may take warfare next, for military history and military affairs are emphatically not matters to be put on one side or, worse, ignored. In warfare the Normans undoubtedly excelled, and their excellence is the direct explanation of their political achievements and indirectly of much else. We must accept, and in accepting understand, a love of warfare for which the knight was born and bred if we are to understand our Normans and indeed their peers and rivals elsewhere in France.

I love the gay Eastertide, which brings forth leaves and flowers; and I love the joyous songs of the birds, re-echoing through the copse. But also I love to see, amidst the meadows, tents and pavilions spread; and it gives me great joy to see, drawn up on the field, knights and horses in battle array; and it delights me when

the scouts scatter people and herds in their path; and I love to see them followed by a great body of men at arms; and my heart is filled with gladness when I see strong castles beseiged, and the stockades broken and overwhelmed, and the warriors on the bank, girt about by fosses, with a line of strong stakes, interlaced . . . Maces, swords, helms of different hues, shields that will be riven and shattered as soon as the fight begins; and many vassals struck down together; and the horses of the dead and wounded roving at random. And when battle is joined, let all men of good lineage think of nought but the breaking of heads and arms; for it is better to die than to be vanquished and live. I tell you, I find no such savour in food, or in wine, or in sleep, as in hearing the shout 'On! On!' from both sides, and the neighing of steeds that have lost their riders, and the cries of 'Help! Help!'; in seeing men great and small go down on the grass beyond the fosses; in seeing at last the dead, with the pennoned stumps of lances still in their sides.

Thus the poet Bertrand de Born,[45] from Périgord in the second half of the twelfth century, in verses which, although a century later, catch entirely the spirit which we want and which the Normans had. Compare, perhaps, William duke of Normandy and Geoffrey count of Anjou in 1051 exchanging through envoys near Dom-front, which the former was besieging, details of their horses, shields and arms that they might recognize each other and put their quarrel to the test of combat in battle the next morning;[46] or compare, again, the song of Bertrand with the more famous Song of Roland, nearer in time and place but where the same spirit is made equally manifest.[47]

The warfare of the mid-eleventh century in France, especially with the Normans who were in the van of military development, turned increasingly upon knights, *i.e.* heavy cavalry, and castles. The two instruments were combined, as we shall see. The very purpose of the knight, though of course he could fight on foot as necessary, was to fight on horseback. For this his splendid *destrier* had been bred, and most of his expensive equipment developed— hauberk down to below the knee, long kite-shaped shield, lance and sword, the latter used when the former broke. Add the conical helmet with nose-piece and one has a heavy cavalryman whose ultimate weapon and function was the charge in concert with his peers. It is clear that the medieval technique of couching the lance, as opposed to the overarm or underarm thrust of a spear inherited from classical antiquity, was already developed in this period.[48] By this method, the lance held rigid and locked or couched under the arm, the whole momentum (weight × velocity) of horse and horseman, aimed directly at the enemy, was concentrated in the point. The shock tactic of the charge was made technically possible by the stirrup,[49] worn long to give the rider a necessarily firm seat in the saddle which was also built up fore and aft to keep him there. All this—the long stirrup leathers, the built-up saddles, the long lances, some with cross-pieces to prevent over-penetration, some with *gonfanons* or pennants and obviously not meant to be thrown, and the use of the lance in the couched position—is vividly shown on the

Primitive carving (eleventh-century from an earlier church ?) of knights jousting, from the south transept of St. Georges-de-Boscherville, Normandy.

Bayeux Tapestry.[50] The *Song of Roland* is full of individual feats with the lance evidently couched.[51] This is what Anna Comnena had in mind when she declared that the charging Frankish knight would pierce the walls of Babylon;[52] and certainly the charge of Frankish chivalry carried all before it in Italy and on the First Crusade. But, to be fully effective, the charge had to be delivered in concert and combination (whatever the size of the unit employed) and timed to the right moment, which, duly done, gives the lie, like so much else, to the persistent myth of lack of discipline in feudal armies—of which in these pages the least said the better.[53] The truth is that the knight, whether of the eleventh century or the twelfth or later, was as professional as the age could make him, born, we may almost say, in the castle and bred in the saddle.

Medieval armies were in any case small by modern standards, but something of the supremacy of knights in their warfare is reflected in the comparatively very small numbers of them which we meet in the chronicles of the time. The total of 2,000 or more knights whom we may guess to have fought at Hastings under the Conqueror's command[54] is altogether exceptional, yet even so was beyond the effective resources of Normandy and contained large numbers of volunteers from other lands.[55] Elsewhere at other times it is clear that a hundred knights could be a lot, while much smaller contingents and mere troops are frequently found attacking with success formations much larger than themselves on occasions which should not be dismissed as the enthusiastic exaggerations of proud contemporary reporters. Though analogies can be false, the aerial warfare of the Battle of Britain in 1940 may be cited again as possibly illuminating—the comparatively small numbers of aircraft, and therefore men, taking part on both sides though great issues are at stake; and, within that context, the very small numbers of aircraft, mere squadrons or less, from Fighter Command frequently attacking successfully much larger bomber formations.[56] In both cases one may suggest, albeit from opposite ends of time, it is a question of the élan of an élite, social as well as military, with confidence in the best equipment that money can provide, and the particular spirit that is bred within the small band of happy and exclusive warriors. Certainly the Norman knights (like those, of course, of other lands), fought in the small groups of the *conrois*,[57] presumably identical with or drawn from the households of their lords in which the young men, at least, not only trained but lived. There are glimpses in the chronicles[58] and something more in the early pages of Gilbert Crispin's *Life of Herluin*[59] (Herluin was a household knight of count Gilbert of Brionne), while on the Tapestry we may watch the Norman chivalry and its young bloods, not only in action at Hastings and on campaign under the *gonfanons* of their lords, but also on their lords' honourable business, as envoys, for example, or as escorts, and almost always mounted.

NVN TII : VVILLELMI

Young knights riding on their lord's business, from the Bayeux Tapestry. On such occasions neither helmet not hauberk are worn.

The fact that cavalry had come to dominate Frankish and Norman warfare by the middle and later eleventh century as the military élite and *force de frappe* does not mean that infantry was despised, in the military sense of any failure to appreciate the value of its rôle—though no doubt the innate superiority in his own eyes of the cavalryman, and his patronising contempt for the flat-footed infantryman, dates from this period. The sheer facts that the cavalry-charge must be withstood, on the one hand, and held back until the tactically exact moment on the other, ensured the importance of foot-soldiers, to say nothing of their missile weapons of bow and (whenever adopted) crossbow. In set-piece battles the proper use of cavalry depended upon the proper use of infantry, and accordingly the skilful combination of horse and foot was a feature of Norman tactics whether at Hastings (where the Norman infantry outnumbered their knights) under William the Conqueror or on the First Crusade under Bohemond, in spite of the myth of feudal warfare propagated by Oman and others.[60] Obviously, infantry were also of crucial importance in defending and besieging fortresses, when even the knights had to dismount. The point is of some importance, for if cavalry dominated battlefields, castles dominated campaigns.

Of castles two things must be said.[61] The first is that they are, if we seek to define them, the fortified residences or residential fortresses of lords, and as such are both unique to the feudal period and of the essence of feudalism. The second is that the military rôle of the castle was at least as much offensive as defensive. The castle was an armed base from which, impregnable to anything but a full-scale and prolonged investment, the knights, the horsemen, who formed so large a proportion of its inmates, could and did ride out to control the surrounding countryside. The range of the castle

Ste. Suzanne, Maine. The keep shown here is held to be of the time of the Conqueror, who besieged the castle in c. 1084–6.

was the range of the mounted men within it, ten miles or more there and back in one day. Castles thus, no less than knights, dominated contemporary warfare because they dominated the land, and those who would hold the land must first hold, or take, or build, the castles. Normandy by the mid-eleventh century was already studded with the castles of the duke and his vassals, and the Norman conquest and settlement of England was made permanent by a castle-building programme the like of which can seldom if ever have been seen, save (though we have less information) in the Norman conquests and settlements of Italy and Sicily and Antioch, or in the establishment of the other crusading states by the Franks in Outremer.

Military organization and tactics are an integral part of any given society, as significant for its type and nature as any other feature. Castles, the fortified residences of lords, are feudal, the symbol and much of the substance of feudal lordship. Knights are feudal, their production indeed, we may say, what feudalism and feudal tenure are almost all about.[62] Nor, of course, was Normandy in the mid-eleventh century wanting in those other fundamentals of feudalism, which are vassalic commendation and the fief. For the former, Rollo, according to Dudo of St Quentin, was constrained to do homage to Charles the Simple in the beginning at St-Clair-sur-Epte.[63] More clearly, William of Poitiers, the jurist, writing in the 1070s, goes out of his way when necessary carefully to describe the full feudal commendation ceremony of homage by the *immixtio manuum* (whereby the vassal places his joined hands between those of his lord and thus became his man), the oath of fealty, and, as appropriate, investiture with the fief. Most notably, he thus describes the homage, fealty and investiture of Harold's commendation when the earl totally committed himself to duke William in 1064.[64] He also tells us how, for example, a few years earlier, Geoffrey of Mayenne commended himself to the duke, 'giving his vanquished hands to him and swearing the fealty which a vassal owes a lord';[65] and how Herbert, count of Maine 'gave himself to him by his hands, and received all that he had from him, as a knight does from his lord'.[66] Feudal tenure, *i.e.* the benefice or fief, land held of a lord by homage and fealty and in return for services of which knight-service is the chief, was well established in Normandy by 1066; while the inescapable implication of the introduction of feudalism into Italy and England by the Normans is that it was already prevalent in Normandy before they went.[67] To read Norman histories and charters of this period is to find C. H. Haskins' words still true, that 'vassalage and dependent tenure meet us on every hand'.[68] In short, Norman society was feudal by the mid-eleventh century—'one of the most fully developed feudal societies in Europe',[69] indeed—and, after Christianity itself, feudalism is arguably the most important adoption by the Normans from the neighbouring Franks. For these are the bonds of secular society, holding the whole together in a hierarchy culminating in the prince, and providing the motivation of attitudes and responses. Nor are they secular only: many abbots and most bishops were also vassals of the duke by 1066, owing knights to his service from their lands, while the oath of fealty was of course made sacrosanct, as Harold swears to William on the Tapestry with one hand on the relics and the other on a portable altar with the consecrated Host.[70] It is impossible to do justice to a social system and, indeed, a way of life, in the narrow confines of a few pages, but it is imperative to insist that feudalism was both socially and politically a positive force, cohesive and not divisive as so often wrongly represented. In it lies much of the strength of Normandy in the great period of Norman achievement. Further, it was exportable. The Normans took feudalism with them wherever they went, and it is a large part of the explanation not only of their conquests but also of their permanent establishment as a ruling class in England, Italy, Sicily and Antioch.

Feudalism also added mightily to the powers of princes, not least of the duke of Normandy who, like others of his kind, was feudal suzerain of his duchy, the lord of lords. The growing power of the duke is one of the central themes of early Norman history, and one which undoubtedly begins in 911. Of the duke as feudal suzerain we have already spoken, and of the great power of patronage which thus accrued. To this we add the knights, the counsel and the attendance at his court which his vassals owed him, the financial as well as political potential of feudal lordship,[71] the centripetal (not centrifugal) workings of feudalism, and the institutionalized, indeed compulsory, loyalty it enjoins. Not for nothing has the feudal prince been called the New Leviathan.[72] The duke of Normandy also controlled his Church within his duchy. He appointed and invested his bishops, who were also his vassals, and could on occasion dismiss them, as the Conqueror, with papal sanction, dismissed Archbishop Mauger in 1054 or 1055.[73] Many of the greatest and all the oldest abbeys were ducal foundations and their abbots equally under his control,[74] while the evidence suggests that private religious houses were scarcely free from ducal intervention: the Conqueror is known to have dismissed Robert of Grandmesnil, abbot of St Evroul,[75] and, at one time, Lanfranc, prior of Bec.[76] The Conqueror, too, was evidently accustomed both to summon and preside over synods of the Norman church, and to intervene in ecclesiastical jurisdiction as he thought fit,[77] nor is there any evidence to suggest that such procedure was an innovation. None of this accorded at all well with the ideal embodied in the Gregorian papacy—so named after Gregory VII (1073–85) its principal champion—namely, that the Church must be free from secular interference; but with William, like his predecessors a proven faithful son of Holy Church, and with otherwise impeccable reformist credentials, little was or could be done.

Something, too, has been said already about the prestige of the ducal house and its unique antiquity in a province where almost everything was new—achieved in practice by a *de facto* hereditary succession as the heir was recognized and accepted in his father's lifetime.[78] The Scandinavian and Carolingian inheritances have also been noted, the latter in due course contributing especially to the power of the duke and to the emergent state.[79] The successors of Rollo, in common with neighbouring feudal princes, adopted the title of count, which remains down to 1066 almost the preferred title of those whom we consistently call dukes of Normandy.[80] By it, they acquired status and respectability.[81] With it, they also acquired many of the regalian powers which had once pertained to the Carolingian office, including a monopoly of the coinage, rights of toll and of calling upon the military service of all free men by the *arrière-ban*, and, most important of all, widespread lands, domains and fiscs which ensured their pre-eminent wealth and thus their supremacy in the duchy. It is notable also that the dukes in their official written deeds or *acta* often used the title of marquis (*marchio, marchisus*) as well as count,[82] which may echo the 'march' or unified frontier district established and centred upon Rouen in the mid-ninth century[83], and perhaps even perpetuated at St-Clair-sur-Epte since Charles the Simple later referred to his grant there to Rollo as 'for the security of the realm' (*pro tutela regni*).[84] Such things, moreover, gave identity, coherence, even unity, as well as at least potential powers, to the prince, and so, of course, did those comparatively precise frontiers which Normandy achieved at least by the mid-eleventh century and their near-coincidence with the ecclesiastical boundaries of the metropolitan province of Rouen.[85] In Normandy you knew where you were and where you belonged, to a degree unusual in the early feudal period when the bonds of personal lordship were often stronger than territorial affiliation; while the near-identity of church and state, both dominated by the duke, was given another dimension of reality by the near-identity of their circumscriptions as duke and archbishop sat side by side, so to speak, at Rouen. That unity and coherence of mid-eleventh-century Normandy, which is not the least element in its strength, was completed by the Conqueror himself who finally amalgamated and sealed the breach between Upper Normandy, the early sphere of ducal influence and Gallicized at an early date, and Lower Normandy, more lastingly and independently Scandinavian and more subject to Breton intervention than to the duke's control. In 1047 the last rebellion of the young duke's minority was largely an affair of Lower Normandy, yet in 1066 more men followed the duke to England from the west than from the east.[86] The attachment of the west was brought about partly by a typical and long-term Norman process of aristocratic colonization, by lordship and lordships with castles and monasteries (*e.g.* Mont-St-Michel initially by Richard I, Cerisy-la-Fôret by Robert the Magnificent, Lessay by Turstin Haldup, lord of La Haye-du-Puits), and finally by William's great victory at Val-ès-Dunes in 1047 and its aftermath. In 1049 the duke's half-brother Odo was appointed to the see of Bayeux with its rapidly expanding city, and at the same time

Caen, castle. The huge walled enclosure is that of William the Conqueror after 1047, with towers added later.

Caen was developed almost as a new town, with its castle and two abbeys, to be a ducal centre second only in importance to Rouen itself.[87]

By the mid-eleventh century the Norman state had emerged, and there is evidence to see it as perhaps the most powerful feudal principality in France. By the standards of the age it was strong, unified, centralized and advanced in its administrative techniques[88]—as indeed we should expect, for it must be absurd to suppose that the Normans in the period of their expansion, whatever their powers of adoption and adaptation, could create and rule states exceptional for their good government in England, Italy Sicily and Antioch without experience and knowledge of their own.[89] At the centre was the duke with his court, the latter varying in size upon occasion to encompass anything from the minimum itinerant household to the occasional full councils of vassals and officials to discuss great matters. The itinerary was of course the key to medieval personal government, whether by kings or princes, and Normandy was small enough to ensure effective unity by this means as by others. In addition, the *vicomtes* administered their *vicomtés* or districts as ducal officials in the provinces and thus, to modern and anachronistic minds at least, were a more effective means of direct ducal control than the bishops and the counts. A fundamental duty of contemporary kings and princes was the maintenance of good peace and the giving of good justice. In this the Norman dukes were most effective, through their own court,[90] their *vicomtes*, their judicial commissioners sent to hear pleas, and through the necessary cooperation of their magnates and their bishops, so that the duke's firm peace in Normandy was not the least of reasons for the economic prosperity of the eleventh-century duchy.[91] Further, in the Conqueror's reign at least, there was a rapid development of a uniform law and custom, without which true political cohesion is scarcely possible.[92] Within this essential framework of the duke, his court, council and itinerary, his *vicomtes*, bishops, counts and other vassals, and the maintenance of his peace, there are signs by the mid-eleventh century, and before, of other developing administrative machinery indicative of an evolving state, entirely characteristic of the age and place. Thus Norman fiscal organization was advanced, as was necessary to handle the ample ducal revenues derived from broad demesnes, tolls and customs upon trade, direct taxation, feudal dues, the profits of justice, a monopoly of the coinage, and all other perquisites of lordship and regality.[93] Indeed, though the thought remains anathema in England, some historians are prepared to give some credence to the belief of Richard fitz Nigel, Henry II's treasurer in late twelfth-century England, that the vaunted procedures of the Anglo-Norman Exchequer were derived in part from eleventh-century Normandy.[94] So, too, on the secretarial side of government, the duchy before 1066, it may and should be argued, showed little if any inferiority even to England in the production of diplomas and other forms of charters, and, *pace* Stevenson, Galbraith and very many other scholars, there are before that date documentary references both to the duke's chancellor and his seal—the one sometimes to supervise the writing of his documents, the other occasionally to authenticate them.[95]

Three other fundamental facts have still to be added in any analysis of mid-eleventh-century Normandy, namely wealth, an expanding population, and the character and capacity of William the Conqueror. Wealth, of course, underlies everything and all Norman achievement, whether it be cultured monks singing in the choirs of new and magnificent churches, or military campaigns and victories. We are dealing also, in modern parlance, with an expanding economy, made manifest by, for example, the development of towns and a vigorous trade and commerce. Two particular features of Norman wealth especially concern us. One is the presence of a money economy which, though land (or, rather, lordship over it) gave the upper ranks of society their ultimate power and status, nevertheless enabled the duke and other lords to hire stipendiary forces—knights as well as other ranks—when necessary, and which accounts for all those volunteers and auxiliaries from other lands who reinforced William's army in 1066.[96] The other is the degree to which the wealth of Normandy was accumulated in and channelled through the hands of the duke, thus ensuring his pre-eminence and creating a loyal and closely-bound aristocracy by the fecundity of his patronage.[97] As for an expanding population, this no less obviously underlies Norman territorial aggrandisement, seen as emigration and the export of younger sons, than it does, for example, the astonishing growth of monasticism. The pages of Orderic Vitalis are full of the prodigious families of the Norman magnates and knightly class, and if, as we are told, some of them prayed for sons,[98] their prayers were surely answered. The classic instance is the twelve sons (by two wives) of Tancred of Hauteville, eight of whom went off to Italy with results that changed the world;[99] but Orderic tells us also of the seven sons (and four daughters) of Giroie, who were 'a race of knights',[100] of the five sons and four daughters of Roger de Montgomery and Mabel de Bellême,[101] and of the forty knightly kinsmen of Robert de Vitot.[102]

And so, finally to William the Conqueror himself, one of the few historical characters of whom almost everybody has heard and of whom Macaulay's schoolboy knows. In William's time all the powers and potentialities of Normandy and *Normanitas* so far analysed reach their culmination. Nor is this a matter only of that good fortune which always attended him, for in all things he was the leader. In fact he won the inheritance of his duchy in the teeth of adversity and in spite of the appalling difficulties of his minority, when his guardians and friends were slain about him, sometimes in his presence.[103] In the long deathbed speech put into his mouth by Orderic Vitalis (itself no bad summary of his life and reign by a well-informed writer of the next generation, steeped in the history and tradition of Normandy) the duke is made to say, 'When my father decided to go on a pilgrimage and committed the duchy of Normandy to me I was still a young boy, only eight years old; from that day to this I have always borne the burden of arms'.[104] Master of his duchy at the age of 19 after overcoming his opponents at his first great victory, at Val-ès-Dunes in 1047, he came to rule over his principality with a close-to-sovereign power, greater than that of any of his predecessors, and with the assistance of a hand-picked aristocracy closely bound to him by his prestige, by kinship and by interest, and not least by feudal ties. He presided no less certainly over a Church which was also his, and in his time and by his example that Church reached the apogee of its revival, both secular and monastic. His bishops were distinguished and his monks excelled. 'I have never harmed the Church of God, which is our mother, but have always been glad to honour her as our duty requires . . . 'With God's help I further enriched the nine abbeys of monks and one of nuns[105] which my ancestors founded in Normandy, so that they grew yet greater in renown through the abundant gifts I gave them. Further, while I was duke, seventeen abbeys of monks and six of nuns were built,[106] where every day full offices are performed and abundant alms are given for love of the most high King. These are the fortresses by which Normandy is guarded (*Huiusmodi castris munita est Normannia*)'—thus the dying duke in the words again of Orderic Vitalis.[107] As the age required of its lords and princes, he was also a warrior of renown and a consummate general who, when he rode onto the field of Hastings in October 1066 at the age of 38, had never fought a battle which he had not won, nor besieged a castle which he had not taken ('I was brought up in arms from childhood, and am deeply stained with all the blood I have shed').[108] He overcame his enemies, notably his hereditary foe the count of Anjou (Geoffrey Martel), and the French king (Henry I, who turned against his vassal and former protégé after Val-ès-Dunes) at the battles of Mortemer in 1054 and Varaville in 1057.[109] Under his rule the expansionist forces within Normandy and *Normanitas* were more widely effective than ever before, as in the final colonizing of Lower Normandy,[110] the strengthening and extension of the southern frontier by the acquisition of Alençon, Domfront and the Passais,[111] the exertion of Norman overlordship or influence upon Brittany, Ponthieu, Boulogne and Flanders, or the absorption of the county of Maine in 1063, three years before the absorption of the English kingdom in 1066.[112] One may feel that in Normandy in the mid-eleventh century William the Conqueror, otherwise William the Bastard, son of Robert the Magnificent and Arlette the tanner's daughter, was all the place and time required. He even had, this Fortune's favourite, a near-perfect wife in his diminutive duchess, Mathilda, daughter of the count of Flanders.[113] Certainly he was to become after 1066 as great a king in England as he was duke in Normandy. There are not many who have permanently and radically changed the fate of nations; and with this reflection William of Poitiers' favourable comparison of his hero with Caesar, though commonly derided, may seem something less than absurd.[114]

The outstanding features and fundamental characteristics of mid-eleventh-century Normandy thus appear to be: a religious revival of a particular kind; a new and energetic aristocracy loyal to the duke; an overlapping upper class of knights; the feudalization of society, chivalry and a love and mastery of war; a precocious unity

expressed in an emergent and potent state effectively governed by a powerful duke; great wealth concentrated in the hands of a few, the duke especially; and an expanding population. It may be hoped that we have in them also the elements of an explanation of Norman achievement both past and yet to come, and the elements also which when fused make for *Normanitas*. Of course there are complications, for few things are straightforward in history. For example, few of the features listed are wholly unique to Normandy but would be found, albeit to a lesser degree, in most of her neighbours and rivals in a period marked generally by religious reform, economic expansion, the development of feudal society and of feudal states. If some are indeed unique, like the very newness of the Norman aristocracy,[115] others such as an expanding population, chivalry, the cult of knighthood and the love of war, most certainly are not. Further, we cannot be merely mathematical, add up all these elements and so use them *en masse* to explain all Norman achievements right across the board. The outstanding qualities of duke William, for example, and the precocious strength and unity of the Norman state, may go some way to explain the conquest of England but are of little if any direct relevance to the conquest or colonization of southern Italy, Sicily and Antioch; nor, for that matter, did the new Norman aristocracy play much part in those latter enterprises in spite of the participation of duke Robert Curthose and some of his lords on the First Crusade. Yet to take and

The walled hill town of Ste. Suzanne in the county of Maine which was annexed by the Normans in 1063.

Eighteenth-century drawing of the tomb of Queen Mathilda (d. 1083) now in the choir of her church of the Holy Trinity at Caen. (Bodleian Library, Oxford, MS Gough drawings—Gaignières, f.2).

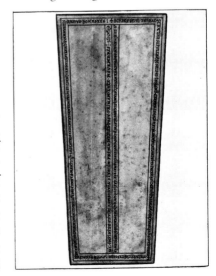

fuse them together to make *Normanitas* is perhaps another matter, and they certainly all contribute to that supreme and sovereign Norman confidence which meets us everywhere, whether crossing the Channel with their warhorses at night in open boats on course for England, or roofing in stone rather then wood the great churches of Durham or Lessay, or piercing the walls of Babylon with their charge in Anna Comnena's memorable phrase.

All the characteristics of mid-eleventh-century Normandy listed are also expansionist or make expansion possible as well as likely, and feed the high-vaunting ambition of Norman nobles, knights and clerics too. Here, then, we surely come close to the heart of Norman territorial aggrandisement and political achievement in this age. An expanding population, in particular the production of surplus and therefore landless knights in search of fiefs, is obviously expansionist, and so too can be their love and mastery of war to which they were born and bred. Feudalism also is expansionist if looked at from the top downwards at this particular stage of its development. For the eleventh century is *par excellence* the age of the feudal princes (at the end of it they, not kings and emperors, lead the First Crusade) and of the development of their feudal principalities, inevitably expansionist and therefore aggressive and competitive.

Lessay, vaulted nave and choir (late eleventh century).

The rivalry, by the 1050s already hereditary and traditional, between the dukes of Normandy and the counts of Anjou is very much a case in point, and resulted in war for the county of Maine which lay between them.[116] The ambitions of the princes for the extension of lordship were shared by their vassals who, with their knights, gave them effect and, also with their knights, received the rewards of further fiefs and lordships. Even the Church in Normandy can be seen as expansionist and the Norman religious revival of the eleventh century as expansionist in its tendencies. It was, after all and characteristically in this period, the *Norman* Church, presided over by the Norman duke and his archbishop at Rouen, and was in practice governed and largely staffed in its upper echelons by the same ruling families who ruled the rest of Normandy. In an age when men called upon their local saints as well as God for aid, the Church provided identity as well as inspiration, while the Norman association with and championship of the general contemporary movement of reform within Latin Christendom gave them a sense of mission and fed their notions of superiority, as well in England as in Italy and Antioch.[117] Certainly by the second half of the eleventh century the Norman Church had much to boast about, and by this route too we reach not only that ebullient self-confidence which lies at the heart of *Normanitas*, but also that most heady of all feelings, that God is on our side. Of course Orderic Vitalis was proud that the chant of St Evroul was sung in the Norman monasteries of Venosa, St Eufemia and Mileto in Capua and Calabria;[118] William the Conqueror could see Hastings as a triumphantly vindicated appeal to the judgement of God; and in the early twelfth century Ailred of Rievaulx could write of victory itself as a fief held of the Most High by the Normans.[119] There are also more prosaic considerations. The astonishing number of monasteries founded in Normandy in the first half of the eleventh century cannot have been over-endowed in spite of the wealth of most of their founders, and were therefore glad of endowment outside Normandy whatever the difficulties of management,[120] just as most Norman clerics, including monks, were willing to take preferment in their Norman commonwealth like nineteenth-century Oxford graduates in their Empire. There were also pilgrimages, a general feature of the eleventh-century religious revival, yet, like so much else, especially cultivated by the Normans.[121] These without doubt focussed attention upon far-flung opportunities, whether in Italy, on the long ride to Jerusalem, or in Spain en route to Santiago. Indeed, we may end this chapter with the observation that however long and close the analysis of Norman society in pursuit of an explanation of Norman achievement, not a little of that explanation must remain in a facility to grasp, and even to create, the opportunities that made it possible. Assuredly, if there is a tide in the affairs of men, the Normans took it at the flood.

Chapter 4 The Norman Conquest of England

The Norman Conquest of England did not come out of the blue as an arbitrary attack by an external enemy after the manner of the invasions intended by Napoleon in 1804 or Hitler in 1940 or launched by Swein Forkbeard in 1013. William the Conqueror, in his own eyes and others, sailed in 1066 as the legitimate heir to the English throne, and the sequence of political events leading directly to that situation began in 1002 with the marriage of Ethelred II, king of the English, to Emma of Normandy. Beyond that there is, of course, the context of Scandinavian conquest and settlement common to both countries,[1] wherein the invasion in 1066 by Harold Hardrada of Norway as well as that by William of Normandy are to be placed. Beyond that again, on the Norman side, there is an even broader context in which the conquest of England is to be seen and thus better understood. This is the thesis of the late John le Patourel to which reference has already been made,[2] that Norman expansion is not something confined to the later eleventh century and the great period of Norman territorial aggrandizement in England, Italy and Antioch, but in fact begins in the beginning as from 911 and moves inexorably to its climax through the conquest, settlement and expansion of Normandy itself and, at the same time, through a constant and largely successful expansionist pressure north-east towards Flanders via Ponthieu and Boulogne, south against Anjou via Maine, and south-west against Brittany. Further, this dynamic of expansion, given effect at first by the crude and basic Viking method of attack, and later by the more sophisticated processes (common to the developing feudal principalities of France[3]) of marriage, homage, suzerainty and aristocratic penetration, all backed up by force as necessary, not only created the Normandy of the 1050s but also a system of external relationships which made possible the events of 1066. By then Normandy's immediate northern neighbour, Ponthieu, from which the invasion fleet in the event set sail (from St Valery-sur-Somme), was in the duke's *mouvance* or suzerainty, and its count, Guy, was his vassal, as may also have been count Eustace of Boulogne, who was certainly his ally and a participant at Hastings. Count Baldwin of Flanders, as William's father-in-law, was also his ally—and was, besides, the guardian of the young French king, Philip, then a minor. The great county of Maine fell to William in 1063 by conquest to vindicate his right through a marriage treaty, and his eldest son Robert, who had been betrothed to the heiress, was made count thereof. By 1066, further-more, the unremitting efforts of the Norman dukes to impose their suzerainty upon Brittany had become so far successful that a particularly large contingent of Bretons fought (on the left wing) at Hastings,[4] in addition to the Flemings and the men of Maine. Throughout all this we may also see the Norman method and pattern of expansion, in an almost exclusively aristocratic coloniz-ation, of lords and knights, prelates and monks, by means of castles, monasteries and churches, as evident in the absorption of Lower Normandy, for example, as it is in the conquests of England, Italy and Antioch.

The fateful marriage in 1002 of Ethelred II to Emma, daughter of Duke Richard I, to which reference has already been made,[5] must be regarded as the beginning of any political history of the Norman Conquest of England. It was, in Freeman's words, 'the first act of the drama'.[6] From it there sprang, of course, the eventual Con-queror's kin-right without which there could have been no con-quest. From it there also sprang the Norman sympathies and preference of Edward the Confessor, son of Ethelred and Emma and long in exile in his mother's land, which led him to nominate his kinsman William as his heir. Without that, again, there could have been no conquest, for it is the very bedrock of the Norman case. Here we must note before proceeding further the controversy which has always surrounded the Great Matter of the English succession in 1066. Some of the most telling facts in William's favour, notably his formal recognition as King Edward's heir, and Harold's 'oath' in 1064,[7] are found only in the Norman sources, and have in consequence often been questioned, sometimes to the point of denial, as propaganda, a mere 'Norman version of events'. It needs therefore to be firmly stated at the outset that while, of course, one makes allowance for a natural Norman bias when studying William of Jumièges, William of Poitiers and the Bayeux Tapestry,[8] there is no good reason to reject the actual events they relate, or repudiate their unanimous testimony. If, indeed, they were telling the truth, so would they also all say the same thing. In any case, their unanimity can be exaggerated: unlike William of Jumièges' history, William of Poitiers' biography, at least as we have it, scarcely begins before the Conqueror's accession in 1035, and the Tapestry begins only in 1064. Further, they can disagree on important minor points such as the place of Harold's oath.[9] It must be emphasized also that there is no English version of events to counter the Norman. The English literary sources, consisting for the most part of the various recensions of the Anglo-Saxon Chron-icle, 'Florence' of Worcester[10] and the *Vita Edwardi*, do not in fact deny the Norman account but, rather, may be held to confirm it, either positively by the few relevant statements which they do make, or—it may be thought—negatively by the enigmatic and suspect silences of the Chronicle especially. Finally, and by contrast, it is to be noted that the strongest point that can be made in Harold's favour, the death-bed bequest of the kingdom by the dying Edward, is in fact accepted by William of Poitiers, normally considered the most prejudiced and panegyric of the Norman writers,[11] and also evidently by the Tapestry.[12]

The marriage of Ethelred and Emma also brought Normans to England in the new queen's household, the first known Norman penetration of the country, we may say,[13] to be significantly reinforced when Edward succeeded to the throne in 1042.[14] Emma herself, of course, queen of two kings of England and mother to two more, clearly requires at least a mention in this respect.[15] As for Edward's exile at the Norman court, the first point to note about it is its length. Born probably in 1005,[16] he was therefore only some

Queen Emma, being presented with the *Encomium Emmae* by its author: on the right, two of her sons, king Harthacnut and the future king Edward the Confessor (Mid-eleventh-century MS of the *Encomium*, BL Add.MSS 33241 f. 1v).

eight years old when, in 1013, Ethelred sent him and his younger brother Alfred 'across the sea', with the bishop of London to 'take care of them', to follow their mother to Normandy.[17] When he finally returned to England in 1041 to share the kingdom with his half-brother Harthacnut and become full king on the latter's death in 1042,[18] he was approaching forty and (save for his abortive visit or expedition of 1036 on Cnut's death)[19] had been absent for nearly thirty years from the realm of which he can have had almost no personal recollection. Nor is there any evidence to suggest that during those long years he had spent any length of time anywhere else but Normandy.[20] Nor in such circumstances need we doubt Norman official support for the cause of the aethlings, made manifest by their constant presence at the ducal court; nor Edward's lasting gratitude for it, not unreasonably emphasized by William of Poitiers especially; nor Edward's Norman sympathies and predilections, which are the context of his naming William as his heir. Especially if we recall the compelling attraction of contemporary Norman society which adopted so many immigrants,[21] by 1041 and 1042 the Confessor must have been in many ways more Norman than English. Moreover, he was to find himself in a land dominated not by an English but by an Anglo-Scandinavian aristocracy, descendants of or collaborators with those who had driven out his family. The most prominent among them was Godwin earl of Wessex who was implicated in the murder of his brother Alfred, yet who (according to Florence of Worcester), was particularly instrumental in Edward's own succession to the throne and whose daughter, Edith, he was required to marry. The banishment of earl Godwin and his sons overseas, and of Edith to a nunnery in 1051, is surely sufficient commentary on King Edward's personal and political situation in his realm in the first decade of his reign.[22]

Cnut's marriage to Emma in his turn, after the death of Ethelred, may have been intended, as suggested above,[23] to neutralize Norman support for Edward and Alfred, her sons by Ethelred, and may have succeeded in so far as the Norman sources make no reference to any activity in this respect by Richard II beyond the shelter afforded them at his court. Under Robert the Magnificent, however, positive support for the aethlings' cause seems certain. William of Jumièges records even the launching of a great expedition (about 1033 or 1034) to reinstate the princes in England, prevented from crossing the Channel only by the weather, stormbound at Jersey and diverted to Mont-St-Michel.[24] These events are also referred to by the later writer William of Malmesbury,[25] who himself may have derived the information from William of Jumièges, but was also a careful historian. A year or two later Jumièges also records the arrival at the ducal court of an embassy sent by Cnut, then very ill, offering half the English kingdom to the aethlings, though nothing came of this because of duke Robert's departure for Jerusalem, on which pilgrimage he died,[26] and because of Cnut's subsequent death also. There is, in addition, the scarcely less dramatic evidence of two surviving Norman ducal charters emanating from these last years of exile, both accepted as genuine by their latest editor, in which Edward is given the title of

Here duke William commanded ships to be built. Bishop Odo sits on the duke's left.

The construction of the invasion fleet

Here they drag the ships to sea.

Here they carry arms to the ships.

And here they drag a cart with wine and arms. Note the hauberks.   The embarkation. *Here William in a great ship*

crossed the ocean

(note the transportation of the war horses) *and came to Pevensey.*

king of England. The first is a grant by Edward himself, described as *Dei gratia rex Anglorum*, of land in England to Mont-St-Michel, whereon the first subscription is appropriately that of *regis Edwardi* and the second of *Roberti comitis*, *i.e.* duke Robert. It is dated by Marie Fauroux as probably 1033–4 because it seems to fit exactly the abortive expedition at that time.[27] The second is a grant by Robert the Magnificent to Fécamp, dated between 1031 and 1035 and with the subscription again of *Edwardi regis*.[28] Soon after the death of Cnut and probably in 1036 both Edward and Alfred in turn made unsuccessful expeditions to England.[29] They did so presumably with Norman aid, though the fact is not stressed either by William of Jumièges[30] or William of Poitiers[31], and the time was unpropitious in the circumstances of Duke Robert's absence and death (in July 1035) and the troubled succession of the young William his son, a minor. The most important result for the future was the murder of Alfred in England on the orders of Harold Harefoot, Cnut's successor, and with the complicity of earl Godwin whom, there is reason to believe, Edward never forgave for the crime.[32] We do not know the precise circumstances in which Harthacnut, son of Cnut and Emma, invited his half-brother Edward from Normandy to share the English kingdom with him in 1041—and so to succeed him when the former died, 'standing at his drink' at Lambeth the next year.[33] The Anglo-Saxon Chronicle, as usual, is enigmatic on such matters, and of course we, as usual, must discount the obvious exaggerations of William of Poitiers in making duke William, then aged about thirteen,[34] personally responsible by his diplomacy and threats of force.[35] Nevertheless we can scarcely doubt that when the middle-aged Confessor crossed to England with a small Norman escort (which in fact is all that William of Poitiers gives him) in 1041, and became king in 1042, he was and had long been the official candidate of the Norman court, was not likely to forget it, and found himself a stranger in his own country.

From then on there is, again, an overall consistency and coherence in the pattern of known political events which leads to 1066 and the Norman Conquest of England. Edward's coming to England and his accession to the throne were inevitably the occasion for a second phase of Norman aristocratic penetration of the country[36] through the medium of his so-called 'Norman favourites'—those he brought with him or who followed him to England—whose importance is neither to be exaggerated nor denied.[37] The matter is most reasonably and naturally stated by the anonymous author of the *Vita Edwardi*: 'When King Edward of holy memory returned from Francia, quite a number of men of that nation, and they not base born, accompanied him. And these, since he was master of the whole kingdom, he kept with him, enriched them with many honours, and made them his privy counsellors and administrators of the royal palace'.[38] Thus established in England, their numbers included one earl, Ralph count of the Vexin, Edward's nephew and made earl of Hereford, in which shire he and his Norman and French followers characteristically built the first castles in England and Wales;[39] Ralph the Staller and Robert fitz Wimarc, the former probably a Breton and the latter also probably the founder of a castle, at Clavering in Essex;[40] and three bishops, Ulf at Dorchester and Robert of Jumièges at London, the latter succeeded by William when he himself was translated to Canterbury in 1051. The *Vita Edwardi* leaves no doubt that Robert, abbot of Jumièges, was the most influential of these men as the closest confidant of the king. Further, according to the same writer, Robert's promotion to Canterbury in the teeth of a rival candidate who was both a kinsman and a protegé of earl Godwin, and Robert's hostility to the earl, and raking up of the smouldering embers of the scandal of the murder of the king's brother Alfred, leads straight into the crisis of 1051–2.[41]

The scene next shifts to 1051, in which year earl Godwin and his sons defied the king, and the kingdom was brought to the brink of civil war, both before and after their ensuing exile (the Scandinavian *ullac*, it would seem, being as prevalent in England as in Normandy).[42] Of that undoubtedly serious crisis,[43] it seems both impossible to be satisfied with the inadequate cause given by the Anglo-Saxon Chronicle—that Godwin refused to obey the royal order to harry Dover as punishment for a *fracas* between the townsmen and the men of Count Eustace of Boulogne when the latter was making a visit to the king—and impossible not to believe that the Great Matter of the succession, and more particularly of Edward's promise of it to duke William, was already the real issue. The Norman chroniclers, of course, William of Jumièges and William of Poitiers, insist upon that promise and formal recognition of the duke as Edward's heir, subsequently confirmed by Harold, Godwin's son, in Normandy in 1064.[44] The promise was made with the agreement upon oath of the English magnates including Godwin, notification was taken to the duke in Normandy by Robert of Jumièges, and hostages (Wulfnoth his son and Hakon his grandson) were sent to Normandy as surety for Godwin's good faith. Further, if this is accepted—and we have almost nothing save silence to set against it on the English side—the date can only be 1051, notably because of the participation of Robert of Jumièges as archbishop of Canterbury, presumably en route to Rome for his *pallium*, and driven from the kingdom in 1052 on the triumphant return of Godwin and his sons. Count Eustace, whose visit requires an explanation not afforded by the Anglo-Saxon Chronicle,[45] then most probably becomes an emissary in the matter—a role for which he was well suited as the friend and ally of duke William, and as Edward's brother-in-law. (He was the second husband of Gode, Edward's sister, whom he had married through Norman ducal patronage). The *fracas* at Dover itself may well have arisen as the result of Eustace's attempt to take over the fortress as further surety for the duke's succession.[46] Curiously enough, while never explicitly admitting that the question of the succession to the throne was at the bottom of the affair of 1051, the English sources may be thought dramatically to confirm it by a statement unique to two of them. After the banishment of earl Godwin and his sons and the dismissal of queen Edith to the nunnery of Wherwell, the 'D' version of the Anglo-Saxon Chronicle states: 'Then forthwith count William came from overseas with a great force of Frenchmen, and the king received him and as many of his companions as suited him, and let him go again.'[47] Florence of Worcester, having added significantly that Edith was sent to Wherwell without honour and with only one female attendant, renders the passage in Latin thus: 'When these things were done, the Norman count William came to England with a large body of Normans, and the king received him and his companions with honour, and sent them back to Normandy in due course with many and great gifts.'[48]

By 1052, however, what must surely be seen as king Edward's bid for political liberty and mastery in his own house had failed; earl Godwin was back in arms and reinstated in the kingdom with his sons, and his daughter the queen restored to her husband's side.[49] Their triumphant return evidently meant also the triumph of an anti-Norman faction, for many (not all) of Edward's Norman friends were driven from the kingdom, including Robert of Jumièges, who was replaced at Canterbury by Stigand, a creature of earl Godwin and whose uncanonical and flagrantly political appointment to the archiepiscopal see, which he held in plurality with Winchester, was to furnish the Norman duke and champion of ecclesiastical reform with an invaluable propaganda weapon in 1066 and after. An attack upon the Confessor's Norman preferences, hopes and plans must also be the context of the arrival in England in 1057 of Edward 'the Exile', son of Edmund 'Ironside' (son of Ethelred II and his first wife, Ælgifu), sent for by the king in 1054 specifically to be proclaimed as heir to the kingdom, according to Florence.[50] The prince, however, died on arrival, and the Anglo-Saxon Chronicle 'D' makes the situation more confused by more than hinting at foul play—'We do not know for what reason it was brought about that he was not allowed to see [the face?] of his kinsman king Edward'.[51] Unless we suppose the promotion of the aethling Edward to have been imposed upon the king, it stands out as inconsistent in an otherwise consistent series of events. Stenton thus suggested long ago that the Confessor may never have recovered from 'his humiliation before Godwin in 1052', and that while keeping in touch with public affairs 'he abandoned the attempt to control them', devoting his energies instead to his foundation of Westminster Abbey[52]—though that, one may add, is dramatic evidence enough of the continuing preference of his heart, as it is a Norman church before the Norman Conquest, completely un-English and with affinities especially with Jumièges.[53] After Godwin's death in 1053, earl Harold, with his brothers, inexorably rose to a position of dominance in England greater even than that of his father—he himself as earl of Wessex augmented by Herefordshire, his brothers Tostig (until the rebellion against him in 1065) earl of Northumbria, Gyrth earl of East Anglia with Oxfordshire, and Leofwine with a new earldom of Essex, Hertfordshire, Middlesex and Buckinghamshire.[54]

The next event in the series leading to 1066 is Harold's visit to Normandy, at a date which can only be 1064, sent by Edward to confirm his promise of the succession—an event insisted upon by William of Jumièges and William of Poitiers as central to William's case, portrayed on the Bayeux Tapestry, and completely ignored

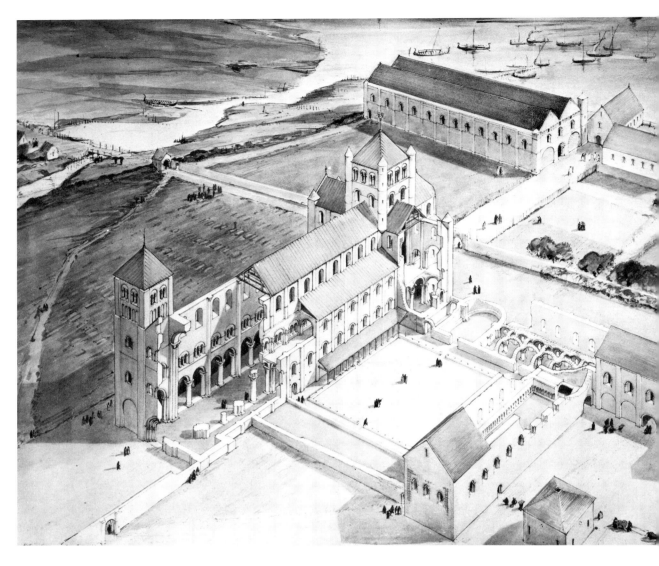

by the English sources. Indeed, the Anglo-Saxon Chronicle has no entry for the year 1064 in any of its versions.[55] William of Jumièges is brief in his relation, as is his habit, but William of Poitiers gives a detailed account which is followed by and large on the Tapestry (where, however, Harold's oath follows, rather than precedes, the Breton expedition, and takes place at Bayeux, not Bonneville-sur-Touques).[56] Poitiers, as might be expected, lays emphasis upon every obligation under which Earl Harold (*secundus a rege*) was placed—his release from imprisonment in Ponthieu by the duke's good offices; the honour done him by the duke in taking him upon the Breton expedition as a companion in arms; the release to him of Hakon, his nephew, one of the two hostages taken from Earl Godwin in 1051; the rich gifts with which he was laden on departure[57]—while the well-known scene upon the Tapestry wherein William bestows arms upon Harold must surely represent his knighting and is thus a further honour done him.[58] The centrepiece of Poitiers' account, however, as of the Tapestry,[59] is Harold's oath to William, and it must be stressed that the former is the only contemporary detailed written version that we have. In it Harold's

Westminster Abbey church, from the
Bayeux Tapestry.

Jumièges, east end (dedicated 1067).

57

oaths touching the succession to the English throne are separate and additional clauses or codicils added to a formal oath of fealty, and the swearing is only the first part of the full ceremony of feudal commendation. The duke next receives Harold as his vassal by homage and subsequently invests him with all his lands and honours in England.[60] Here, then, is the Norman technique of feudal penetration and the imposition of lordship as the means of expansion employed at the highest level, to be compared with the homage taken from Herbert count of Maine between 1058 and 1060 which led to the occupation of that county in 1063.[61] It may also be noted that Harold's investiture safeguarded his position as the pre-eminent magnate in England; it is therefore possible that at this stage he had not yet decided to seize the crown himself on Edward's death.[62] As for Harold's oaths in confirmation of the duke's succession, they may be summarized as follows: that he would be the representative (*vicarius*) of William at the English court during Edward's lifetime and do all he could to ensure his succession after the king's death; and that he would meanwhile hand over to William's knights the fortress of Dover and other castles in other places where the duke should wish them to be raised.

In the event, of course, Harold did seize the throne as the penultimate act in a drama which was to reach its denouement at Hastings, and was crowned on Friday 6 January, 1066, the day after the old king's death and the very day of his funeral, the two ceremonies following each other in the Confessor's great new church of Westminster. Further, he was evidently crowned by the uncanonical and schismatic Stigand,[63] which fact the Normans used as one more nail in the coffin of his reputation as perjurer and usurper. On the Tapestry the scenes of Harold's coronation are accompanied in the upper border by the comet, 'the long-haired star', foretelling doom, and the ghostly ships of the coming Norman invasion in the lower.[64]

On the eve of Hastings William of Poitiers has the duke send to Harold by a monk of Fécamp a formal statement of his claim which is a useful summary of the Norman case.[65] King Edward, his kinsman, had made William his heir in gratitude for the benefits which he and his brother Alfred had received from the Norman court, and because Edward thought him the most worthy member of the royal stock. This was done with the assent of the English magnates, and with the counsel specifically of Stigand and earls Godwin of Wessex, Leofric of Marcia and Siward of Northumbria, who had sworn to receive William as lord after Edward's death and do nothing against his succession during the king's lifetime. As surety, Edward gave William the son and grandson of Godwin as hostages, and finally sent Harold to Normandy to 'swear to me there in my presence what his father and the above named had sworn in my absence'. The duke had obtained Harold's release from captivity in Ponthieu, and Harold had done him homage and confirmed the duke's succession to the English kingdom. On these grounds William was prepared to plead his case by the law either of Normandy or England, or, if Harold refused, to wage single combat against him to prove his better right to the crown.

As for Harold,[66] he had, of course, his *de facto* coronation, and he may well have received before it recognition or acceptance as the rightful successor by the magnates assembled in London for the dedication of Westminster and the Christmas feast. He had, however, no kin-right, no drop of royal blood from the ancient house of Wessex, and had, in Norman eyes at least, both perjured himself and gone against the declared wishes of the dead king in an age when perjury was an appalling offence against both God and man and the will of the reigning king of paramount importance in the selection of a royal heir. The main point in his favour, and the central fact in his case, was the alleged death-bed bequest of the kingdom to him by Edward. To this all the English sources refer, though in the nature of things we can never know what happened as the king lay dying, whether any bequest he made was extracted or freely given, or whether he was in any condition to know what he was doing. The only detailed account is that given in the *Vita Edwardi*, and there Edward's words as reported scarcely seem to bear the interpretation of anything so momentous as a grant of the succession, the throne and the kingdom.[67] Edward's first concern is for his wife and queen (the work, of course, was written in honour of Edith and under her patronage): the kingdom comes second, and after that the king's Norman friends in England. All three are put without distinction under Harold's protection, and if a precise interpretation is to be made one is reminded chiefly of Harold's oath in 1064, that he would be William's *vicarius*, representative or proxy in England, *i.e.* until the duke should take up his inheritance.[68] 'And stretching forth his hand to his governor (*nutricium*), her brother, Harold, he said, "I commend this woman and all the kingdom to your protection, that you may serve and honour her with faithful obedience as your lady and sister, which she is, and do not despoil her, as long as she lives, of any honour got from me. Likewise I commend those men who have left their native land for love of me . . . that you may protect and retain them or . . . send them safely home"'. But be that as it may, William of Poitiers, the jurist and Norman apologist, accepted the death-bed bequest to Harold as a fact,[69] though holding it invalid against the earlier donation to his lord and master. In Poitiers' account, however, Harold takes the contrary view—'For since the time when the blessed Augustine came into this country', Harold is made to say, 'it has been the common custom of this nation that a gift made at the point of death is valid.' If indeed there is a conflict of custom here as between England and Normandy, and therefore of understanding, then a further dimension is added to the drama of 1066.

After Harold's coronation that drama swiftly unfolds. The Tapestry shows a ship bearing the news to Normandy and thereafter vividly depicts the preparations for the expedition which are, necessarily, no less impressive than the conquest itself.[70] Councils had to be held to obtain the consent of the Norman magnates and arrange for the government and security of the duchy in the absence not only of the duke and most of his vassals but also the majority of their fighting men. A whole fleet had evidently to be constructed (Wace gives the number of ships as 696) able to transport the horses as well as the warriors,[71] and a great army assembled supplemented by contingents of volunteers from other lands, since the enterprise was beyond the resources of Normandy alone.[72] They came, especially landless knights, the characteristic product of the age and place, attracted by the lure of adventure, loot and fiefs in conquered lands, and by William's good pay, well-known generosity and, above all, his victorious military reputation. Also, William of Poitiers assures us, they were attracted by the justice of the Norman cause—a point that probably should not be under-estimated amongst the conscience-stricken as well as bellicose chivalry of northern France.[73] The total Norman fighting force which sailed for England in the autumn of 1066 can be estimated at perhaps some 7000 men, made up of 4–5000 infantry and 2–3000 knights and mounted esquires, each surely with more than one horse.[74] Such numbers, to be matched by a roughly equal total by Harold at Hastings inspite of the haste of his movements and the preceding battle of Stamford Bridge, are prodigious by contemporary standards,[75] and it is worth noting that the Anglo-Saxon Chronicle says of Harold's own preparations in the summer that he mobilized forces by land and sea 'larger than any king had assembled before in this country'.[76] Further, duke William kept his force together without loss of discipline nor substantially of morale[77] for six weary weeks of waiting, first at Dives-sur-Mer and then at St-Valery-sur-Somme, from 12 August until at last he got the wind he prayed for on 27 September.[78] Then, on the evening tide, his armada was launched, deliberately and as planned, at the Sussex shore and the heartlands of the Godwinson patrimony.[79] Meanwhile on the other side of the Channel the long delay had proved too much for Harold's military system, thus throwing duke William's organization into sharper relief. The English forces which all through the summer were stood-to along the south-east coast had to be dismissed at the end of the first week in September. 'The provisions of the people were gone, and no one could keep them there any longer'.[80]

Duke William also, again apparently in marked contrast to Harold, included a veritable diplomatic offensive amongst his preparations, which won over what may be called the public opinion of Europe to his side. Alliances of some kind were concluded with the imperial court of the young Henry IV of Germany and even with Swein Estrithson of Sweden, himself a potential claimant to the English throne through descent from Swein Forkbeard and kinship with Cnut. Most important of all, the duke obtained the approbation of the Papacy and papal blessing and a papal banner for the enterprise, thus winning recognition of the justice of his cause from the highest court in Latin Christendom.[81] Nor did the Normans as faithful sons of Holy Church omit to make their peace with God before they embarked upon their great adventure, led in this as in all things by their duke who was submitting his claim to the arbitrament of the Just Judge. In June 1066 William and his duchess Mathilda presided over the dedication of her church of the Holy Trinity at Caen and gave their daughter Cecilia to religion in that place, while a well-known charter of the

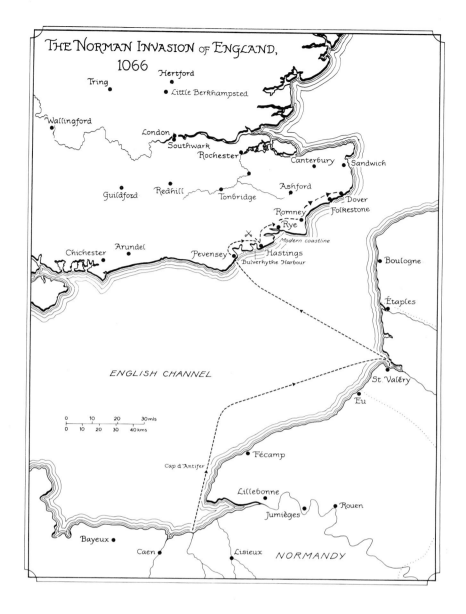

THE NORMAN INVASION OF ENGLAND, 1066

duke dating from this time records the grant to his abbey of Fécamp of the land of Steyning in Sussex to take effect 'if God should give him victory in England'.[82] Indeed it must often have seemed that God was on their side and victory held as a fief from Heaven.[83] Modern historians have pointed out the good fortune which attended the Norman venture against England, which could scarcely have been undertaken before 1066 when king Edward died. By then both William's principal enemies, the French king Henry and the Angevin count Geoffrey were dead, while in the event, in 1066, the English kingdom was to be invaded first by Harold Hardrada of Norway, and severely weakened at Gate Fulford and Stamford Bridge, while the Norman fleet was land-locked at St-Valéry-sur-Somme.[84]

Nevertheless, the Norman Conquest of England is not to be explained away by the luck of Fortune's favourites, for in these matters we may see the characteristic Norman gift for seizing

61

Holy Trinity, Caen, dedicated in June 1066. The church was by no means then finished and the west front was (badly) altered in the seventeenth and nineteenth centuries.

St-Valery-sur-Somme, the estuary from which the Norman fleet sailed on the night of 27–28 September 1066.

opportunities and bending circumstances to their will.[85] We must also surely see more weakness in the Old English kingdom than modern English historians are often ready to admit although to exaggerate its strength will not help us to understand its defeat in 1066. Conquered by Swein Forkbeard and Cnut only 50 years before Hastings, far from united (especially as between north and south), presided over by a weak king and an over-mighty earl representing the Anglo-Scandinavian ascendancy whose dominance was resented by the surviving Old English house of Leofric (earls Edwin and Morcar of Mercia and Northumbria respectively), old-fashioned in its organization and not least its military system, England on the eve of the Norman Conquest presents to the neutral historian plenty of internal reasons to explain a Norman victory in what was in effect one more disputed succession to the throne.[86] Of the two principal contenders in that dispute, it also seems probable that William knew his man and exploited his pride and impetuosity as well as his assailable legal position. He certainly succeeded in drawing Harold, on whose side time ran, to the quick and decisive battle that he needed, without himself leaving his base and ships on the Sussex coast; and he may have done so by the deliberate provocation of invading Harold's patrimony and ravaging the lands about Pevensey and Hastings.[87]

On the night of 27–28 September 1066 the Norman fleet crossed the Channel from St-Valery-sur-Somme and landed unopposed at Pevensey the next morning.[88] The English defence force in the south-east had been dismissed on 8 September and Harold was by now with his army in the north where he had won his great victory over Harold Hardrada (with his ally Tostig, Harold's brother) at Stamford Bridge on 25 September. The ancient Roman fort of Anderida was then probably defensible as an Anglo-Saxon burgh or

The castle of Pevensey within the old English burgh and former Roman fort of Anderida. The present castle of mainly thirteenth-century date occupies the site of the Norman castle of 1066.

fortified town, but the main Norman force, having raised a castle in it, moved on to the similar fortress at Hastings, where they established an even better base and raised another castle.[89] Harold received news of the Norman landing on or about 1 October at York and at once set off on his last campaign. It seems clear that his intention was to repeat his strategy and tactics of Stamford Bridge, when the rapidity of his movements, and especially his great march of 190 miles from London to York, had enabled him to take the Norwegian Harold's forces by surprise. Now within the space of thirteen days at most he had covered again the distance between York and London with all those who could keep up with him, paused in the latter city as short a time as possible to raise more forces, and gone on another 50 or 60 miles into Sussex to be approaching Hastings by the evening of Friday 13 October. This time, however, the advantage of surprise attack was taken from him. Norman mounted reconnaissance informed the duke of his enemy's approach on that same Friday. That night the Normans stood to arms in case of night attack, and at first light moved off in the known direction of the enemy, thus turning the tables, seizing the initiative and, in the event, in the words of the Chronicle, coming against Harold 'by surprise before his army was drawn up in battle array.'[90] The Normans first saw the English from Telham Hill, and the English the Normans from the ridge at what has ever since been Battle,[91] where Harold was constrained to fight his defensive engagement in a position admirably chosen on the spur of the moment but yet with disadvantages. There was no way of withdrawal save the narrow isthmus along which he had come, which is now Battle High Street, and the space was too confined even for the reduced forces to which his haste had condemned him.[92]

And so at 9 a.m. on Saturday 14 October the battle began, with numbers roughly equal on both sides, at some 7000,[93] the English, all dismounted and on foot, occupying the ridge of Battle where the Norman monastery now stands (the high altar of the church on the spot where Harold fell), the Norman army below with the lie of the land against them. The duke disposed his forces in three divisions with Bretons on the left (west), Normans in the centre, and 'French' (everyone else) on his right. Each division was in three lines, with archers and perhaps crossbow-men in front, then heavy infantry, and third the chivalry and heavy cavalry of knights to deliver the hoped-for *coup de grace* by the shock tactic of their charge. Their enemy, the English, were densely massed in the close formation poetically known as the 'shield-wall', seemingly short of archers[94] and their élite troops at least, the housecarls of the king and earls, armed with the dreadful Scandinavian weapon of the two-handed battle axe. They stood, wrote William of Poitiers, as if rooted to the soil, with scarcely room for the slain to fall or the wounded to remove themselves from the line, and he comments on the strange kind of battle, as it was in Norman eyes, with all the mobility on one side.[95] All day long the battle raged, the English impenetrable even to the knights who were repeatedly hurled against them. At

Aerial view of the site of the Battle of Hastings at Battle, Sussex. The abbey occupying the centre of the English position on the ridge is top centre. The line of Harold's approach is from top left, and of William's from top right.

65

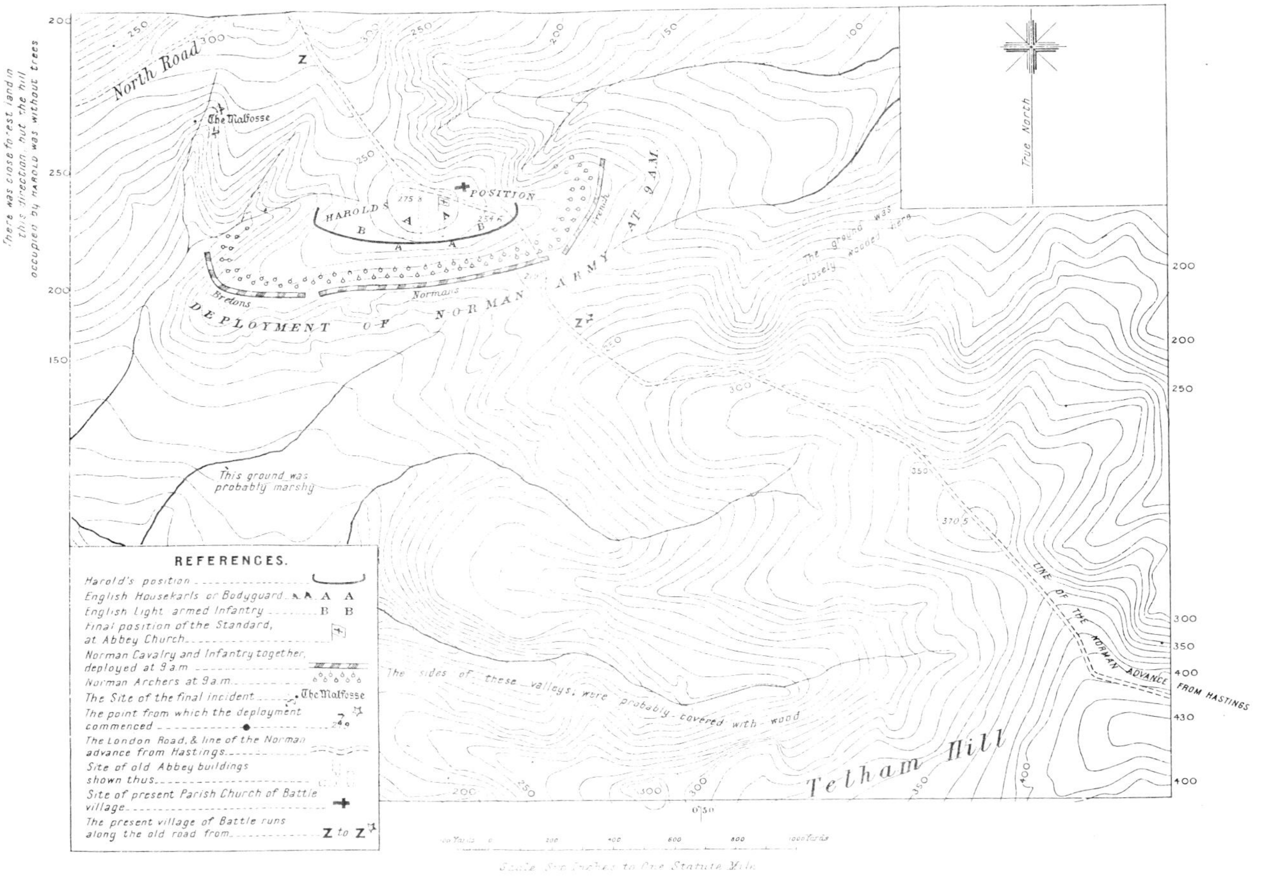
North Road
The Malfosse
There was close forest land in this direction, but the hill occupied by Harold was without trees
Harold's Position
Bretons
Normans
Deployment of Norman Army at 9 A.M.
The ground was closely wooded here
True North
This ground was probably marshy
The sides of these valleys were probably covered with wood
Telham Hill
Line of the Norman Advance from Hastings
REFERENCES.
Harold's position
English Housekarls or Bodyguard
English light armed Infantry
Final position of the Standard, at Abbey Church
Norman Cavalry and Infantry together, deployed at 9 a.m.
Norman Archers at 9 a.m.
The Site of the final incident
The point from which the deployment commenced
The London Road, & line of the Norman advance from Hastings
Site of old Abbey buildings shown thus
Site of present Parish Church of Battle village
The present village of Battle runs along the old road from Z to Z

Plan of the Battle of Hastings by General E. Renouard James, from F. H. Baring, *Domesday Tables* (1909). The position of the Malfosse is best ignored.

one quite early stage a crisis developed. The Bretons on the left began to give way, the English to pursue them. The movement spread across the whole Norman army, fanned by the rumour that the duke was dead. The rot was stopped by William himself, in a scene vividly portrayed on the Tapestry[96] as the duke bares his head to show his face, Count Eustace of Boulogne points him out to those in doubt, and Odo bishop of Bayeux, brandishing his mace of authority, turns back the young esquires (*pueros*) who are fleeing. 'Look at me. I am alive, and, by God's help, I shall win. What madness puts you to flight . . .': thus in William of Poitiers' account the duke, who straightway leads a counter-attack to cut down the pursuing English.[97]

In William of Poitiers' account it is now also that the Normans, noting how the English had broken ranks to follow up the previous retreat and then been easily cut down, successfully applied the well-known tactic of the 'feigned flight' repeatedly to draw down and destroy considerable numbers of their opponents who were otherwise still immovable as the long day wore on.[98] Finally, as the autumnal dusk descended, an all-out assault by Norman horse and foot at length achieved the objective: the English position was penetrated at its centre, and Harold slain at the foot of his standard. It seems fitting to leave the epilogue to William of Poitiers, the former knight and chaplain of the Conqueror, whose prose, even in translation, rises elegiacally to the occasion.

'Now as the day declined (*Jam inclinato die*) the English army realized beyond doubt that they could no longer stand against the Normans. They knew that they were reduced by heavy losses; that the king himself, with his brothers and many magnates of the realm had fallen; that those who still stood were almost drained of strength; that they could expect no help. They saw the Normans not much diminished by casualties, threatening them more keenly than in the beginning, as if they had found new strength in the fight; they saw that fury of the duke who spared no one who resisted him; they saw that courage which could only find rest in victory. They therefore turned to a flight . . .'[99]

The Norman knights, hot with the fire of victory, pursued them far into the dark and broken countryside (though the well known incident of the Malfosse is less than certain)[100] and when the duke, who had led them in this as in all things, returned to the battlefield, he found it, literally we may well believe, strewn with 'the flower of English nobility and youth'.[101] The strength of England, or perhaps we should say the strength of Harold, lay dead.

After the battle the duke rested in his camp at Hastings five days, evidently to await submissions, which never came, from the remaining English leaders. Then he went straight to Dover, which surrendered to him, and stayed eight days while a castle was raised within the existing burgh.[102] There followed, delayed by dysentery in his army and the duke's own sickness, the slow, intimidating and encircling advance upon London (after the manner of that upon Le Mans in Maine three years before) where in the confusion the aethling Edgar, son of that aethling Edward who had died mysteriously in 1057, was elected king. The cities of Canterbury and Winchester submitted, and the Thames was crossed at Wallingford

Dover castle, Kent, air view from the north. The site of the first Norman castle of 1066 was in the vicinity of the church (centre rear) and the thirteenth-century earthwork about it. The subsequent taking-in of the entire area of the old English burgh and former Iron Age fortress is mainly the work of the twelfth and thirteenth centuries.

where Stigand the archbishop came in and did homage to the duke, denying Edgar. At (Little) Berkhampstead,[103] at a date which must be December, many other surviving English leaders submitted, including the young Edgar himself and the citizens of London. An advance party was sent into the city to prepare both fortifications, *i.e.* castles, and the Conqueror's coronation, and soon afterwards the duke rode in without opposition. He was crowned king of the English, by Archbishop Ealdred of York and not the uncanonical Stigand, on Christmas Day 1066, in the Confessor's new and prophetically Norman church of Westminster, which thus witnessed two coronations in the first memorable year of its existence.

Though Hastings is undoubtedly one of the decisive battles of Western history, the issue cannot have seemed so certain to contemporaries and even we can scarcely call the Norman Conquest finished before 1071. At the time of his coronation the new king directly controlled only a fraction of his kingdom. After it and the Christmas festivities, he himself withdrew from London to Barking in Essex, where further submissions were made to him including it seems, those of earls Edwin and Morcar,[104] and while fortifications against the fickle and savage population were completed in London—presumably the three early castles there of Montfichet, Baynard's Castle and the future Tower.[105] Thence he moved on into East Anglia and raised a castle at Norwich which he put in charge of his closest friend, William fitz Osbern, soon to be earl of Hereford and lord of the Isle of Wight.[106] Next came celebration, more heartfelt even than that which followed his coronation, as the king-duke in March 1067 made his triumphant return to Normandy in thanksgiving for his victory.[107] Many English notables were taken with him—Edgar aethling, earls Edwin and Morcar, earl Waltheof the son of earl Siward, Stigand of Canterbury and others—partly as trophies, partly as hostages and to ensure peace in his absence, but nobly treated. The fleet which bore the glittering company from Pevensey in commemoration had white sails as symbols of peace and victory. In Normandy, though it was still winter the sun shone as if it were summer, and though it was still Lent the churches brought forward Easter in the king-duke's honour.[108] Amongst the joyful round of mainly ecclesiastical festivities recorded were, characteristically, the dedications of two great new abbatial churches at St-Pierre-sur-Dives and Jumièges.[109]

Already, however, there had been trouble in his absence—a rising in the west led by the dissident Edric the Wild in alliance with Welsh princes, and the curious affair of an unsuccessful attack upon the new castle of Dover by William's erstwhile ally Count Eustace of Boulogne.[110] A new and more serious dimension of danger was given to such piecemeal hostilities by the threat of intervention by Swein of Denmark, himself a claimant to the English throne, though he had stood aside in 1066.[111] The king returned to England early in December 1067, and after the Christmas festivities in London, was forced upon a winter campaign in the south-west where Exeter stood against him. The city was besieged and taken

Here duke William exhorts his knights

William bears a mace here as an emblem of authority.

to prepare themselves courageously and wisely for battle against the English army

Note the gonfanons on some lances, and the lances used overarm, underarm and couched (only one is certainly thrown).

Though the knights dominate the scene, note also the archers.

The English are drawn up in the close formation of the shield–wall.
Note the two–handed battle–axe (and the single archer).

Here fell Leofwine and Gyrth, the brothers of king Harold. Note again the couched lance
and the dreadful two–handed battle–axe capable of felling both horse and rider.

Here Bishop Odo holding a mace puts heart into the young men.

Here English and French fall together in battle. This scene
may be the origin of one tradition of the *Malfosse*.

ere is duke William   Eustace (of Boulogne).
    For this scene, see p.66

Here the French fight on

and those who were with Harold have fallen.

The death of Harold. *Here Harold is slain*

and the English have turned to flight.

The chapel of St John, part of the royal suite in king William's White Tower of London.

and a castle planted in it, whence later the Normans moved on into Cornwall. In the spring of 1068 it was possible to bring the duchess Mathilda from Normandy to be crowned queen of England on Whitsunday by Ealdred of York in a splendid ceremony at Westminster. 'Then the king was informed that the people in the north were gathered together and meant to make a stand against him if he came'.[112] The English earls Edwin and Morcar had fled the court and were finding support in Northumbria and York, while the aethling Edgar with his mother and sisters had also fled and gone to Scotland. There followed the Conqueror's first northern expedition, of 1068, 'a military promenade',[113] with peace and fealty obtained from Malcolm king of Scots, the renewed submission of Edwin and Morcar and castles founded all the way—at Warwick, Nottingham and York (on the site of what is now Clifford's Tower), Lincoln, Huntingdon and Cambridge.

The thirteenth-century Clifford's Tower on the Conqueror's motte at York.

Two further northern expeditions were required within a year, however, before the ancient northern resistance to royal government from the south was broken by the dreadful devastation of the winter of 1069–70. The first involved the swift relief of York and the planting of a second castle there on the right bank of the Ouse. The second was an altogether different matter, to overcome the one major crisis of Norman rule after Hastings. In the autumn of 1069 a great Danish fleet sent by Swein Estrithson sailed up the Humber (having first raided Dover, Sandwich, Ipswich and Norwich) to be joined by Edgar aethling, earl Waltheof, and Cospatric, the recently appointed earl of Northumbria, 'with the Northumbrians and all the people'.[114] At the same time spontaneous but uncoordinated risings flared up in Cheshire, Dorset, Somerset, Devon and Cornwall. The king concentrated upon the north and the Danes, leaving the rest successfully to his lieutenants. In the course of his campaigns that winter in dreadful conditions he spared himself and his army nothing. He also brought up to York for Christmas his court and his regalia from Winchester that his majesty might be displayed in those parts and his wrath made more terrible. 'Then in his anger he commanded that all crops and herds, chattels and food of every kind should be brought together and burned to ashes with consuming fire, so that the whole region north of Humber might be stripped of all means of sustenance'.[115]

With these campaigns of 1069–70 and the devastation of the north the Norman conquest militarily was over and two postscripts only followed. The first was the affair of Hereward the Wake and Ely where the remnants of the Old English party and the Danes held out in 1070 and 1071 until the king broke in along a specially constructed causeway two miles long from Aldreth to the Isle. There earl Morcar was captured, (his brother Edwin was already dead) to be imprisoned for the rest of William's reign.[116] The second was the great expedition by sea and land against Scotland in 1072, whose outcome was the submission of Malcolm king of Scots, the harbourer of English exiles and by now married to the aethling Edgar's sister Margaret, and the exile thence of Edgar to Flanders.[117]

At this stage, therefore, the historian's interest shifts from the Norman conquest to the more long-term process of the Norman settlement, though the two should not be sharply distinguished, for they overlap so much that the former may be thought subsumed within the latter. Indeed, in official Norman eyes, no doubt, the military conquest was undesirable and unnecessary, and it may be that the high drama of Hastings and 1066 encourages us too easily to regard 'the Norman Conquest of England' as different from the other instances of Norman expansion both within and without eleventh-century Normandy. Certainly Norman penetration of England begins long before 1066[118] and what we think of as the Norman settlement begins immediately after Hastings as the victor distributed the lands of those who had fallen or stood against him in the field to those who had followed him to England from Normandy and elsewhere on the promise of rich rewards. Whatever may have been the Conqueror's first intentions of ruling over a truly Anglo-Norman realm as the legitimate heir of his kinsman Edward the Confessor, in the event, as is well-known, only two Old English landlords of the first rank, Thurkell of Arden and Colswein of Lincoln, remained by the time of the Domesday survey as recorded in 1087.[119] The extinction and disappearance, in death, in exile[120] and by social suppression, of the Old English aristocracy is one of the few non-controversial results of the Norman Conquest which, sociologically, is the imposition of a new and alien ruling class upon the land. Nor, necessarily, were matters any different in the Church, where the change of personnel in its upper echelons was equally complete, so that by the Conqueror's death there were left only one Old English bishop (Worcester) and two abbots of any consequence (Ramsey and Bath).[121] Here, then, is the imposition of lordship, secular and ecclesiastical with little distinction, on a vast and comprehensive scale, and the instruments of its establishment as always were castles and churches, monasteries not least. At every step the Norman settlement of England is marked by the castles which were raised, from Pevensey, Hastings and London to York and Durham, from Colchester and Norwich to Chepstow and Chester.[122] The take-over of the Old English Church was no less vital to the new régime, while such particular instances of new monastic foundations as Battle itself, set up as one more among the

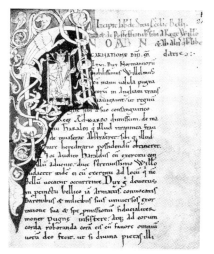

'The most noble William, duke of the Normans'. Illuminated capital letter 'A' (*Anno ab incarnatione Domini . . .*) from the twelfth-century Chronicle of Battle Abbey, f.21 (BL MS Cotton Domitian A II).

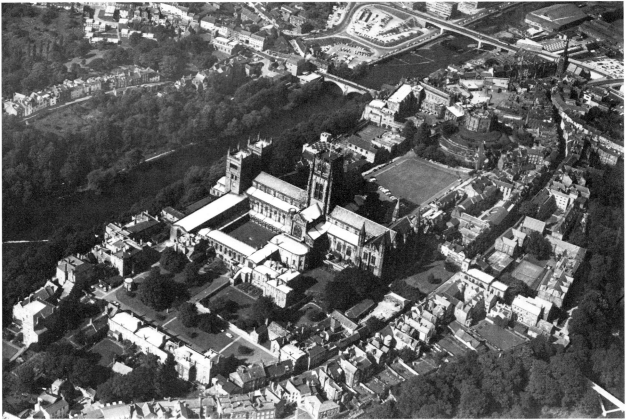

72

Chepstow, Monmouthshire, from the air. The keep of William fitz Osbern, the Conqueror's closest friend, stands at the centre and narrow waist of the castle but was heightened in the thirteenth century.

Durham, Norman cathedral priory and castle from the air. Here the Two Swords of spiritual and secular authority were both in the hands of the bishop.

The mid-twelfth-century keep of Rochester castle.

compact lordships of the Sussex rapes, or the replanting of monasticism in the north after 1070, are characteristic examples of Norman aristocratic colonization, to be compared with their colonization throughout the eleventh century of Lower Normandy as a whole, or the district of the Cinglais south of Caen.[123]

If finally we turn to the results of the Norman Conquest of England, and attempt to summarize a subject which requires a book to itself rather than the tail-end of a chapter, we may, indeed, begin with the word 'colonization', or the phrase 'the Norman settlement', for almost everything else follows from this. Sociologically the Norman Conquest was aristocratic colonization, the imposition upon a pre-existing kingdom of a new, alien and different ruling class, overwhelmingly Norman and, though liberally interlaced with Bretons, Flemings and others,[124] all the more Norman for that, given Norman society's attraction and tolerance of immigrants and its eclecticism. The new ruling class in Church and state included, of course, a new ruling house of princes, the Norman kings of England and subsequently their Angevin and 'Plantagenet' kinsmen and successors. About them and their magnates, the latter changing a little as time passes through the vicissitudes of fortune and continuing settlement from France—Clare, Bohun and Bigod, Mowbray and Mortimer, Mandeville, Warenne and Vere—future English history has to be written, as indeed does most of the history of Wales, Ireland and Scotland. In a sense, the continuous political history of England begins in 1066. So sweeping a change of personnel at the top was crucial in an age of personal kingship and personal lordship, with immense power concentrated in the hands of the few—especially after 1066 since a greater concentration of wealth in the hands of fewer than before is itself one of the results of the Norman settlement.[125] For a start the very nature of society changed to become what we call feudal, as the new lords and their new king naturally and automatically transplanted to England those forms of social organization, custom, tenure, military organization and tactics which were prevalent in Normandy and northern France.[126] The law changed in consequence, not least the land law, and so did the dispensation of justice to accommodate feudal notions of jurisdiction and the dynamic energies of Norman and Angevin monarchs. The power of the monarchy was vastly increased as the monarch became the New Leviathan,[127] not only a divine and Old Testament king but the feudal suzerain, the lord of lords, the greatest magnates of the realm his tenants, and conditional tenants at that. The essential sinews of his power grew also, with a greater endowment of royal lands, more widely dispersed about his kingdom, and all the very considerable financial perquisites of feudal lordship especially, together with the profits of an expanding royal justice. The chief trouble of English medieval history, one might say, is not overmighty subjects but overmighty monarchs, and the trouble begins in 1066, as witness Magna Carta. The unity of the realm, itself a measure and condition of royal power, achieved new dimensions, in, for example, the obliteration of the ancient distinction between the Danelaw and English England, or in the imposition of effective control upon the north, or in the rapid

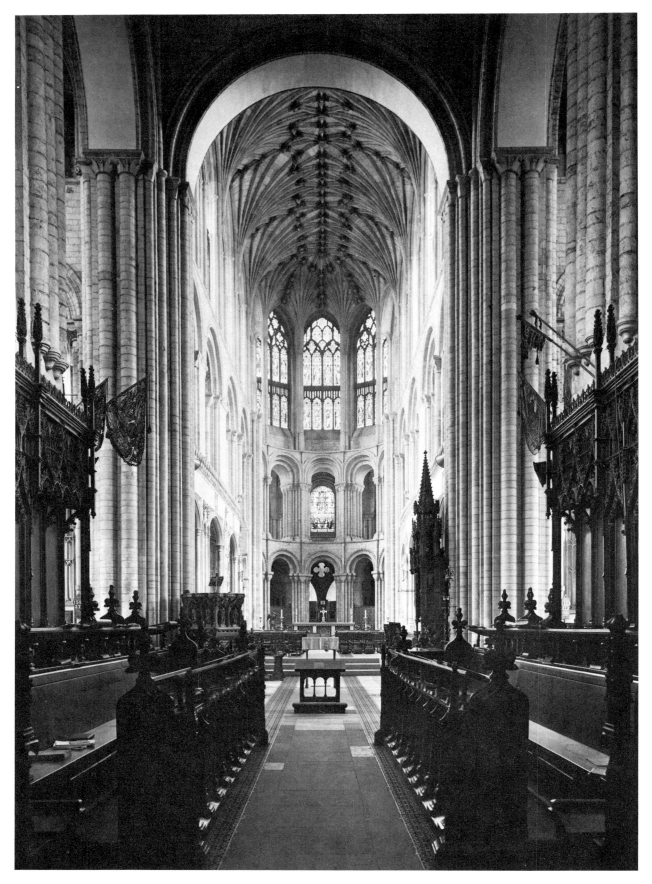

74

Norwich cathedral, interior, choir,
transepts and chancel. Only the high
windows and vaults are substantial
alterations from the Norman church
of bishop Herbert Losinga (late
eleventh century).

development of the coherence and discipline of feudalism. The
machinery of royal government also developed rapidly after 1066.
Whatever the degree of its development before, and whatever
controversy surrounds this subject in particular,[128] it simply is
significant that only in Norman England do we hear of a chancellor
and chancery, treasurer and treasury, and (very soon) of that
medieval wonder, the Exchequer; while the shire-reeve or sheriff
becomes the Norman *vicecomes*. As for the Domesday survey of
1086 that, too, is a post-Conquest achievement of royal administration unparalleled until the nineteenth century.

The Church, as we have seen, was no less under new management than the state well within a generation after 1066, and changed
accordingly—in a word, was Normanized. It was placed under the
direction of Lanfranc, appointed archbishop of Canterbury in place
of Stigand in 1070, formerly abbot of the Conqueror's new foundation of St Stephen's, Caen, his principal ecclesiastical counsellor in
the duchy and, like so many of the new Norman clerics in England,
a former monk of Bec. The ecclesiastical changes wrought thereafter are very much more than organizational, important though the
re-organization was—unity and discipline under Canterbury as the
primatial see, separate church councils and synods, separate church
courts and the development of canon law, organized cathedral
chapters, archdeacons and the rest.[129] The changes included also a
new sense of purpose, a new dynamism, a recharged spirituality, all
derived from Normandy whose own Church was then at the apex
of a great revival. At the same time, through the agency of the new
Norman prelates above all, England was brought culturally and
intellectually into the mainstream of the new learning of northern
France.[130] Such judgements, of course, are qualitative, involving an
element of personal preference, and are thus particularly emotive.
Perhaps the most emollient statement to make, which yet comes
very close to the truth, about the Old English Church, as of Old
English society as a whole, is that both were old fashioned by the
standards of northern France, features of a surviving Carolingian-
type realm still in full working order in spite of the Danes. It is not
unfair to say that in England at Hastings in 1066 the Old World
went down before the New.

Much of all this can still be seen and appreciated in English
architecture, contemplated with a moment's thought. Clapham
argued long ago for an architectural revolution resulting directly
from the Norman Conquest as profound as the political and
social:[131] the claim must be sustained, and of course the two things
go together. The Normans introduced castles into England and
thereafter Britain (significantly some before as well as most after
1066[132]) and castles stand above all for feudalism and the new
society. They also rebuilt almost every major church in England in
the decades after Hastings, the exceptions being Edward's Westminster which, significantly again, was a new Norman church
already, and Harold's Waltham Holy Cross.[133] Those majestic
buildings, reaching their culmination in the present cathedral of
Durham, above all monumental, integrated, organized, and larger
even than their prototypes in Normandy, certainly express what

the Normans regarded as the necessary reformation of the English church, but they also express the new order and the new lordship of a confident and rich society, in ways thought pleasing to God. In Norman England as in Normandy we may cite the psalmist's words put by William of Malmesbury into the mouth of that great building prelate, Roger bishop of Salisbury, 'Lord, I have loved the

St Stephen's, Caen, in which the Conqueror was buried. The crossing and tribunes (vault a twelfth-century addition).

Norwich cathedral from the south, showing the immense length of the nave of fourteen bays (late eleventh—early twelfth centuries).

glory of thy house'.[134] The churches and the castles also express more than changes, however profound, brought about within England, just as the total result of the Conquest will not be so confined. Castles and churches, of course, will be the means of subsequent Norman penetration into Wales and Scotland and Ireland, but they are witnesses also to the integration henceforth of England in the wide Norman world. Further yet, and lasting far beyond the disappearance of that Norman world itself, the most important single result of the Norman Conquest of England must be that it broke this country's close but barren ties with Scandinavia, and replaced both them and the affiliations with the increasingly obsolete German world by the closest bonds of absolute integration with northern France. Nothing could be of greater importance at a time when the Brave New World of northern France was rapidly becoming the centre and inspiration of a new version of medieval and European civilization.

Chapter 5 The Normans in the South: Italy and Sicily

The Norman conquest of southern Italy and Sicily was perhaps not only the most impressive but also the most romantic of their political achievements. This is the stuff of which fairy-tales, and legends, are made, as dusty, hard-riding warriors from the north become kings and princes in the sun and in near-Oriental splendour. The stuff, too, of films one would have thought—though perhaps it is as well there was no epic by Cecil B. de Mille.[1] Undertaken in the teeth of the four greatest powers of contemporary Christendom—the Eastern Empire of Byzantium, the Western German Empire, the Moslems and the Papacy—the achievement was yet, unlike the conquest of England, entirely the result of private enterprise, as individual knights and companies of knights rode out of Normandy to seek their fortune in the south. Most in the event won fiefs, some principalities, and the son of one a kingdom. But in the beginning, though there were many captains, there were no princes and certainly no kings. They were lesser men for the most part, many of them younger sons for whom there seemed no room at home, others political exiles from a Normandy which was beginning to become an ordered duchy and a state, many of them impoverished, at least in their own estimation, but all seemingly ebullient in their knighthood. Amatus, or Aimé, of Montecassino has given us an unforgettable glimpse of them, riding gaily 'through the meadows and gardens—happy and joyful on their horses, cavorting hither and thither'.[2] Of course there was a reverse side to this idyllic picture, bloodshed and cruelty as well as chivalry, and at least that ruthless exploitation without which fortunes are seldom made in any age. Amatus adds that 'the citizens of the town [Venosa] saw these unfamiliar knights, and wondered at them, and were afraid',[3] and Geoffrey Malaterra has the Haute-ville brothers leaving their inadequate patrimony in Normandy *per diversa loca militariter lucrum quaerentes* ('seeking wealth in arms in many places')—though he adds that it was God who led them at

Monreale, Sicily, the cloister (1172–89) and fountain (monastic lavatorium); the perfect blend of Norman and Arabic in Sicilian Romanesque.

length to Apulia (*Deo se ducente*),[4] for the Hautevilles especially were to become the allies of the Papacy, and all the Norman chivalry came to be seen, not only in their own eyes but also in those of many others, as *milites Christi*, the knights of Christ.

It is impossible to conceive of this extraordinary saga or *geste* as happening in any other period of European history than the eleventh century ('Present promise and wealth of the future beyond the eyes' scope') nor does its marvellous irresponsibility detract from its importance in the history of Italy, and thence of Christendom and the world. Nor is it possible easily to think of its being carried out by any other people than the Norman. In it we surely see the ultimate exercise in that aristocratic penetration, colonization and settlement, by means of the imposition of lordship both secular and ecclesiastical, through castles and churches, not least monasteries, all made effective by sheer military prowess—all of which may not be unique but is peculiarly Norman, to be seen again in Antioch,[5] as it was also in the creation of the duchy of Normandy itself;[6] but which in the affair of England is obscured by the drama and almost nationalistic confrontation at Hastings.[7] There are other, related, differences between the Norman conquest of southern Italy and that of England. While Norman penetration of the latter can be seen as beginning in 1002 with the marriage of Ethelred II and Emma,[8] and the Norman settlement even in terms of new arrivals and immigration does not end until at least the early twelfth century, yet we can also speak of the Norman Conquest as something which occurred between 1066 and 1070 if not in 1066 itself, and this concentration, combined with the central direction and unified command of the Conqueror as duke and king, produced something of a *tabula rasa* for the Norman leadership to work upon. By comparison, the Norman conquest of southern Italy and Sicily is different. There, too, about a century elapsed between the first known party of Norman knights in action at Salerno in 999[9] and the fall of the last Moslem stronghold in Sicily at Noto in 1091, but within it there was no one short period of concentrated or outright conquest, and no one battle to decide the fate of nations. Indeed, in mainland Italy the conquest—if that word is even appropriate[10]— was piecemeal in a double sense: territory and lordship were acquired over a long period of some 70 years (reckoned to the fall of Bari in 1071), and by a number of different Norman leaders. There was no unity until 1130 and, in the beginning, no concerted plan nor even any conscious design of conquest beyond the universally held ambition to be *militariter lucrum quaerentes*. The affair of Sicily was, it is true, more a straightforward conquest, more or less under the single command of Roger of Hauteville, the 'Great Count', who was only occasionally joined and helped by Robert Guiscard his suzerain and brother; yet, even so, it took thirty years from 1061 to the completion. A further difference arises from the respective dates of the two enterprises in Italy and England. The first Norman adventurers in the former, and some of their successors, were well established (if, indeed, they were not already slain or dead) before their compatriots in Normandy set sail for England in 1066, by which year almost the entire south of Italy was under Norman rule.

The conquests of and in Campania, Capua, Apulia and Calabria were thus by far the earliest of Norman expansionist enterprises beyond the homeland of the duchy and its neighbours in France, and the fact needs to be stressed if we are to enquire what the Normans took with them and introduced into Italy. So much of what we in England especially think of as 'Norman' is in reality the product of the rapidly developing Normandy of that same first half of the eleventh century, and thus dates from after the departure to the south of many of her sons.

With the nature of the sources and the evidence for the early history of the Normans in Italy and Sicily the English historian is, so to speak, on familiar ground.[11] That is to say, there is a sufficiency, if not an abundance, with at least three first-rate, mutually independent and near-contemporary histories which, though written from the Norman point of view, are not necessarily the worse for that and certainly not less important. They are, first, the *History of the Normans* (*Ystoire de li Normant*), written between *c.*1071 and 1080 by Aimé or Amatus of Montecassino, a Lombard monk of that great abbey which was very closely involved with the Normans. The original text is unfortunately lost and the work survives only in a fourteenth-century Italianate French translation, but is generally thought the best source for the early period down to *c.*1078.[12] Next is *The Deeds of Robert Guiscard* (*Gesta Roberti Wiscardi*), written *c.*1095–99 by William of Apulia,[13] who may or may not himself have been a Norman, and whose Latin epic poem is dedicated to Roger 'Borsa', Guiscard's son and successor in Apulia. The third is Geoffrey Malaterra's 'Sicilian History' (*Historia Sicula*), written soon after 1098 on the instructions of Roger I, count of Calabria and Sicily.[14] Geoffrey was evidently a Norman monk from St Evroul, before he moved to its daughter house in Italy of St Eufemia and subsequently to St Agata at Catania, and his work is of especial importance for the conquest of Sicily. The partisanship of these three sources can, to a degree, be checked by reference to others, not least the first redaction of the Montecassino Chronicle, by Leo of Ostia, another monk of that great house, writing between *c.*1099 and 1105—a work which may almost count as a fourth major source because of the role of Montecassino in the history of the Normans in Italy—and some other literary sources from outside Italy like Raoul Glaber and Adémar of Chabannes.[15] There is also the abundant charter evidence of a highly literate contemporary Italy, and this of course includes papal documents as well as such great collections as those of Montecassino and La Cava.[16] Finally, for Norman Italy and Sicily, as for England and Normandy itself, we have the surviving artistic evidence, and, above all, a great series of splendid monuments, churches especially but not exclusively, all of which have as much to tell as ever anything that was written, however much their message may be quarrelled over, and even misinterpreted, by architectural and art historians.[17]

Norman involvement in southern Italy evidently began at the close of the tenth century.[18] The earliest known incident is that recorded by Amatus, 'before the year 1000' (*i.e.* 999[19]), when a party of 40 Norman pilgrims returning from Jerusalem were staying at Salerno when it was attacked by Saracens.[20] Shocked by the lack of any resistance from the citizens—and doubtless finding the dishonour to themselves intolerable—they obtained horses[21] and arms from Gaimar [IV, 999–1027], the prince of Salerno, and drove the infidels away. Refusing the invitation of the delighted Gaimar to stay in his service, they returned to Normandy, taking with them his envoys laden with gifts to recruit others 'to come to this land that flows with milk and honey and so many beautiful things'. After this, however, Amatus' account becomes chronologically impossible, for he says that amongst those who then came to Italy was Gilbert Buatère who had slain William Repostellus and in consequence fled from the wrath of the Norman duke Robert (i.e. 1027–35) with his four brothers, Rainulf, Asclettin or Anquetil, Osmund and Rodulf, all of whom were taken into the service of Melo[22] for his Apulian rebellion against the Greeks (i.e. 1017–18). Another and different story is related by William of Apulia[23] who, at a date somewhere between 1012 and 1017 and probably 1016, has a party of Norman pilgrims visiting the shrine of the Archangel Michael (Sant'Angelo) at Monte Gargano, where they met a Lom-

Bronze doors with silver inlay at the shrine of St Michael the Archangel, Monte Sant'Angelo, Apulia (late eleventh century).

bard noble from Bari called Melo and, to them, strangely attired as a Greek. He explained that he was a political exile and sought to recruit them for his revolt to free Apulia from Byzantine rule. They promised to return bringing others with them, and did so, meeting Melo in Campania. He supplied them with arms and led them into Apulia in the spring (of 1017) against the Greeks. Thereafter both Amatus and William of Apulia continue with the story of Melo's rebellion until its disastrous end at Cannae in October 1018.[24] Meanwhile a third account of early Norman involvement in Italian politics and Melo's rebellion is given by Leo of Ostia, Raoul Glaber (Burgundy, c.1035–44) and Adémar of Chabannes (western Aquitaine, before 1034).[25] The most informative is Leo who says that while Melo was in exile in Capua (1011–16) a party of some 40 Normans arrived there 'fleeing from the wrath of their lord, the count of Normandy' and seeking military service. They were tall, handsome and exceptionally skilful in arms (armis experientissimi). Chief among them were Rodulf (II) de Tosny,[26] Gosmannus, Rufinus and Stigandus. All were recruited by Melo, who then 'hastened to Salerno and Benevento to unite the many who out of hatred of the Greeks as well as for his own sake were disposed to join him', and immediately invaded Apulia. Raoul Glaber and Adémar de Chabannes specify the Norman count or duke as Richard (II, 996–1026) but name only Rodulf or Ralph (de Tosny) and have him directed to join the Apulian Lombard rebels by Pope Benedict (VIII, 1012–24).

It is impossible to reconcile these three distinct stories or traditions and conflate them into one occasion as the beginning of Norman penetration into Italy; nor should we expect to do so, since it is clear that in the beginning, and for some time thereafter, we have to deal with separate groups and individuals severally involved in Italian politics. Further, the process evidently begins about the millennium, 1000 AD, and in it there is no need to doubt the role of pilgrimage in introducing Norman knights errant to the opportunities Italy offered, as the best known traditions of Amatus and William of Apulia have it.[27] The Normans were notably enthusiastic participants in the growing cult of pilgrimage at this time,[28] which opened men's eyes to wider horizons. The grandest centres of pilgrimage were St James of Compostella, Rome and Jerusalem. Pilgrimages to Jerusalem led directly to the armed pilgrimage of the Crusade. The pilgrimage to Compostella led to Frankish participation in the wars against the Infidel in Spain, though in the event less by Normans than by knights from Burgundy and France south of the Loire.[29] Southern Italy, which was to become the main Norman theatre of operations and their land of opportunity, lay, in its upper reaches where their activities began, close to Rome itself and across the favoured route to Jerusalem and the Holy Places,[30] the most challenging and therefore rewarding of all pilgrimages. There is also a ring of truth in William of Apulia's story of Norman pilgrims at Monte Sant' Angelo, a major pilgrimage centre in its own right, for the Normans had a particular cult of Saint Michael, as witness their own shrine at Mont-St-Michel, St Michael-in-Peril-of-the-Sea, to which Saint Aubert had brought a fragment of the

Archangel's cloak from Monte Gargano at the beginning of the eighth century.[31] Of course we must not overdo the piety of the first Normans in Italy nor of their successors, but we must not discount it either. It is also clear that political exiles played as large a part in the penetration of Italy as former pilgrims.[32] Nevertheless, the two roles are not incompatible, and nor, for that matter, are piety and violence. William of Apulia adds, without pause (save to note omens) or comment, to his account of the recruitment of Norman knights by Melo at the shrine of Saint Michael on Monte Gargano the statement that all Apulia feared them when they came and many perished as the victims of their cruelty.[33]

Certainly southern Italy at this time was ripe for infiltration and exploitation and presented the kind of golden opportunity for the acquisition of riches and fiefs which the Normans were so adept to create and grasp, a fertile and rewarding field for their military prowess which was evidently recognized at once, wide open to the ruthless enterprise of the hired lance and the sword for sale. Settled like most of Italy by the Lombards long ago, it was now at the highest level subject to the competing claims of the great powers of the age. Still officially part of the Eastern or Byzantine Empire, Apulia and Calabria were governed with greater or lesser effectiveness from Constantinople and Bari. The Papacy, which in any case could not be indifferent to the political situation south of Rome,

St. Michael the Weigher of Souls, eleventh-century sculpture at Monte Sant'Angelo.

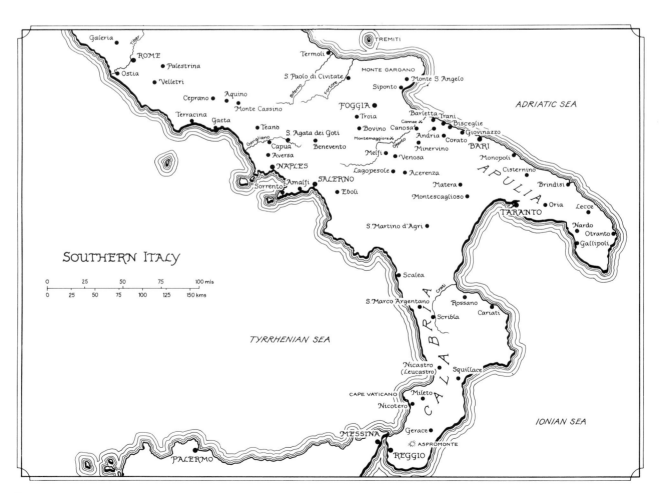

SOUTHERN ITALY

The west front of the abbey church of St Mary at Jumièges (dedicated 1067). (Photo Zodiaque)

Domesday Book. Entry for Herefordshire, showing the list of landholders.
The red lines are the equivalent of underlinings.

(*Public Record Office*)

claimed dominion from the mythical 'Donation of Constantine' which placed all Italy under its rule, and from the more specific grant by Charlemagne of the whole of Spoleto or Benevento which then comprised most of southern Italy. In addition there were the papal claims to supremacy over a universal Christian Church, now sharpened by the growing schism between the two Churches of reality, East and West, Greek and Latin. The Western Emperors also, now kings of Germany and of Lombardy and still at this time the protectors and the allies of the Papacy, claimed suzerainty as the heirs of Charlemagne, who with his Lombard kingdom had claimed all Benevento. From time to time they came south with their armies to give expression to their lordship. Sicily belonged to Islam, as it had done since the ninth century, and the Moslems, though divided amongst themselves, were stepping up their raids on the mainland at the turn of the tenth and eleventh centuries (*e.g.* Salerno in 999). Closer to the grass roots, so to speak, the three great Lombard principalities of Capua, Salerno and Benevento were autonomous and usually at loggerheads with each other. On the west coast the four small duchies of Amalfi, Sorrento, Naples and Gaeta were quasi-autonomous but attached in sympathy and politics to the Byzantine 'catapanate of Italy' based on Bari. To all this we must add another unit, the great Benedictine abbey of Montecassino, rivalling even Rome in sheer prestige as the foundation of Saint Benedict,[34] whose lands, the *terra Sancti Benedicti*, formed another principality in themselves. Montecassino, Lombard in personnel, has been called 'the bastion of Latinity' towards the south, [35] and the Lombards themselves were ecclesiastically Romans, but the Byzantine 'catapanate' or province was inevitably Greek or Orthodox in religion, looking to Constantinople not Rome, and Calabria especially was heavily 'Hellenized' in terms of Greek bishops and Greek or 'Basilian' monasteries. Three worlds, Latin, Greek and Moslem, thus met and overlapped in what was to be Norman Italy and Sicily, ethnic differences fortified inevitably by wide and widening cultural and religious divisions. The Normans were to become the champions of Latinity and *Romanitas*, but on their first arrival, when in practice they added to the divisions which they exploited, they profited most from the wars between Greek and Lombard and between the Lombard princes themselves—charging, we may say, into the 'incessant and fratricidal strife which was the substitute for political endeavour in Lombard Italy'.[36]

The Norman knights recruited by Melo for the liberation of Apulia from Byzantine rule were at first a great success, and contributed to a series of five victories in a row (according to Amatus) before the disastrous defeat at Cannae on the right bank of the Ofanto in October 1018.[37] Heavily outnumbered by a powerful Byzantine army under the catapan Boiannes, they and their Lombard masters were cut to pieces and Melo's dream of a free Apulia was shattered. Amatus wrote that the Greeks swarmed over the battlefield like bees from an overfull hive and that of the Normans only 10 survived out of a total of 250—no doubt an exaggeration but one of the innumerable indications of the very small numbers of

Normans who actually took part in the whole enterprise of Italy and Sicily, on the battlefield and off it, from the beginning to the end. After this, for about a decade, we know nothing save the bare but exciting, if as yet undistinguished, truth of troops of Norman knights, their numbers frequently reinforced by new arrivals from the north, selling their military prowess to any of the many bidders for it—the princes of Salerno and Capua, the duke of Naples, the abbot of Montecassino to defend the *terra Sancti Benedicti*, even the Greeks to garrison their new Apulian fortress of Troia. When, true professionals as they were, they met on opposite sides, the victorious party took care to obtain favourable terms for their defeated brethren. At this stage their activities were chiefly confined to the west, to Capua and what is now the Campania, and it is here that what we can see as the first milestone towards Norman domination of the south is reached when, in 1030, one Rainulf 'Drengot' became lord of the town and territory of Aversa. It was the first Norman lordship established in Italy, and Rainulf was evidently one of the first Norman adventurers in Italy (in Amatus' account one of the brothers of Gilbert Buatère) who had survived the disaster of Cannae to be elected leader of that depleted Norman company.[38] He had obtained Aversa by changing sides from Pandulf prince of Capua to that of Sergius duke of Naples, and now confirmed his new status amongst the Lombard nobles by marrying Sergius' sister, widow of the duke of Gaeta. He was to switch his support twice more, back to Pandulf (whose niece he married after the death of his first wife) and then to Gaimar, prince of Salerno, but he was confirmed in his lordship and formally invested as count of Aversa by the German Emperor Conrad II in the summer of 1038. He had arrived, and in due course he will be duke of Gaeta as well as count of Aversa, and his successor Richard I will become prince of all Capua in 1058. Rainulf died in 1045, and Amatus describes him as 'a man adorned with all the virtues which become a knight'.[39]

Meanwhile, about the year 1035, the first Hauteville brothers, the first members of that family destined to rise to the pinnacle of power and fame in Norman Italy and Sicily, had ridden into Aversa amongst other new arrivals. They were William, Drogo and Humphrey,[40] three of the twelve sons (by two wives) of Tancred of Hauteville (which may or may not be the village of Hauteville-le-Guichard), a Norman lord of moderate standing in the Cotentin.[41] All twelve sons, Malaterra informs us, were trained and educated as knights from their adolescence,[42] and, their patrimony in Normandy obviously being insufficient, eight of them eventually went off to seek their fortunes abroad, God leading them (as we have seen) eventually to Apulia.[43] Soon after the first Hauteville arrivals, Fate if not God may seem to take a hand and point to the future. In 1038 the new Greek Emperor at Constantinople, Michael IV, launched a great expedition led by the larger-than-life general George Maniakes against Moslem Sicily, and called upon Gaimar, the Lombard prince now of Capua and Salerno, for military aid. Gaimar sent 300 of his Norman knights from Aversa, and amongst them were the Hautevilles. The expedition in the end was not a

The sadly neglected east end and apses of the cathedral of St Paul at Aversa (mid-twelfth-century).

great success, but the Normans distinguished themselves before they left (disgusted by mismanagement and inadequate distribution of loot), and young William of Hauteville unhorsed and slew the Moslem emir of Syracuse in single combat, for which feat of arms he has ever afterwards been known as William of the Iron Arm, *i.e.* William Bras-de-Fer. Soon after that a more immediate prospect

beckoned. In 1041 Arduin, a Lombard rebel against Byzantium in Apulia, obtained another contingent of 300 Norman knights from Aversa and established them in the fortified hill-town of Melfi. The Hautevilles were amongst them and in due course Apulia, then Calabria, and ultimately Sicily, will be theirs.

Spectacular successes were immediate. Within days of the Norman arrival at Melfi, neighbouring Venosa fell, followed by Lavello and Ascoli. There were three major victories in pitched battles against the Greeks in the first campaigning season of 1041—near Venosa on the banks of the Olivento on 17 March; at Montemaggiore near Cannae on 4 May; and at Monte Siricolo near Montepeloso on 3 September. The second avenged the defeat which the first Normans had shared with Melo on the same field twenty-three years before:[44] this time they were led to victory by the indomitable William Bras-de-Fer (who was suffering from a fever at the time) and the loot, Amatus tells us, was prodigious.[45] We are also assured that the Normans were heavily outnumbered in all three engagements and we may be sure they were, as they always were to be in Italy and Sicily, whether as mere auxiliaries as now or whether as the *corps d'élite* and master-race of lords and knights hereafter.

Then in 1042 we reach a second milestone in the *gesta Normannorum* in the south, and may see it also as a turning point as the Normans move closer together, take the initiative, and hammer out a policy which is something more than acting as richly rewarded mercenaries and entrepreneurial knights. In 1042 the current Lombard leader in Apulia against the Greeks, Argyrus, son of Melo, went over to the enemy and made peace. The Normans of Melfi were thus without an employer and increasingly exasperated by what they saw as Lombard duplicity. There were by now three principal Norman groups, entrenched at Aversa, at Melfi, and also at Troia where they had been installed by the Greeks some twenty years before.[46] In 1042 all the leaders met at a great council at Melfi, including Rainulf I of Aversa, and his Lombard lord and patron of the Normans, Gaimar prince of Capua and Salerno. The outcome was what we may perhaps call in crude modern terms a carve-up, and one with characteristic Norman audacity concerned as much with the future as the present. William Bras-de-Fer was recognized as the leader of all the Normans in Apulia, *i.e.* of Troia as well as Melfi, and proclaimed count of Apulia, no less. As such he became, like Rainulf of Aversa, the vassal of Gaimar, who was himself proclaimed duke of Apulia as well as of Capua and Salerno. William also obtained a new and proper dimension to his elevation by marriage to Guida, Gaimar's niece and daughter of the duke of Sorrento.[47] And then the land of Apulia, 'acquired and to be acquired' (*aquestées et à aquester*), was distributed by Gaimar as suzerain to the chief Norman lords—for lords they certainly now became—Ascoli to Count William Bras-de-Fer himself, Venosa to Drogo of Hauteville his brother, Siponto and part of Monte Gargano to Rainulf count of Aversa and now also duke of Gaeta, and so on.[48] In 1047 the Western Emperor, in the person of Henry III, made one of his periodic descents into Italy and, after his own imperial coronation at Rome, came with the new Pope Clement II to Capua. By no means all of the *ad hoc* arrangements of 1042 received his confirmation, without which, in his view, they had no validity. Thus Gaimar was demoted to mere prince of Salerno once more, Pandulf being restored to Capua. The Normans, however, moved further into established and official respectability, Rainulf II (nephew and successor of the first Rainulf who had died in 1045) being confirmed as count of Aversa, and Drogo of Hauteville (brother of William Bras-de-Fer who had just died) formally invested as 'duke and master of Italy and count of the Normans of all Apulia and Calabria' (*dux et magister Italiae comesque Normannorum totius Apuliae et Calabriae*).

From now on the principal momentum in the conquest of southern Italy was to come from the Normans of Melfi and Apulia, and from the house of Hauteville in particular; though the Norman counts of Aversa were to wax also and become princes of Capua from 1058. In 1046 there arrived in Italy among the swelling crowd of Norman immigrants two young men, Richard, nephew of the reigning count of Aversa, and Robert, future 'Guiscard' (the Wary), another Hauteville brother and the eldest son of Tancred by his second wife. The former came with forty knights and attendants and will become count of Aversa and prince of Capua—

Richard, Asclettin's son, well-formed and of fine lordly stature, young, fresh-faced and of radiant beauty, so that all who saw him loved him; and he was followed by many knights and attendants. It was his habit to ride a horse so small that his feet nearly touched the ground.[49]

The latter, who rode almost alone, was to prove himself perhaps the greatest of the Hautevilles, and his career was to bend and dent the history of Christendom. One must make one's own choice as to the greatest of this extraordinary family. In the first generation the rival claimants must surely be Robert Guiscard and Roger I the 'great count'; in the second, Roger II king of Sicily and Bohemond prince of Antioch. There are many descriptions of Guiscard, who on his tomb was *terror mundi*, but the best known and most interesting for its combination of high-born feminine malice and sensual attraction is that written later by Anna Comnena, daughter of the Eastern Emperor Alexius Comnenus who had met and even contained his high-vaulting ambition:

> This Robert was a Norman by birth, of obscure origin, with an overbearing character and a thoroughly villainous mind; he was a

Squillace, site of one of the earliest Norman castles in Calabria, founded by William Bras-de-Fer.

> brave fighter, very cunning in his assaults on the wealth and power of great men; in achieving his aims absolutely inexorable, diverting criticism by incontrovertible argument. He was a man of immense stature . . . he had a ruddy complexion, fair hair, broad shoulders, eyes that all but shot out sparks of fire. In a well-built man one looks for breadth here and slimness there; in him all was admirably well-proportioned and elegant. Thus from head to foot the man was graceful (I have often heard from many witnesses that this was so). Homer remarked of Achilles that when he shouted his hearers had the impression of a multitude in uproar, but Robert's bellow, so they say, put tens of thousands to flight. With such endowments of fortune and nature and soul, he was, as you would expect, no man's slave, owing obedience to nobody in all the world. Such are men of powerful character, people say, even if they are of humbler origin.'[50]

At first on his arrival in Apulia Robert was disgruntled not to be given the fief and preferment which he expected from the count, his brother Drogo. Instead he was sent south to desolate Greek

Calabria, as yet scarcely penetrated by the Normans save for William Bras-de-Fer's castle at Squillace. He was allowed free rein or took it, and, abandoning the castle of Scribla[51] first assigned to him, established himself in another of his own choice at San Marco Argentano, thence to set about with a will to enrich himself and subdue the province. Here in his early days, with few or no resources, he acquired his nickname of the Wary. It was now, too, that he married his first wife Aubrey (Alberada), a mere girl but the aunt of an established Norman lord in Apulia, Girard of Buonalbergo. Girard offered Robert his alliance in the conquest of Calabria, Aubrey's hand in marriage, and two hundred knights. Aubrey's dowry of those two hundred knights effectively launched Guiscard on his career,[52] though he later found it necessary to repudiate her in favour of a then more politically advantageous marriage, to Sichelgaita, sister of the reigning Lombard prince of Salerno, in 1058.

San Marco Argentano, site of the first castle and base of Robert Guiscard in Calabria.

Aubrey, however, had borne him a son, Bohemond the mighty warrior and future prince of Antioch. She lies now in the old church of the abbey of the Trinity at Venosa, built by her husband and his brothers, and though she seems to have harboured no ill-will, and took two more husbands after Robert, there is perhaps poetic justice in the fact that hers is the only original Hauteville tomb remaining in what was meant to be a family mausoleum. It bears the evocative but later inscription: 'In this sepulchre is buried Aberada wife of Guiscard. If you seek [our?] son, he lies at Canosa' (*Guiscardi coniux Aberada hac conditur arca. Si genitum quaeres, hunc Canusinus habet*).[53]

The tomb of Aubrey (Alberada), first wife of Robert Guiscard and mother of Bohemond, in the old church of the abbey of the Holy Trinity at Venosa.

As the Normans from Melfi continued inexorably with the take-over and colonization of Apulia, and Robert Guiscard, brother and vassal of the Norman count, with the acquisition of land and lordship in Calabria from his stronghold of San Marco Argentano, we approach another milestone in the form of the great battle and victory of Civitate in 1053. Local opposition to the Normans grew with their success, which was expansionist, exploitive, domineering, and devastating to any resistance. Count Drogo of Hauteville himself was assassinated in 1051 in the chapel of his own castle at Montello, probably by Byzantine agents. He was succeeded at once by his brother Humphrey and the terrorist gesture brought no change, but it was not only the Greeks now who were opposed to the Normans in Apulia and elsewhere. Their strong-arm methods, which too often failed to respect either age or sex or churches, aroused what Chalandon calls 'an explosion of hatred' against them at this time.[54] For the Lombards, those who had come as liberators were now oppressors, worse than the Greeks, worse even than the Saracens. Complaints poured in to the Papacy as well as other centres of authority, some of them from high places. Merely to be Norman was an invitation to be assaulted if opportunity offered, and this in a land frequented by pilgrims en route to Rome, Monte Gargano and Jerusalem.[55] John, abbot of Fécamp, thus wrote to the

Pope after suffering such an attack on his return from a pilgrimage to Rome: 'The hatred of the Italians for the Normans has now reached such a pitch that it is almost impossible for any Norman, albeit a pilgrim, to journey in the towns of Italy, without being assailed, abducted, robbed, beaten, thrown in irons, even if fortunate enough not to die in a prison.'[56] The new reforming Pope, Leo IX, felt called upon to intervene, was in fact called upon to do so, and was urged on by his radical cardinal, Hildebrand, the future Gregory VII. He was concerned also for the state of the Church in the troubled provinces, and for the Norman threat to the patrimony of Saint Peter itself, and not least to Benevento. He therefore summoned an army, called upon the oppressed to rise, and made an alliance with Constantinople to drive the Normans out of Italy.

In the face of so formidable a threat, the Normans once more drew together, Count Richard of Aversa[57] joining Count Humphrey of Hauteville and the latter's brother Guiscard riding in from Calabria. 'They were outnumbered and without allies . . . Ranged against them were not only two armies, the Papal and the Byzantine, but also the entire indigenous population of Apulia . . .'[58] They assembled all the forces they could muster and moved first to Troia and then north to prevent the combination of the Papal and Byzantine armies planned to occur near Siponto. They made contact with the Papal army on 17 June 1053 by the city of Civitate.[59] The next day, with reluctance, negotiations having been spurned, the Normans attacked the forces of Saint Peter. With Humphrey in the centre, Richard of Aversa on the right, and Robert Guiscard on the left and acting also as a reserve, they won a famous victory, under the eyes of Pope Leo watching from the ramparts of the city. Guiscard especially distinguished himself with lance and sword, and according to William of Apulia was three times unhorsed (like William the Conqueror at Hastings).[60]

As a decisive battle in the history of the Normans in Italy, Civitate has been compared to Hastings in their conquest of England.[61] The comparison is a little far-fetched, but there are military similarities as the old world of Germanic infantry tactics went down before the new chivalry of heavy cavalry, the Suabian élite of the Papal army resisting stoutly to the end with their great two-handed swords like Harold of England's housecarls with their battle axes. By virtue of its consequences, Civitate can be seen as not only a milestone but also as a watershed in Norman fortunes in the south. The immediate results were the withdrawal of the Greek army, of which we hear no more, and the humiliation of the Papacy in the person of Leo IX. Though William of Apulia assures us (as we may well believe) that after the battle the Normans knelt before Leo for forgiveness and kissed his feet,[62] he was a virtual prisoner in their hands, and the inevitable outcome was the recognition by the Papacy of the Norman acquisitions in Italy, as the Western Emperor had recognized them in 1047.[63] Further, though Leo himself died in Rome the next year, the papal defeat at Civitate in 1053 led straight to the alliance of the Papacy with the invincible Normans, launched at Melfi in 1059. This diplomatic revolution meant henceforth (though Gregory VII in the early years of his pontificate felt it

Western portico of Sant 'Angelo in Formis, near Capua, built by abbot Desiderius of Montecassino between 1058 and c. 1073. The whole interior is painted in the Cassinese style.

necessary to excommunicate Robert Guiscard three times) that the Italian Normans had not only the support but also the approbation and ultimately the blessing of the highest moral authority in Latin Christendom, now going from strength to strength as the leader of a great movement of ecclesiastical reform. It was brought about by the same Cardinal Hildebrand (the future Gregory VII) largely responsible for Civitate, and also by the influence of the great abbot Desiderius of Montecassino, who had sought Norman friendship from the time of his succession to the abbacy in 1055, and who had to live even more closely with the Normans after Richard of Aversa finally took all Capua in 1057, thus ending Lombard rule there. In 1058 Richard, now prince of Capua, was received in triumph at Montecassino 'like a king' (come roy), and, with the church decorated as if for Easter, *Laudes* were sung before him so that the courtyard rang with praise, and the abbot washed his feet.[64] In the next year, 1059, it was in fact Richard who sent 300 knights to Rome when Hildebrand requested aid for the reforming Pope Nicholas II against the anti-Pope Benedict X, and in the same year Nicholas himself came to Apulia, by way of Montecassino and with abbot Desiderius in his train. At Melfi he held a synod for the reformation of the south Italian church, and he also formally confirmed Richard as prince of Capua, and Robert Guiscard as duke of Apulia and Calabria—and, for the future, Sicily. Both princes evidently swore him fealty though only the text of Robert's oath survives, his sonorous titles a far cry from his dusty beginnings freebooting at San Marco Argentano—'I, Robert, by the grace of God and of Saint Peter, duke of Apulia and of Calabria and, if either aid me, future duke of Sicily.'[65]

Also during his visitation of Apulia in 1059 Pope Nicholas II consecrated the abbey church of the Holy Trinity at Venosa, the first Norman and Benedictine monastic foundation in their principality, significantly not far from their original headquarters at Melfi, founded by Drogo of Hauteville soon after 1043 and completed after his death in 1051 by his brothers and successors William and Robert Guiscard.[66] To this church, small and not very distinguished by later Norman standards,[67] as is commensurate with its early date, Duke Robert moved the bodies of his brothers, William Bras-de-Fer, Drogo and Humphrey, for grandiose burial, and here he himself was brought after his death in 1085. It was to be, in short, the mausoleum and monastic chantry of the house of Hauteville (as the great houses at this time rising everywhere in Normandy were the mausoleums and chantries of their founders) and was placed under Norman abbots from the start, the second of whom was Berengar from St Evroul.[68] Richly endowed, its properties included Greek monasteries made subordinate in Calabria.[69] Nothing

Sant 'Angelo in Formis, detail of doorway in western portico. Above is St Michael Archangel: the inscription over the door commemorates abbot Desiderius of Montecassino who built the church.

could be more symptomatic of the permanent intentions of the new establishment and of the Hautevilles, now ranked among the princes of Latin Christendom, not only in terms of grandiose tombs and prayers and masses for their souls and policies, but also in terms of true Norman colonization by means of religious foundations as well as fiefs and sub-enfeoffments.[70]

After Melfi in 1059 the expansion of Norman domination, especially from Apulia, and especially to the south but also west, inexorably continues. The once independent duchy of Amalfi[71] was acquired by Robert Guiscard in 1073, and Salerno in 1076. The fall of the latter marks the end of the great Lombard principalities in southern Italy,[72] and the ancient city with its famous medical school became henceforth the principal pride of Duke Robert's Apulia, with (as at Amalfi) a splendid new cathedral to express new lordship. It was built on the model of abbot Desiderius' new church at Montecassino by archbishop Alfanus, the abbot's lifelong friend, and was consecrated in 1084 by Gregory VII, who still lies within.[73] To the south, the capture of Reggio in 1060 marked the end of Byzantine rule in Calabria and the virtual completion of the Norman conquest of that province, while the capture of Bari in 1071 after a three-years' siege by land and sea, saw the end of any Byzantine presence in Italy and the fall of their Italian capital city which had been imperial and 'Greek' since the time of the Emperor Justinian. The warriors who achieved these and other triumphs, and who launched the Norman attack on Sicily in 1061, were chiefly Robert Guiscard and his younger brother Roger. Guiscard had succeeded his elder brother Humphrey on the latter's death in 1057, first as regent and then as count despite the rights of Abelard, Humphrey's infant son,[74] and in 1059, as we have seen, had been elevated to the vaunting heights of duke of Apulia and Calabria, and, in future, Sicily. Roger was the eighth, the last and youngest of the Hauteville brothers to arrive in Italy, aged 26, in about 1056.[75] He was handsome, tall and well-proportioned, eloquent, clever and prudent in counsel, intrepid in arms, 'agreeable and courteous in all things'—thus his admiring biographer, Geoffrey Malaterra.[76] Guiscard sent him off at once with only sixty knights into Calabria to gain experience,[77] and almost from the beginning he became his brother's trusted and trusty principal lieutenant, in Calabria and in Sicily and elsewhere. Side by side, with very little friction,[78] on almost all the great occasions of Guiscard's remaining reign, they were brothers-in-arms indeed, though increasingly Roger was left free to manage the affair of Sicily of which he was made count, as his brother's vassal, in 1072.

The conquest of Sicily began in May 1061, after two exploratory raids by Roger the previous year. Long dreamt of, there can be no doubt the attempt would have in any case been made, though the occasion was presented by divisions between rival Moslem emirs within the island. It was not to be completed for thirty years, a fact which, for so ambitious an undertaking, should cause no real surprise. The length of time required can be further explained by the fact that the enterprise was itself an extension of the remarkable Norman conquest of the mainland, where there continued to be

Salerno, cathedral (consecrated 1084); atrium and campanile (twelfth century).

troubles and diversions; by a shortage of manpower which, while it did not prevent great victories and amazing feats of arms by Norman knights especially, was a bigger problem when it came to occupation of territories won; and by a more formidable resistance from the Arabs than anything the Norman chivalry had met in Italy from Greek or Lombard. Not the least impressive feature of the campaign of 1061 was the invasion itself, which was most carefully

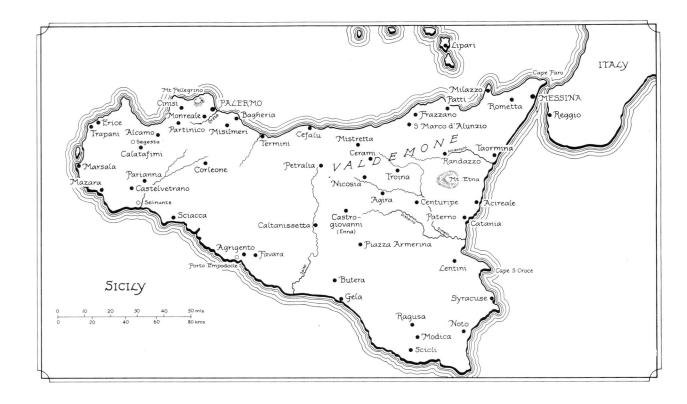

prepared. It was necessarily amphibious, but for the Norman knights, their war horses were essential, and so they took them with them. They may have acquired the difficult art of transporting horses by sea from the Byzantines and the sailors of the formerly Greek ports of mainland Italy, though they were to repeat the exercise on a much larger scale for the invasion of England across the Channel five years later in 1066.[79] The crossing was made from Santa Maria del Forò to a land-fall south of Messina, thus throwing off guard the defenders of that city who were patrolling the coast to the north in expectation of the shorter passage. No doubt because of a lack of sufficient transports the whole army of perhaps some two thousand could not be taken across the Straits of Messina in one operation, and the first party of 270 knights in thirteen ships, under the command of Roger of Hauteville, made the crossing by night under cover of darkness. At daybreak they armed and mounted and promptly attacked and slew a Moslem supply-train moving towards Messina. Next they were joined by a further contingent of 170 knights as the fleet made its second crossing, and with this force of under 500 horsemen Roger took the city of Messina before his brother Robert had even sailed with the main army.[80] When the duke arrived a triumphal entry was made, and during the next eight days the city was fortified and garrisoned. Then the Norman army rode into the interior, led and supported by their Sicilian Moslem ally, the Emir Ibn at-Timnah, towards the hostile territory of his rival and their enemy, the Emir Ibn a-Hawas. (In the words of the Arab proverb, 'My enemy's enemy is my friend'; and the Normans were past-masters of that other ancient adage, 'Divide and rule'). The 'superb natural stronghold' of Rometta[81] was taken without resistance, and so in the event was Paternò. They came at length to the foot of al-Hawas' mountain fortress of Enna[82] in the centre and heart of Sicily. That was to prove impregnable, in the heat of summer on a first and dangerously extended campaign with a depleted army, and after a two months' siege the Normans withdrew, but not before, in the early stages, they had deliberately engaged and heavily defeated a vastly larger army of Ibn al-Hawas in what was the first major battle between Normans and Saracens, a foretaste of the Crusades. Malaterra gives the figures as 700 Normans and 15,000 Moslems, and neither may be an exaggeration either way.[83] According to Amatus, duke Robert Guiscard, in his speech to his army before battle began, cited not inappropriately Matthew xvii,20, that faith will move mountains. 'Be not afraid, for we have Jesus Christ with us, who sayeth "If ye have faith as a grain of mustard seed, ye shall say unto this mountain, Remove hence to yonder place; and it shall remove; and nothing shall be impossible unto you."' They were to make their confession and partake of the Holy Sacrament, and God would give them the victory. This they did, and raised their gonfanons, and went into

Rometta, Sicily.

Sicilian lunar landscape near Enna, outside which the Normans fought and won their first major battle against the Saracens in 1061. 'If ye have faith as a grain of mustard seed, ye shall say unto this mountain, remove hence to yonder place; and it shall remove. . . .

battle, in two divisions with Roger in the van 'as was his custom' (*sicuti sibi moris erat*).

The campaign of 1061 ended in the autumn when the Normans returned to Italy, but leaving Messina behind them as a fortified base and bridgehead for their return. In addition to this and other bases they also raised the first castle on the island, at San Marco d'Anunzio, where it still is, close to the north coast near classical Aluntium, and so named by Robert Guiscard after his castle and base of San Marco Argentano where his meteoric career had begun only fifteen years before. But while the duke celebrated Christmas in Apulia with his second wife Sichelgaita, Roger accompanied them only as far as Mileto[84] (increasingly henceforth his preferred residence in Calabria) and before the year was out was back again in Sicily with 250 knights.[85] The mountain citadel of Troina was surrendered to him by the Greek Christians within it, and there he held his Christmas. The next year he took leave, on news of her arrival, to ride to Italy (*multum exhilaratus . . . quanto celerius potuit*— full of joy . . . as fast as his horse could carry him) to marry his Judith, with a wedding at Mileto especially marked by its music (*cum maximo musicorum concentu*), but was soon back again, 'in no way to be detained by the persuasions of his tearful wife'.[86]

Unfortunately we cannot follow the stirring but long story of the subsequent piecemeal conquest of Sicily with the detailed narrative that it deserves. It became increasingly the affair of Roger of Hauteville, and Guiscard himself never returned to Sicily after the capture of Palermo, the capital, in January 1072, after which he made Roger count of Sicily as his vassal. There were battles won, invariably against seemingly hopeless odds—Cerami, west of Troina, in 1063, where Roger had only 130 knights and whatever infantry went with them against a Moslem army numbering thousands;[87] and Misilmeri, south of Palermo, in 1068, 'which broke the back of Saracen resistance in Sicily'.[88] Palermo, as we have seen, fell in 1072, and, of the last two major Saracen strongholds, Trapani, in the west, was taken in 1077 and Taormina in the east in 1079. Syracuse fell in 1085; the great mountain fortress of Enna, first attacked in 1061, fell at last in 1087; and the fall of Noto in 1091 marks the completion of Norman domination over the whole island. For the historian, three features of it all especially deserve note. One is the increasing use of sea power by the Normans, hired, acquired and adopted, no doubt, from the Greeks in Italy, essential for the logistics of campaigns in Sicily launched from Italy and against the Moslem fleets, and employed, for example, in such great sieges by sea and land as those of Palermo and Syracuse. A second is the aura of Holy War that increasingly attends the campaigns. Men will always see their cause as just and pray to their God or gods for victory: the attributes of the Christian God as the God of victory were an important factor in the spread of Christianity in the West; but a new dimension comes when the Normans who are allies of the Papacy fight Paynims and Unbelievers who can be represented as the enemies of Christ. The Normans in Sicily, we are told, confessed and received absolution of their sins in preparation for the battles of Enna and Cerami; and during the latter desperate engage-

Bronze doors from the cathedral at Trani.
(*Hirmer Fotoarchiv*)

Trani cathedral, Apulia, from the west (begun 1098)
(*Hirmer Fotoarchiv*)

Cefalù cathedral, Sicily: Christ in majesty, apse mosaic.

(*Scala, Milan*)

ment a vision of St George shone before Roger's hard-pressed knights and led their charges—appearing, of course, as a knight, superbly armed and mounted on a white horse, bearing a white gonfanon on the end of his lance with a splendid cross thereon.[89] After Cerami, Pope Alexander sent a papal banner to Roger to go with him in his battles, and proclaimed absolution for all who joined him and duke Robert in their wars against the heathen. This, we can see with hindsight, makes the war in Sicily a crusade. Yet the third feature of the conquest and the colonization of Sicily is the tolerance of necessity displayed, when the fighting was over, by the new Norman lords to their Saracen subjects, which has so hypnotized historians.

So by 1091 and indeed before, less than a century after the first known appearance of Norman knights in action at Salerno, the whole southern half of the Italian peninsula—Capua, Apulia and Calabria, the former principalities also of Salerno and Benevento (except the city and some territory left to the Papacy), the duchies of Amalfi, Gaeta and Sorrento (with Naples in theory autonomous until 1139)—all this, and Sicily too, were under Norman lordship. Nor was this all, for Malta also was taken by Roger I in 1091, and his son and successor, Roger II, held, from c.1123 for more than twenty years, a section of the North African coast which by 1148 extended from Tunis to Tripoli.[90] Nor is even this all, for Robert Guiscard before he died not only cemented his alliance with the Papacy by turning back the German Emperor from Rome in 1084 and rescuing Gregory VII from the city (in the process Rome was sacked by Guiscard's troops to blacken the Norman reputation in the eyes of many), but also turned his presumptuous arms against the Eastern Empire and the Byzantine mainland across the Adriatic. It is an extraordinary commentary on the heights to which these once undistinguished Norman knights had risen that Pope Gregory died as Guiscard's guest at Salerno in 1085 and lies buried in his new cathedral there, while in 1081 the same duke Robert had defeated the Eastern Emperor Alexius Comnenus himself at Durazzo, the imperial Varangian guard notwithstanding, still failing to exact revenge for Hastings in 1066.[91] What might have happened next we cannot say, for to this man all things seem possible, but Guiscard died of typhoid on 17 July 1085, on the Ionian island of Cephalonia, aged 70 and still on campaign against Byzantium.[92] His body was brought back for burial in his abbey of the Trinity at Venosa beside his only less distinguished brothers William, Drogo and Humphrey of Hauteville. Their original tombs were destroyed in the sixteenth century, but the epitaph inscribed on that of the great duke was preserved by William of Malmesbury and began: '*Hic terror mundi Guiscardus* . . . Here lies Guiscard, terror of the world . . .'[93]

Robert, duke of Apulia, Calabria and Sicily died in 1085; Richard, count of Aversa and prince of Capua, had died in 1078; Roger, 'Great Count' of Sicily was to die, aged 70, in 1101. With their passing, and the death of Guiscard perhaps especially, a whole and almost unbelievable era passes, of that first generation of Norman knights riding into Italy to win their spurs and so much else. There was a century yet of glory to come, but it was, so to speak, an established glory and the glory of establishment: never glad, confident morning again, when all the world was young, and everything yet to be won. In Capua Richard I was duly succeeded by his sons, grandsons and great-grandsons. In Apulia, Guiscard was succeeded by his son (by Sichelgaita) Roger 'Borsa' ('Money-bags') and grandson William, each of whom is generally considered an anticlimax—as who would not be? As count of Sicily, Roger I was succeeded by his son by his third wife, Roger II, at first a minor (he was born in 1095 when his father was sixty-four), who eventually brought all the Norman-Italian principalities together under his rule and was recognized and made king thereof by Pope Anacletus, to be crowned on Christmas Day 1130 in Palermo. With the history of that glittering, polyglot kingdom until it passed to the German Emperor Henry VI in 1194 by marriage, with its dazzling civilization a blend of Latin, Greek and Moslem yet created by the Normans, we are not concerned—which, one may add, makes a change, since historians have generally been fascinated by it to the detriment of the preceding century of high endeavour and also to the point of misinterpretation. Suffice it to say the splendid Norman Sicilian monarchy was fundamentally a feudal monarchy like

The tomb of Roger II (d.1154) in Palermo cathedral. The porphyry sarcophagus is or was imperial purple in colour.

Christ crowns Roger II king of Sicily. Mosaic in the church of the Martorana at Palermo (mid-twelfth century).

that of France or England or ultimately Germany, stemming also from the Carolingian experience and Latin Christianity. We should not be misled by the obvious oriental trappings of its court, nor even by certain Byzantine traditions in its art, into seeing it (still less welcoming it) as an anticipation of the modern bureaucratic state, derived from Byzantine concepts of theocratic absolutism and Roman Law.[94]

If, finally, we try briefly to summarize and explain the Norman achievement in Italy, it is *par excellence* a classic, perhaps the classic, exercise in *Normanitas*.[95] It is true that the duchy of Normandy considered as a state, the power of its duke, and the new Norman aristocracy, contribute little save indirectly as propellants of determined exiles, though it is also true that each of those elements was only at an embryonic stage when the penetration of southern Italy began. That aside, the perception and grasping of opportunities was characteristically Norman, as were the far-flung pilgrimages which did so much to generate the enterprise. Next, and first amongst the attributes which brought such devastating success, we must place sheer military expertise. Here, however, something more is needed than mere martial prowess to account for so many amazing feats of arms and victories almost invariably achieved by small companies of outnumbered knights, and the explanation must surely lie in the impact of heavy cavalry and the shock tactic of the couched lance, hitherto beyond the experience of Lombard, Greek or Moslem.[96] While any serious military study of the Normans in Italy is lacking (like so much else in the neglected field of medieval military history), it is clear that infantry, the *pedites* of the chronicles, played

Knights jousting; doorway of the church at S. Marcello Maggiore, Capua (early twelfth century). With the increasing cult of chivalry, knights became a decorative motif second only to saints and bible stories.

Knights in action; north door (*porta dei leoni*) of St Nicholas at Bari (twelfth century).

their part in Norman campaigns, but that part was subsidiary. Contemporary sources give all publicity to mounted knights, and rightly so; for the knights made victory possible—indeed, we may say with hindsight, seemingly inevitable—and the Norman immigration into Italy, not least in the beginning, was above all an influx of knights and an export of chivalry. In fact from the beginning we hear very little of anybody else, save clerks and monks, and the whole affair is a supreme example of Norman aristocratic colonization. Not too much should be made in this respect of the poverty of these knightly immigrants of the first generation or thereafter: their poverty is of the comparative kind, of younger sons and exiles from the upper stratum of society, unable without enterprise to live at the standard to which they wished to become accustomed. Assuredly in Italy, and subsequently in Sicily, this military élite became the social élite which they aspired to be, and, if they did not lose their lives, they soon won the fiefs and lordships of their ambitious dreams. Marriage, too, as in Normandy or England, was a chosen means of consolidating newly won positions, as Rainulf of Aversa married first the sister of the duke of Naples and next, on her death, the niece of Pandulf, prince of Capua; or Robert Guiscard put aside on grounds of consanguinity his Norman wife Aubrey to marry Sichelgaita, sister of the prince of Salerno.[97] The result, sociologically, as in England and as in Antioch, was the imposition of a new ruling class upon a pre-existing society, the imposition of lordship in the characteristic Norman manner.

Of course this lordship was feudal, and the Normans introduced what we call feudalism into Italy and Sicily as they did everywhere they went; for at this level the new lords inevitably brought with them those social attitudes, assumptions and institutions with which they were familiar at home. In southern Italy and Sicily, however, the new lordship was spread very thin because of the small numbers of the new lords, and in the former case there could be no question of the total displacement of the native Lombard aristocracy to be compared with that of the old pre-Conquest ruling

Knights in action, from a capital of the cloister of Monreale, Sicily (late twelfth century).

class in England. In consequence, feudalism in Norman Italy was not and could not be total either, and among and beneath the new establishment there were enclaves of surviving but demoted Lombard lordship and substrata of indigenous society little affected by the new régime.[98] In Sicily also, there were differences from any text-book pattern of feudal society, caused by a numerous Moslem and thus entirely alien population. Yet none of this, any more than the too-well known borrowings of Moslem and Byzantine administrative techniques and institutions by Norman kings and princes,[99] should blind us to the fundamentally feudal nature of the new and dominant society which they established or of the monarchy which ruled over it from 1130. 'The feudal character of the Norman monarchy could not be, and never was, altered by the fact that the newcomers adopted both Arab and Byzantine institutions and methods of administration.'[100] There never was anywhere a perfect and exclusive feudal society or state because in the time-scale of European history, in the vital centuries between the fifth and twelfth, feudalism came late, to be grafted on the stock of what had gone before. England was no less feudal because the Normans there inherited a Carolingian-type monarchy and imposed their lordship upon the existing Anglo-Scandinavian society, and so, *mutatis mutandis*, it is with southern Italy and Sicily. One may add also, for good measure, that it is most unlikely that Roger II, any more than William the Conqueror—or (dare one say?) Henry I or Henry II, his closer contemporaries—were primarily interested in administration and governmental techniques, as so many modern historians, imposing their wholly anachronistic concepts upon the past, would have us believe.

The use of that other instrument of Norman colonization and lordship, the Church, is as much in evidence in southern Italy and Sicily as it is in Normandy itself or England. Nor because, thus analyzing, one speaks of the use, conscious or unconscious, of the Church and Latin Christianity, is there any need to doubt the sincerity of Norman piety. Motives are usually mixed except perhaps with saints, and if the cult of chivalry involved the cult of violence as well, it also enflamed the consciences of its practitioners. In fact in Italy after Civitate[101] the Normans soon became the champions of the Latin Church as the allies of the Papacy and the allies and patrons also of the great existing Lombard and Latin monasteries such as Montecassino, Volturno and La Cava.[102] Further, though this situation was brought about by the radical thinking of such great churchmen as Cardinal Hildebrand and abbot Desiderius, we can also see the inevitability of it as the Normans became a power in the land; for while the Lombards were Romans in religion, Greek influence was predominant in the south at a time when the Greek and Roman churches were moving rapidly into schism, and it was against the Greeks especially that Norman warfare was directed. Sicily of course was Paynim, and there the fighting could be seen as Holy War and a version of the *gesta Dei per Francos*. The consequence was that everywhere the Normans were established the Church was Latinized, as indeed had been promised by Robert Guiscard at Melfi in 1059.[103] In Calabria the Latinization

King William II 'the Good'
(1166–89) offers his new church of
Monreale to the Virgin; mosaic in
Monreale cathedral (late twelfth
century).

of the ecclesiastical hierarchy was carried out as quickly and completely as possible by Robert Guiscard and Roger I, Greek bishops being replaced by Latin save in one or two places for political reasons.[104] In Sicily the organization of the Christian Church after so long a Moslem occupation had to be recreated, and, again, the new hierarchy was Latin, French bishops being appointed by Roger I, for example, at Troina, Syracuse, Mazara, Catania and Agrigento as well as to the archiepiscopal see of Palermo.[105]

So, too, the new Norman lords planted Latin monasteries as soon as they became established—though again the time-scale of the Norman enterprise has to be remembered, in that it took time for even the Normans to become established, and when the first of them left Normandy William of Volpiano had not yet come to Fécamp.[106] The first new Norman foundation in Apulia, Holy Trinity at Venosa, by the Hautevilles soon after 1043, and dedicated by the Pope in 1059, has already been mentioned. In 1063 it was placed under St Eufemia, and Berengar son of Arnald, a monk from St Evroul in Normandy, was appointed as its second abbot.[107] St Eufemia itself, put in charge of abbot Robert of Grandmesnil and

St Evroul, Normandy, ruins of the thirteenth-century abbey church which replaced that of Orderic Vitalis.

colonised from St Evroul, was founded by Robert Guiscard in 1062 in Calabria as soon as the conquest of that province was more or less complete.[108] Also in newly won Calabria, Guiscard, with his wife Sichelgaita, founded Santa Maria della Mattina, near his original base at San Marco Argentano, in expiation of Norman misdeeds in the region, and Roger I founded at his favourite Calabrian residence of Mileto the abbey of Holy Trinity, which again was given a monk from St Evroul as its abbot and placed under St Eufemia.[109] In Sicily also the foundation of Latin monasteries followed in the wake of the conquest—Lipari before 1085, Catania (another daughter-house of St Eufemia) in 1091, Patti in 1094, Messina (Santa Maria della Scala) in 1095. By the end of the Norman period there were more than fifty Latin religious houses in Sicily, including the three monastic cathedrals of Monreale, Catania and Lippari-Patti, and the cathedral of Cefalù served by Augustinian canons.[110] The great majority of these foundations in Norman Italy and Sicily were of course Benedictine, but the Carthusians came to settle in Calabria in 1091 in the person of St Bruno himself, the Augustinians were brought from Calabria to be installed in architectural splendour at Cefalù by Roger II in the 1130s, and the Cistercians came at length when Saint Bernard eventually brought himself to make peace with his 'tyrant of Sicily' in 1140. Each and all of these monastic houses mark personal devotion and the establishment of Norman lordship, but they also mark the advance and triumph of Latin Christianity and *Romanitas* in southern Apulia and Calabria which had been largely Greek, and in Sicily which had been Moslem. On the mainland Greek or 'Basilian' monasticism, far from enjoying a renaissance and an Indian Summer under Norman rule, as has sometimes been alleged, was slowly but inexorably suppressed by the foundation of Latin monasteries endowed with the former property of Greek houses, or by the subordination of those houses and their property alike to such established Latin abbeys as Montecassino or La Cava.[111] The concept of the Norman kings and princes of the south as sympathetically inclined to Greek religion—let alone Islam—is as much a myth, it seems, as that of their un-feudal, oriental and half-modern despotism.[112]

The Norman aristocratic colonization of southern Italy and Sicily was characteristically accompanied by a great series of buildings and rebuildings which can only be compared to the building programmes carried out in England after 1066 and, indeed in Normandy itself during the eleventh century. The castles still await, at least in England, their survey and their historians (the more remarkable since those raised in Italy and Sicily before 1066 must be directly relevant to any argument about the types of castles raised in pre-Conquest Normandy), but one notes the references to castles raised at once as centres of new lordship in territories acquired in Calabria, for example, and in Sicily, and surmises that the number of castles founded in the long course of the conquest must have rivalled the prodigious number raised in England and Wales in the decades following 1066.[113] The churches, and the secular palace buildings at and around Palermo especially, however, have attracted the enthusiastic attentions of architectural and art historians in this country as elsewhere,[114] and while the former especially have all too often suffered from the depredations of earthquakes, rebuilding and Baroque,[115] no more splendid monuments to Norman achievement in the south could be asked for than, let us say, St Nicholas at Bari, Trani, Cefalù, Monreale, or the Palatine Chapel at Palermo. Nevertheless some strange things have been said about them, to the effect that they are scarcely 'Norman', and therefore the 'Normans'

Bari, St. Nicholas, Apulia (under construction 1089).

who built and commissioned them are scarcely 'Norman' either.

The truth is that Norman architecture was never more Norman than when adopting non-Norman features, whether in Normandy or England, Italy or Sicily. Remembering as we must that the earliest Norman settlers had been in Italy for half a century or more before the evolution of a Jumièges (1067) or a St Stephen's, Caen (1077), it is also an accepted fact that Norman Romanesque in Normandy made use of features from Burgundy, Lombardy, the Rhineland and elsewhere. It could scarcely be otherwise in a country as new as Normandy, which only begins in 911 and develops apace only in the eleventh century. When the Hautevilles built Holy Trinity at Venosa in the 1040s and 1050s we would be lucky indeed to get a building as far advanced in terms of 'Norman' Romanesque as Bernay and it is not at all surprising that we do not.[116] Nor is it surprising to find Norman buildings in the south adopting Byzantine and Arabic features like, for example and respectively, mosaics and grotto ceilings, or almost everywhere following the basilican plan rather than that of the Latin cross. The Normans in Italy and Sicily, like the British in India, were heavily outnumbered by the subject races over whom they lorded it, and there must have been even fewer Norman masons and other craftsmen. Further, the Normans were the most eclectic of races, and there are few more prominent features of *Normanitas* than eclecticism. We do in fact find Norman Romanesque, from Nor-

Cefalù cathedral, Sicily, from the south-east (begun by Roger II in 1131).

mandy at, for example, Bari,[117] Cefalù[118] and Mazara del Vallo[119] (the last two in Sicily), but we also find features from elsewhere in France, like roofs of joined cupolas or domes more likely to come from western France (Loches, Cahors) than Byzantium,[120] or sculpture also from western France and from Provence.[121] A church like St Etienne at Périgueux would not look out of place in Norman Italy. There we must not be seduced by the Greek mosaics and

Palermo, Capella Palatina, interior looking east (Note the grotto ceiling).

San Giovanni degli Eremiti, (1132) interior.

bronze doors everywhere, or the Arab ceilings, columns, arches and arcades of Palermo, Monreale and all Sicily, into supposing that our Normans have somehow gone native and lost their identity. The internal splendour of the Palatine Chapel in the palace at Palermo has recently been called 'a masterpiece of happy eclecticism', and it is indeed a heady mixture of Early Christian, Latin, Byzantine and Arabic.[122] Such buildings in Sicily especially recall the splendour phrase of Jean Décarreaux who writes of their giving expression to 'a spirit of synthesis amounting to genius' ('esprit de synthèse poussé au génie'),[123] and they directly reflect not only Norman eclecticism but also, like all art and architecture, the society which produced them, exciting, polyglot and multiplex— and created by the Norman lords who fashioned it to their will.

Those who achieved the Norman conquest of Italy and Sicily were certainly predominantly Norman and conscious of it (even Roger II, we are told, was always conscious of his Norman origins),[124] as Norman as those who conquered England though probably less numerous, and, like them, joined and reinforced by other French.[125] Their coming may also obviously be seen as a dramatic result of that over-population which is a feature of Nor-

Loches, St. Ours, the nave roof
consisting of two hollow octagonal
spires (mid–twelfth century).

Trani, west front, decorated window
opening.

Aulnay, Poitou, with rich exterior
sculpture and decoration (twelfth
century).

113

mandy (as of other areas in the West) in the eleventh century.[126] The
twelve sons of Tancred of Hauteville of whom eight came to Italy
must be the sovereign paradigm, followed by the nine sons of
Guidmundus des Moulins (Moulins-la-Marche, dep. Orne) who
gave their name to the great county of Molise. As for the wealth and
economic prosperity of eleventh-century Normandy,[127] at first
sight the early emigrants to Italy may seem to make little advertise-
ment for it since their poverty is always stressed by historians, and
was indeed a powerful element in their motivation—*militariter
lucrum quaerentes.* Yet it is to be remembered that they were evidently all knights, save for such servitors as they presumably brought
with them, and the poverty of knights is not absolute.[128] It can
indeed be argued that knights, like monks, are necessarily the
product of an affluent society, since both are elevated above the
mere business of labouring for a living and neither thus contribute
(as we would say but they would not) to the GNP. One is reminded
again of Tancred of Hauteville's twelve sons each trained as a knight
when he reached adolescence.[129] It must have been a very expensive
business, like sending twelve sons to public schools.

The Norman impact upon Italy was scarcely less than that upon
England, though there they took only half the country and not the
whole. To that half at least they brought unity in the end, and the
kingdom established by Roger II in 1130 lasted until the nineteenth
century. In other ways also the Norman enterprise in the south
changed the course of history. They contributed by their exploits to
the fateful schism then developing between the Latin and Greek

Churches and between East and West. At the same time they were responsible for bringing southern Italy and Sicily into the world of Latin Christendom. Further, in so doing they achieved the first substantial gain by the West from Islam, which had once threatened to overwhelm it.[130] Further yet, while the Normans bore a papal banner before them in both Sicily and England, in Italy as the allies of Rome they contributed directly and more than can be measured to the triumph of the reformed Papacy and all that follows from it, even to the virtual destruction of the power of the medieval German Empire in the thirteenth century. These are great matters, but there are at least two others. The first is that which probably attracts

Périgueux, St-Etienne-de-la-Cité (twelfth century)
B. Interior.

modern historians most, the creation (for what other word will do?) of the brilliant and extraordinary culture and civilization of the twelfth-century Sicilian kingdom, the amalgamation, by Norman genius and eclecticism, of three worlds, Latin, Greek and Moslem, plus a fourth which we may surely call Norman. The second, to which we must turn again in the next chapter, is that in Sicily the Normans put into practice the growing concept of Holy War. Out of that, and out of southern Italy also, was to come the Crusade launched by Pope Urban II in 1095.

The 'grotto' ceiling of the Cappella Palatina, Palermo (mid–twelfth century)
(*Scala, Milan*)

Monreale cathedral, Sicily: interior to east (1174–82)

(*Scala, Milan*)

San Giovanni degli Eremiti, Palermo.

(*J. Allan Cash*)

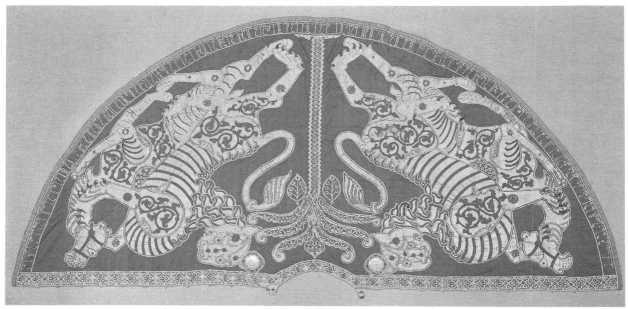

The coronation mantle of Roger II, woven at Palermo.

(Kunsthistorisches Museum, Vienna)

The 'crusading' window from Chartres. The events depicted are Charlemagne's campaigns against the Arabs in Spain.

(Photo Giraudon)

Chapter 6 The Normans on the First Crusade: Antioch

On Tuesday 27 November 1095, at a special and general meeting of the council of Clermont for an advertized public announcement, Pope Urban II launched the First Crusade.[1] The session was so well attended, by both clerk and lay, that it had to be held outside the cathedral and in a field outside the east gate of the city, and the enthusiasm with which his speech was received was contagious and overwhelming. His actual words are lost in the varying versions later published, but he called for the liberation of the East, the Eastern Churches and the Holy Places from oppression and defilement by Unbelievers, and his passionate appeal was greeted with great shouts of *Deus le volt!*—'God wills it!'[2] Adhemar, bishop of Le Puy, with whom the pope had consulted in advance, was the first to take the cross, and everywhere garments were cut in the shape of crosses to be sewn to shoulders as the multitude followed his example in the imitation of Christ—'And he that taketh not his cross and followeth after me, is not worthy of me' (Matthew, x, 38). Throughout France and into Germany and Italy and Britain the fiery message spread and was taken up, by rich and poor alike, fanned in the latter case by popular preachers such as Peter the Hermit and Walter Sans Avoir. Whatever Urban's original intentions may have been, they were soon swept on a tide of popular enthusiasm beyond his control into the simple realities of an armed pilgrimage to the earthly Jerusalem, with the reward of milk and honey in this world and remission of all sin in the next. The resultant pathetic rabble of the People's Crusade led by Peter the Hermit was to be cut to pieces by the Turks at Civetot in Asia Minor, far from Jerusalem and the Promised Land, and other disorganized and popular contingents from Germany never got beyond Hungary, where they too were slaughtered in retaliation for their atrocities and their massacre of Jews along the way.[3] But while these unimagined tragedies were taking place, so far removed from the intentions and the spirit of Clermont, the armies of the

Robert Curthose, duke of Normandy, with couched lance unhorses and kills his Saracen opponent at the Battle of Ascalon (1099). From an early eighteenth century set of drawings of destroyed stained glass windows depicting scenes from the First Crusade, (mid-twelfth century) at St Denis, engraved by Montfaucon in the eighteenth century (*Les monumens de la monarchie francoise*, i, plates l–liv). (Bibliothèque nationale, MS Fr. 15634 (1))

princes were assembling in the West, in France especially, to undertake, and ultimately to achieve, the liberation of Jerusalem.

First of the great Frankish princes to take the cross, and the senior among them, was Raymond (IV) of St-Gilles, count of Toulouse and marquis of Provence, from southern France. Nearly 60 years of age and a veteran of the wars in Spain against the Moslems there, he too had evidently been consulted in advance about Urban's great design on the latter's journey to Clermont (via Avignon and St-Gilles). Now he took with him his wife, the princess Elvira of Aragon, and Alfonso his heir, and vowed to remain in the Holy Land for the rest of his life. With him also were the papal delegate and spiritual leader of the crusade, Adhemar bishop of Le Puy, and many nobles and magnates from southern France including both the count (Rambald) and bishop (William) of Orange, Gaston de Béarn, Gerard de Roussillon and William de Montpellier. Raymond set out in October 1096, with a total strength which has been estimated at ten thousand men including one thousand two hundred knights and cavalry,[4] chose the difficult route via northern Italy down the Dalmatic coast, and himself reached Constantinople on 21 April 1097. Scarcely less elevated in status than count Raymond of St-Gilles was Hugh de Vermandois, a younger son of Henry I, king of the French, and brother to the reigning king, Philip. Aged about forty he was the first of the cruasading leaders to get under way, in late August 1096, but had only a small contingent of perhaps one hundred knights.[5] He travelled to Constantinople by the normal route through Italy, crossing the Adriatic from Bari

to Dyrrachium or Durazzo and suffering an unfortunate shipwreck in so doing.

Also from northern France (and also aged forty) came Robert 'Curthose', duke of Normandy, eldest son of William the Conqueror, with the first of two Norman armies taking part, numbering perhaps one thousand knights plus infantry.[6] He was joined by Stephen-Henry, count of Blois, who was the Conqueror's son-in-law through his marriage to Adela, and Robert count of Flanders, each with respectively some three hundred and six hundred knights plus infantry. Amongst the Norman and Anglo-Norman, and also Breton, lords with Robert duke of Normandy were Alan Fergant count of Brittany, Stephen count of Aumale, Odo bishop of Bayeux (the Conqueror's half-brother), Ralph Guader or de Gael (earl of Norfolk but in exile from England since 1075), Pain Peverel (the duke's standard-bearer on the crusade and afterwards a tenant-in-chief in England) and William de Perci (benefactor of Whitby Abbey, Yorkshire, to which by legend his heart was brought back from Jerusalem for burial).[7] This great army and glittering company also travelled via Italy and Norman Italy. There the duke of Normandy passed the winter of 1096–7 with Roger Borsa, Guiscard's son and heir, now duke of Apulia, Calabria and Sicily,[8] took ship from Brindisi in the spring and was the last of the crusading leaders to arrive at Constantinople.

The second of the two Norman contingents was that from Norman Italy itself, under Bohemond of Taranto, the disinherited son of Robert Guiscard by his first wife Aubrey. Comparatively small but most effective, its backbone was five hundred knights amongst whom were many members of the leading Norman families in Italy, including relatives of the ruling houses of Capua and Apulia—not least the Hautevilles who were characteristically strongly represented by Bohemond himself, his nephew Tancred (another nephew, William, Tancred's brother went on ahead with Hugh de Vermandois), his cousins Richard of the Principate, Herman of Canne and Robert son of Girard (the last named Bohemond's standard-bearer) and Geoffrey of Montescaglioso.[9]

Last but not least of the crusading armies was that of Godfrey de Bouillon, duke of Lower Lorraine, with an estimated one thousand knights and seven thousand infantry drawn mostly from Lorraine. He took the legendary route of Charlemagne through Germany and Hungary and arrived at Constantinople on 23 December 1096. In his host were his brothers, Eustace (III) count of Boulogne (who may have travelled separately via Italy) and Baldwin of Boulogne, his cousin Baldwin of Le Bourg, Baldwin (II) count of Hainault and Rainald count of Toul. Of this great company, two, Godfrey himself and his younger brother Baldwin, were destined to rule in Jerusalem, as the same Baldwin and the Norman Bohemond of Taranto were to rule respectively at Edessa and Antioch in the principalities they founded in northern Syria.

Thus in the autumn and winter of 1096, as the direct result of Pope Urban's appeal, a large proportion of the new chivalry of Latin Christendom, and of the Franks especially, were riding east, to assemble at Constantinople and thence to free the Holy Places from the Infidel. With them went many more lesser men to serve under them as infantry, with clergy as was necessary and desirable, and even some ladies and other women as wives and hangers-on, in one of the most remarkable events that even the early Middle Ages can produce. Underlying it was a great spiritual revival, cultural revival, economic revival, and an expanding population, all of which combined to make the crusade both conceivable and possible. It is also clear that the crusade, for which no word had as yet been coined, grew from the stock of pilgrimage, not least to Jerusalem itself,[10] and was provoked by the advent of the Seldjuk Turks in the Middle East[11] whose new hegemony, it was reported, brought further oppression to the eastern Christians, cut off the favourite pilgrimage route through Asia Minor, and even threatened Constantinople itself, whose army and whose Emperor Romanus Diogenes had been disastrously defeated at the battle of Manzikert by Alp Arslan in 1071. Early in 1095, at a papal council at Piacenza which preceded that of Clermont, envoys from the new Byzantine Emperor Alexius Comnenus had even called for military aid from the West,[12] though by then in fact the situation was improving and they sought mercenaries and certainly not the intervention of independent armies. The crusade also and most obviously stands out as the ultimate manifestation of the newly developed concept in the West of Holy War,[13] as a revived Latin Church, a revived monasticism and a revived Papacy sought to channel the bellicosity of knights into approved warfare and the Just War, and found this more effective than earlier attempts to stamp out such bellicosity or curb it in the Peace and Truce of God. And here surely we reach the nub of motivation, which is also explanation, at least for the lords and knights who set the tone and aspirations of secular society and without whom Jerusalem would not have been regained. Born and bred to war, which was their *raison d'être*, stepped often in the cult of violence which in an imperfect world was integral with the cult of chivalry, their consciences could be stilled and their fear of Hell Fire abated in waging Holy War with the promise of indulgence.[14] In many cases also their earthly ambitions could be realized as well. The 'landless knights' and political exiles *militariter lucrum quaerentes*[15] were as prominent on the First Crusade as in any other of the territorially expansionist movements of this age of open frontiers, in Normandy or England, in Spain, southern Italy or eastern Germany, and in Holy War one could achieve both lordship in this world and paradise in the next. On the crusade one could fight the good fight, and even die in peace. Nothing could have better served the needs of the dominant class of contemporary society, and nothing would, even for the highest minded and most altruistic, until the crusading ideal itself brought forth the Military Orders wherein a man might even be at once both knight and monk. 'There was something in the crusade to appeal to everyone',[16] whether warrior or peasant, clerk or expansionist merchant from such Italian trading cities as Genoa and Pisa, Venice and Amalfi. Nevertheless we should rather say that the crusade enabled Everyman to reconcile many mixed motives and give them all expression. 'Stand fast all together, trusting in Christ and in the victory of the Holy Cross. Today, please God, you will all gain much booty'—such was the message passed along the ranks at Dorylaeum, according to the author of the *Gesta Francorum* who was present.[17] Nor is there any call for us, cynically failing to understand the world we have lost, to question the religious motives of the crusaders; nor, which is scarcely more perceptive, to divide them crudely into the two categories of sheep and goats—Count Raymond of St-Gilles, it may be, or Godfrey de Bouillon, as 'good' crusaders, spiritually motivated, and Bohemond of Taranto or Baldwin of Boulogne as each the archetype of the ruthless and worldly adventurer, out only for fiefs and lordship. If the Holy Places were to be liberated, they must also be held against the Infidel. For both, hard fighting would be necessary, and for both the Greeks had seemed to show themselves incapable and unworthy.[17a]

It should occasion no surprise that on this great adventure and pious undertaking the Normans were disproportionately and doubly represented, with contingents from both Normandy and Norman Italy, nor that their military contribution was disproportionate also, not least in the person of Bohemond, who soon showed himself the natural leader in the field and, with his five hundred knights, carved out the principality of Antioch at the very gates of Outremer. The Normans, after all, had so far been the principal begetters and chief exponents of Holy War, in Italy, in England, and in Sicily. The conquest of the last-named had been only recently completed by feats of arms against the very Moslems against whom the crusade was launched. Norman piety is not, or should not be, in doubt; nor is their martial prowess, nor their willingness to apply it to any cause which might to them seem good. The Normans in Italy, moreover, had long been directly involved with the Byzantine Empire which they had driven from the peninsula, while Bohemond (and doubtless others on the First Crusade) had fought against the Greeks in Illyria on his father's campaigns of 1081–5.[18] Clearly their thoughts and ambitions were already irresistibly turning east, as even now at Bari one may long to go on and take the modern car-ferry across the Adriatic to Ragusa or Corfu. The fact that Bohemond and his knights, their infantry and their supporters, on the long march to Antioch, were necessarily operating for once not on their own, but as part of a larger whole, must not obscure the reality that their subsequent foundation and creation of their principality of Antioch was another characteristic exercise in Norman territorial expansion, aristocratic colonization and (in modern terminology) take-over. In a real sense the contribution of the Normans from Italy to the First Crusade can be seen, in Evelyn Jamison's words as 'one more enterprise of the house of Hauteville'.[19]

Of the two Norman leaders on the First Crusade, both of whom were to end their lives in personal tragedy, Bohemond concerns us most, as the proven ablest warrior and the future prince of Antioch. Robert 'Curthose', duke of Normandy, as the eldest but least successful son of William the Conqueror, has inevitably received the more attention from English historians, though his well-known standard biography might by now with advantage be revised. There, as elsewhere in modern histories, his reputation is of feckless weakness as a prince, 'wrong but romantic', so to speak, as opposed to his younger brothers, William 'Rufus' and Henry (I), who are by comparison 'right but repulsive' and neither of whom went on crusade.[20] His frustrated opposition to his father, by no means untypical of his age (or others), led to his disinheritance of England at the Conqueror's deathbed.[21] He was later to lose Normandy to Henry I at the Battle of Tinchebrai in 1106, and end his days a political prisoner in Cardiff castle.[22] To contemporaries, however, he was a fine knight if not, in the end, a successful lord, and he left a reputation behind him as a crusading hero 'whom neither Christian nor pagan could ever unhorse'.[23] Since he mortgaged his duchy to his brother William Rufus to go on crusade, and returned to Normandy immediately after the capture of Jerusalem and the victory at Ascalon, he cannot be made to suffer the charge of gross materialism which in our time seems ineradicable from the reputation of Bohemond.

Bohemond certainly deserves a fuller, up-to-date, and better-known biography.[24] Robert Guiscard's eldest son by his first marriage to Aubrey, he had been disinherited of his birthright in Italy and Sicily after his father's second marriage to Sichelgaita of Salerno, yet evidently loyally served him on attaining manhood, not least in the Byzantine campaigns of 1081–5. The bitter fact was that he alone was a worthy son of the great Guiscard, yet had no worthy future in the Italy of Roger 'Borsa' ('Moneybags'). Anna

Comnena has left us a word-portrait of him to set beside her description of his father.[25] 'Bohemond resembled his father in all respects, in daring, strength, aristocratic and indomitable spirit. In short Bohemond was the exact replica and living image of [him]'.[26] And, as with his father, Anna was attracted in spite of herself by Bohemond's appearance and, in his case, charm.

> 'The sight of him inspired admiration, the mention of his name terror . . . His stature was such that he towered almost a full cubit over the tallest men. He was slender of waist and flanks, with broad shoulders and chest, strong in the arms . . . perfectly proportioned . . . His hands were large, he had a good firm stance, and his neck and back were compact. If to the accurate and meticulous observer he appeared to stoop slightly, that was not caused by any weakness of the vertebrae of the lower spine, but presumably there was some malformation there from birth.'

His skin was white though his face was also ruddy; his hair lightish-brown and short, 'to the ears'. He was clean-shaven, 'his

123

chin smoother than any marble'. His eyes were light-blue and showed his spirit and dignity.

> 'There was a certain charm about him, but it was somewhat dimmed by the alarm his person as a whole inspired; there was a hard, savage quality in his whole aspect, due, I suppose, to his great stature and his eyes; even his laugh sounded like a threat to others. Such was his constitution, mental and physical, that in him both courage and love were armed, both ready for combat. His arrogance was everywhere manifest; he was cunning, too, taking refuge in any opportunism. His words were carefully phrased and the replies he gave were regularly ambiguous.'

Thus the princess Anna, daughter of the Emperor Alexius Comnenus, described long afterwards her sweet enemy.[27]

According to the anonymous *Gesta Francorum*, the earliest and best source for the First Crusade, written, it is thought, by a knight and vassal of Bohemond who accompanied his lord and master to Antioch, the 'great warrior' took the cross [in June 1096] when he was besieging Ponte di Scafati in the course of a campaign with his brother Duke Roger Borsa and his uncle Roger the Great Count of Sicily, against Amalfi.[28] Hearing that a great army of Frankish warriors was moving through Italy *en route* to the Holy Sepulchre and to fight the pagans, he enquired about them and was told they were well armed and bore Christ's cross on their right arm or back and had as their war cry 'Deus vult, Deus vult, Deus vult!' 'Then Bohemond, inspired by the Holy Ghost, ordered the most valuable [red] cloak which he had to be cut up forthwith and made into crosses, and most of the knights who were at the siege began to join him at once, for they were full of enthusiasm, so that count Roger [of Sicily] was left almost alone, and when he had gone back to Sicily he grieved and lamented because he had lost his army'. In his re-working of the same source, Robert the monk of Rheims has Bohemond especially moved by the fact that it is his own kith and kin from France and Normandy who are thus setting out for Jerusalem, for martyrdom and for Paradise, and he appeals to his followers in terms of their Frankish origins which make it impossible for them to stay behind without the certain condemnation of posterity.[29] And so 'my lord Bohemond went home to his own land', *i.e.* Taranto, made careful preparations,[30] and departed, as we have seen, with his five hundred knights for Constantinople via Durazzo, which with his father he had taken from the Emperor Alexius Comnenus fourteen years before.[31]

So in the winter and spring of 1096–7 the crusading armies assembled one after the other at Constantinople. The Emperor Alexius, alarmed and suspicious of their autonomous intentions, extracted from all the leaders oaths of fealty,[32] whereby they also swore to return to him any conquests made from the Turks of imperial territory lost since 1070, before and after Manzikert,[33] and to hold any others only under his suzerainty.[34] Bohemond, who as a marked man and former enemy of Byzantium behaved impeccably in Constantinople and throughout his march there from Durazzo, now, according to Anna Comnena, demanded high office in the imperial army and received a soft but evasive answer.[35] He also, according to the *Gesta Francorum*, made a secret pact with Alexius whereby he was to take, receive, and hold as vassal, a large territory east of Antioch.[36] The latter statement is generally regarded as a later insertion in the *Gesta*, made to justify Bohemond's retention of Antioch at the time of his visit to the West in 1106 to raise his crusade against Byzantium. There is, however, really no reason why it should be.[37] It is clear from the oath imposed upon the crusading leaders that Alexius had no objection to the creation under his suzerainty of buffer states—or, as the crusaders would have seen them, marcher lordships—beyond the 1070 frontiers of the Empire against the Turk, while the city of Antioch itself, whose retention by Bohemond remains a flagrant violation of his oath, is not included in the compact.

These matters having been arranged, the crusading armies were ferried across the Bosphorus and advanced into Asia Minor against the Seldjuk capital of Nicaea in the early summer of 1097.[38] Byzantine guide and engineers went with them, and at this stage Byzantine supplies sustained them, while imperial forces followed behind them to receive and consolidate their conquests. 'Then Bohemond took up his station in front of the city, with Tancred next to him, then Duke Godfrey and the count of Flanders, next to whom was Robert of Normandy, and then the count of St-Gilles and the bishop of Le Puy . . . Our men were all, for the first time, collected together in this place, and who could count such a great army of Christians? I do not think that anyone has ever seen, or will ever again see, so many valiant knights'.[39] At Nicaea they had their

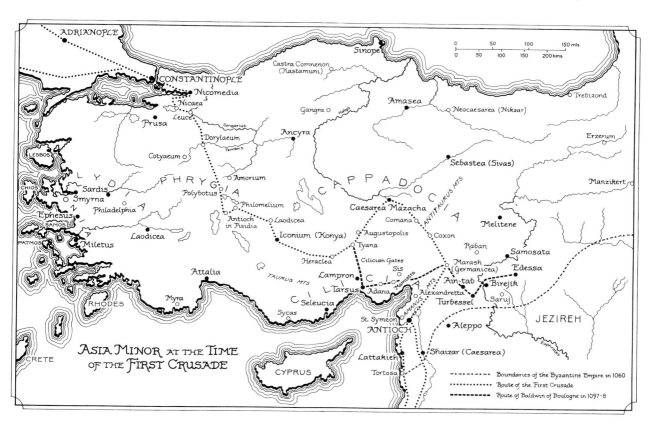

ASIA MINOR at the TIME
OF THE FIRST CRUSADE

---------- Boundaries of the Byzantine Empire in 1060
················ Route of the First Crusade
- - - - - - - Route of Baldwin of Boulogne in 1097-8

Nicaea, the first battle and victory of the Franks against the Turks (1097) from the lost window at St. Denis, mid twelfth-century (Bibliothèque nationale). Note the Turkish mounted archers and the couched lance and gonfanon of the crusaders.

first taste of victory against the Turks, when Kilij Arslan the Seldjuk sultan was beaten off, albeit with heavy losses (including Baldwin of Ghent), on 21 May. The experience was also their first encounter with the worrying Turkish tactics of harassment by mounted archers and extreme mobility. At Nicaea also, its walls strengthened by two hundred towers and where Byzantine ships were necessary to complete the investment of the city on the lake side, they came up for the first time against eastern and imperial fortifications. Nevertheless the city fell, submitting on 19 June, the day for which their final assault was planned, and was duly handed over to imperial emissaries—to the disappointed irritation of the rank and file, and of some of their leaders.

A week later on 26 June, having rested and been richly rewarded by Alexius to mitigate their loss of loot, the crusading armies began to move on along the road to Dorylaeum. They marched now in two divisions, partly to solve the difficulties of supply. The Normans from Normandy and Italy were in the van with the counts of Blois and Flanders and under Bohemond's command, while the rest, including the southern French and Lorrainers under Raymond of St-Gilles' command, marched about a day behind. At dawn on 1 July the sultan Kilij Arslan attacked the vanguard near Dorylaeum, coming down out of the hills upon them, and the first major battle of crusading history between Franks and Turks ensued. It was also a major victory for the Christian warriors, though, in the words of a

The capture of Nicaea (1097) from the lost mid-twelfth-century St. Denis window (Bibliothèque nationale).

later idiom, 'a damn close-run thing'. Bohemond gave orders to pitch camp in the centre where women, children and non-combatants were assembled to be protected by the infantry while the knights tried to attack the enemy. But again they were faced by that dreadful and bewildering mobility as the hordes of Turkish light cavalry rode round them and encircled them, throwing spears and shooting arrows from the saddle[40] (very like Red Indians in a 'Western' film, offering no firm target for the charge. According to Fulcher of Chartres, the entire enemy host were archers and 'all were on horseback . . . such warfare was unknown to all of us'.[41] A costly defensive action was of necessity forced upon the crusaders, and enforced a particular discipline upon the knights, accustomed as they were to the heady glory and shock tactic of the charge, usually carrying all before it. Through harsh, hot hours the battle was thus waged, the women bringing water from the centre to the fighting-men in front, until at last the second crusading army, summoned by Bohemond's urgent messengers ('If any of you wants to fight today, let him come and play the man'[42]), came in sight through the heat-haze and the dust and sweat, while Adhemar, bishop of Le Puy, brought a contingent through the hills to menace the Turks from the rear. Then the offensive could be taken and the knights marshalled, with Bohemond and Tancred, Robert Curthose and Raymond of St-Gilles (and the author of the *Gesta*) on the left, Godfrey de Bouillon, the count of Flanders and Hugh de Verman-

127

VINCVNTVR PERTI

The crusader victory at Dorylaeum (1097), from the lost mid-twelfth-century St. Denis window (Bibliothèque nationale).

dois on the right. The Turks were swept off the field, pursued and slaughtered to their own camp, and the sultan's pavilion taken as a trophy amongst much other loot.[43]

Dorylaeum was a famous victory, hard won (amongst the dead was William of Hauteville, Bohemond's nephew and Tancred's brother), which gave to each side respect for the other's military prowess. 'You could not find stronger or braver or more skilful soldiers', wrote the knightly author of the *Gesta* about the Turks.[44] It also opened the way across Asia Minor for the crusaders. They rested for two days after the battle and then moved on south-eastwards. Their principal opponents now were the conditions, a desolate countryside of mountain and desert in pitiless heat, lack of water (the Turks having destroyed the cisterns), and the loss of horses. For all seemingly avoidable difficulties they blamed the Byzantines, not least the unfortunate Greek general, Tatikios, who with his guides accompanied them. They were able to rest and refresh themselves for a few days in the well-watered fertility of Iconium (Konya), and at Heraclea met and dismissed another Turkish army in a brisk engagement. There Bohemond, 'Like a lion exulting in his might', especially distinguished himself by a charge against Kilij Arslan which, according to Anna Comnena,[45] put the enemy to flight. After Heraclea it was decided to take the long route round north via Caesaria to Antioch, though Tancred and Baldwin of Boulogne, the latter with five hundred knights (and two thousand infantry), the former with a mere one hundred knights (and two hundred infantry), went on direct towards Antioch via the difficult passage of the Cilician Gates, partly to avoid taking Tatikios' advice and partly to see what they could do amongst the potentially friendly Christian princes of Armenia. Little came of this diversion, though a few towns were garrisoned in Cilicia and Tancred took the useful port of Alexandretta. Baldwin was constrained to rejoin the main armies at Marash by the news that his Norman wife, Godvere de Tosny, and their children were dying, but soon set out again, this time with only one hundred knights, riding east into the Euphrates valley. The Christian Armenians welcomed him and in February 1098 he was received in triumph as a liberator at Edessa. In this way, and almost peacefully, the first crusading state was founded, in north-east Syria, while the crusade proper had scarcely entered the Holy Land but was toiling at the walls of Antioch.[46]

Tancred had meanwhile rejoined the main armies at Antioch, which they had reached on 20 October 1097, after an appalling journey in autumn rains across the Anti-Taurus mountains, four months after they had set out from Constantinople to Nicaea. More than seven months passed before they entered the city on 3 June 1098, and after that they were themselves besieged inside. The siege and counter-siege of Antioch, involving two major battles both of which were won, formed by far the greatest single military effort of the First Crusade and more than established Bohemond as its outstanding military leader. And when at last the Latin armies moved on towards Jerusalem in January 1099, Bohemond, with most of his Italian Normans, stayed behind, henceforth prince of Antioch, in evident defiance of the crusaders' oath to the Emperor Alexius at Constantinople.[47]

Antioch, which had been taken by the Turks only as recently as 1085, was for the whole crusade an essential objective, a see of St Peter, a formerly great Christian centre awaiting liberation, and the gateway to the Holy Land from Asia Minor. It was also near-impregnable, not least to a weary and depleted army very far from home. The city is now almost vanished save for the mere line of its defences, but three hundred and sixty towers are said to have studded its walls, themselves pierced with five gates plus posterns, while a powerful citadel on the south side crowned the highest ground in the whole great fortress.[48] Not until the last of three siege-castles ('Tancred's Castle') was raised against St George's Gate in April was the investment of the city effectively complete.[49] Meanwhile the Christian army had to endure the miseries of winter rains, a serious lack of supplies which sent the price of foodstuffs soaring, and an increasing loss of horses. Some supplies came in through St Symeon's Port, which the crusaders occupied, from Cyprus, from a Genoese fleet of thirteen vessels, and from another fleet from England commanded by the 'aethling' Edgar of the displaced Wessex royal house and once a claimant to the English throne.[50] Horses, more especially warhorses, however, could not thus be made good, and only seven hundred were available for action when in early February a Turkish relieving army approached under Ridwan of Aleppo. The ensuing plan and brilliantly executed

victory of the Lake of Antioch on 9 February 1098 were Bohemond's. Leaving behind the dismounted knights and infantry to deal with any sortie from the city, he rode out under cover of darkness on the 8th with the seven hundred horse that he could muster to attack the advancing Turks next day. Soon after daybreak he engaged them from a carefully chosen position between the Orontes river and the lake, so that the mobile Turkish tactic of surrounding could not be carried out and their army could not avoid presenting a target for the charge of the mailed knights. When, even so, the Frankish chivalry was almost overcome by superior numbers, the *coup de grâce* was delivered by Bohemond and his squadrons in reserve. 'So Bohemond, protected on all sides by the sign of the Cross,[51] charged the Turkish forces like a lion which has been starving for three or four days . . . His attack was so fierce that the points of his banner were flying right over the heads of the Turks'.[52] The Turks fled, the loot included vital horses, and the knights rode back in time to relieve their infantry, pressed all day by the Antioch garrison who had seized the opportunity to attack as Bohemond had foreseen.[53]

Nevertheless, as the siege wore interminably on and conditions worsened, and as the expectation of another relieving army under the powerful Kerbogha, 'atabeg' of Mosul, increased, morale began to crack in certain quarters and divisions to appear amongst the Christian leaders. There were desertions, real and suspected, both before and after the battle of the Lake of Antioch. Amongst them were Peter the Hermit (of all people) and William 'the Carpenter' (so-called—he was a knight and lord of Melun) who slipped away in January and were ignominiously caught and brought back by Tancred, Bohemond's nephew. The *Gesta Francorum* gives us a military scene, timeless across the ages, as the wretched William stood in Bohemond's tent at first light, to have strip after strip torn off him by his commanding officer—'You wretched disgrace to the whole Frankish army—you dishonourable blot on all the people of Gaul! You most loathsome of all men whom the earth has to bear . . .' etc.[54] In February Tatikios,[55] the Greek general, returned to imperial territory to try to arrange supplies; but though he left most of his staff behind in good faith, he was held to to have fled from cowardice.[56] By May it was known for certain that Kerbogha was on the march. In fact the crusaders gained a few weeks respite while he sought unsuccessfully first to dislodge Baldwin from Edessa, but his eventual advance upon Antioch led to the most serious and, in the event, fateful desertion. On June 2—and, as it happens the day before the city fell to the crusaders—Stephen count of Blois, a prince and one of the crusading leaders, left for home with a large number of his followers. Further, on his way he met Alexius with the imperial army at Philomelium in Asia Minor, and caused the abandonment of the Emperor's expedition to relieve the crusaders by reporting that their cause was lost already.[57] For that abandonment, in turn, the crusaders never forgave Alexius, and it was thus a principal cause of their rapidly worsening relations with Byzantium.[58] As for Stephen, not even his glorious death three years later, again fighting paynims in the East and against hopeless odds, could save or has saved the reputation of this reluctant crusader, forced into it by his wife, the Norman Conqueror's daughter.[59]

Meanwhile there was also division among the leaders as Bohemond made clear his growing determination to have Antioch, once taken, for himself in spite of their common oath to the Emperor Alexius.[60] At one stage he evidently put it about that he would have to withdraw from the crusade for lack of funds and commitments at home without such compensation, and at another, as Kerbogha approached, he persuaded his peers, except count Raymond, that if his force should enter the city first, and the Emperor himself did not arrive, then he, Bohemond should keep it.[61] In the event it was indeed Bohemond's initiative and Bohemond's plan which brought about the fall of Antioch, by liaison with and the connivance of an Armenian within called Firoux; and it was Bohemond's men and their lord who first entered the city, up ladders into the Tower of the Two Sisters on the west, where Firoux admitted them. The operation, including the preceding feint of marching the army away to lull the Turks into a false sense of security, was carried out in the darkness of the night of 2–3 June 1098, and in the ensuing daylight Bohemond's banner floated over the highest part of the city (where the citadel could not be taken) while the Turks within were slain together with their women, and many resident Christians also by mistake.[62] No sooner were the crusaders exultantly inside the city[63]—empty of the provisions they had hoped for, its walls almost too extensive for them to defend, its citadel still held against them—then the enemy was once more upon them. On 5 June Kerbogha was at the Iron Bridge at the approaches to Antioch, where he slew the garrison, and on the 7th he was encamped before the walls in the Christians' own former lines. After the close-fought failure of an assault from the citadel itself by Kerbogha's forces, probably on 9 June, complete investment of the city was established on the 10th and the siege recommenced with the roles of Christian and Moslem reversed. For the former, in particular those who could not afford the soaring price of food, the torments of famine and despair were renewed also. Deserters again began to slip away, this time over the walls and including two members of the hitherto distinguished Grandmesnil family, one of whom, William, was Bohemond's brother-in-law, who had married his sister Mabel in Apulia before the crusade began.[64] In such circumstances there occurred a miracle in which not all believed, whereby one Peter Bartholomew, guided by repeated visions of Saint Andrew, found in the cathedral of Antioch, buried in the ground, the Holy Lance which had pierced the side of Christ as His crucifixion.[65]

While other visions foretold that a great battle was nigh, Bohemond, undisputed leader at least in military affairs and in the illness of Raymond of St-Gilles, decided that assault and the offensive were their only hope. The consequence was the 'Great Battle' of Antioch, fought on 28 June 1098.[66] The crusading armies

The siege of Antioch (1097–8) from the lost mid-twelfth-century St. Denis window (Bibliothèque nationale). Note the scaling ladders.

came out of the city in six divisions,[67] each of horse and foot, the infantry covering the knights whose numbers were again reduced because of the shortage of horses.[68] Of necessity they marched out in column through the narrow Bridge Gate and had then to deploy in line against the enemy—Hugh de Vermandois and Robert count of Flanders with the French and Flemish; the Lorrainers under Godfrey de Bouillon; the Normans of Normandy under duke Robert; the men of Provence and Toulouse under Adhemar bishop of Le Puy (Count Raymond being ill); the Normans from Italy under Tancred and Bohemond, the latter in reserve. Raymond of Aquilers bore the Holy Lance,[69] and bishops, priests and monks in their vestments accompanied the warriors, while others stood in prayer and blessing upon the walls of Antioch. We are told that Kerbogha allowed all this to happen that all might be destroyed more easily. We are also told that other squadrons, of heavenly knights, joined the Christians, to ensure that those who were so outnumbered should prevail.[70] 'Then also appeared from the mountains a countless host of men on white horses, whose banners were all white. When our men saw this, they did not understand what was happening or who these might be, until they realised that this was the succour sent by Christ, and that the leaders were Saint George, Saint Mercurius and Saint Demetrius. (This is quite true, for many saw it).'[71] Bohemond's tactics also ensured the victory, for he deployed his forces between the Orantes river on his right

The Great Battle of Antioch against Kerbogha (1098), from the lost mid-twelfth-century St.Denis window (Bibliothèque nationale)

BELLVM·INTER·COR̄B̄RAM·ET·FRᴬͦ

and high ground on the left so that again they could not easily be encircled; and the charges of the heavy cavalry in echelon forced the massed enemy to retreat. 'Then we called upon the true and living God and rode against them, joining battle in the name of Jesus Christ and of the Holy Sepulchre and by God's help we defeated them.'[72] When Kerbogha's lieutenant in the citadel of Antioch saw the defeat of his master he at once surrendered the fortress and, after some confusion, placed Bohemond's, not Raymond's, banner upon it.[73]

The Great Battle confirmed that Antioch was a crusading conquest, but the question of what was to be done with it remained and had to be resolved. Bohemond's claims and desires were opposed especially by the would-be leader of the whole crusade, Count Raymond of St-Gilles, and also by the papal representative, Adhemar bishop of Le Puy, though the latter was carried off by the typhoid epidemic which ravaged the army in July and his wise and far-seeing counsels were thus lost. The city had been taken from Byzantium by the Turks as recently at 1085, and there was no question that it should be returned in accordance with the oath of Constantinople. Yet it had been retaken by the crusaders' own immense labours and the grace of God; neither the Emperor nor his representative were present, nor, as time passed, likely to be before the spring;[74] and there was the beckoning precedent of Edessa, already firmly held by Baldwin, whom some crusaders now rode off to join.[75] Not until January 1099, under mounting pressure from the frustrated rank and file[76] ('Jerusalem or bust'), including those of Raymond's own army, was decision reached by action and default. On the 13th the old count, bare-foot as became a pilgrim, now the acknowledged leader of a depleted crusade in Bohemond's absence, set out at last for Jerusalem, leaving his great rival as sole lord of Antioch and future prince of a great principality. Nevertheless, Bohemond (who, in the general distress at the death of Bishop Adhemar of Le Puy, had sworn to carry his body personally to Jerusalem) was to make his pilgrimage to the Holy City in due course, with Baldwin of Edessa;[77] meanwhile some at least of his vassals and members of his relatively small contingent,[78] including his nephew Tancred and the author of the anonymous *Gesta Francorum*,[79] went south with Raymond. And so, of course, did the Norman army of Robert duke of Normandy.

On the march to Jerusalem there was no further opposition to the crusading army, now comprising perhaps one thousand knights and five thousand infantry,[80] and they met with more co-operation than hostility from the native Arab Moslems who had no more love for the Turks than had the native Christians. The valuable port of Tortosa (Tartous) and the inland town of Ramleh were occupied on the way, as was Bethlehem whose entirely Christian population greeted joyfully as deliverers Tancred and Baldwin of Le Bourg with their hundred knights who came to take it over.[81] On 7 June 1099 in the morning the crusaders had their first sight of Jerusalem from the hill they called Mountjoie, and by the evening they were encamped before the walls.[82] The earthly Jerusalem was, amongst other things, one of the great fortresses of the medieval world, and

A twelfth-century map of Jerusalem.
(Stuttgart, Landesbibliothek,
Cod.bibl. 2056, end pastedown).

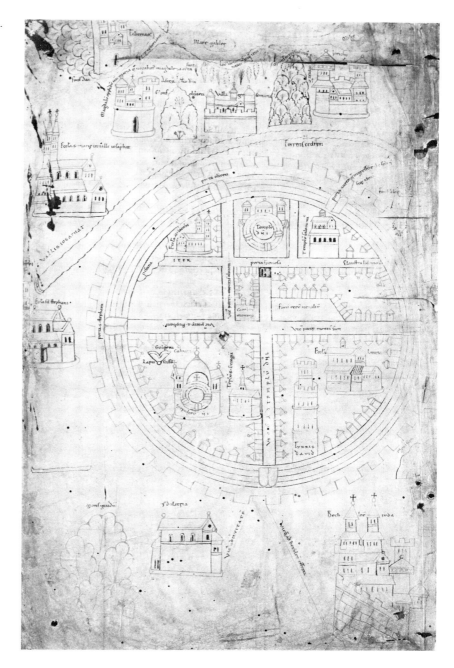

only a few months before had been occupied by the militarily
powerful Fatimids of Egypt.[83] Insufficient manpower, agonies of
heat and thirst (most local wells were poisoned), shortage of food,
and the imminent advent of a relieving army from Egypt, all
seemed to threaten a repetition of Antioch; yet nevertheless the city
was taken by storm on 15 July. Two Flemish knights, Litold and
Gilbert of Tournai were the first to gain the wall-head, followed
closely by duke Godfrey de Bouillon, their lord, and soon after by
Tancred of Hauteville. The entry of the Christians into Jerusalem
was followed by such a massacre, men, women and children, as
none of the leaders could prevent or control, nor Islam in future
forgive or forget. 'Shout unto God with the voice of triumph. For

The siege of Jerusalem (1099) from the lost mid-twelfth-century St. Denis window (Bibliothèque nationale). Note the siege tower.

the Lord most high is terrible'.[84] Exactly four weeks later, on 12 August, the crusaders met and defeated the expected Moslem attack from Egypt at a battle near Ascalon,[85] the Normans in the centre and both Robert Curthose and Tancred of Hauteville particularly distinguishing themselves in the series of charges which were devastatingly delivered.[86] At Ascalon their possession of Jerusalem was confirmed, as that of Antioch had been at the Great Battle.

In September 1099 Robert duke of Normandy, presumably with most of his army, and in company with Robert count of Flanders, left Jerusalem for home, vows fulfilled and duty well and truly done. Their departure did not end the disproportionate Norman contribution to the crusade and the subsequent establishment of the Latin states of Outremer. Tancred remained at Jerusalem with Godfrey de Bouillon, its elected first ruler,[87] and, we are told, with twenty-four knights carved out for himself the lordship of Galilee, based upon Tiberias and Haifa, before being called to Antioch in 1101, at the age of 25, to play a part scarcely less important than that of Bohemond himself in the establishment of the Norman state there.[88] In short, the Normans of the First Crusade, more specifically the Normans from southern Italy, and, more specifically still, the Hautevilles, created at the turn of the eleventh and twelfth centuries the fourth in the extraordinary series of Norman states stretching across the known world—Normandy itself, England, southern Italy and Sicily, and now Antioch. Nor should it surprise us that the principality of Antioch under the Hautevilles—Bohemond and his nephew Tancred (between them 1098–1112), the latter's nephew Roger of Salerno (1112–19), son of Richard of the Principate, and Bohemond II (1126–30) son of Bohemond I—was the strongest of the Latin states of Outremer. So it remained to outlast the kingdom of Jerusalem and endure to the end,[89] still leaving its indelible mark on the land of northern Syria.[90]

The history of the principality of Antioch is ill-served. Few documents could survive the holocaust of the Moslem revival of the later thirteenth century, and the princes do not seem to have commissioned or attracted contemporary historians like their peers in England, Normandy and Italy, except for Walter the Chancellor whose work is confined to a few years of the earlier twelfth century.[91] Furthermore, modern crusading historians save only Claude Cahen[92] have often been not so much disinterested as oblique in their interest, concentrating upon the kingdom of Jerusalem to the detriment of the other crusading states of Edessa, Antioch and Tripoli which are then treated as satellites of the kingdom yet cast in the same mould, which Antioch certainly was not.[93] Outremer, as Cahen insists, had two poles not one, both Antioch and Jerusalem, and about them both crusading politics variously revolved.[94] Antioch was different in that it was a Norman settlement from southern Italy, whereas Jerusalem and Edessa were predominantly the settlement of Lorrainers and Tripoli the settlement of men of Provence. Antioch was also autonomous, as Bohemond's title of prince proclaimed;[95] and the fact that its princes by and large always remained so, in spite of the double threat of Byzantine resentment on the one hand and the resurgence of Moslem power in northern Syria on the other, is not the least of their achievements.

The battle of Ascalon (1099) which assured the crusaders' possession of Jerusalem; from the lost mid-twelfth-century St. Denis window (Bibliothèque nationale).

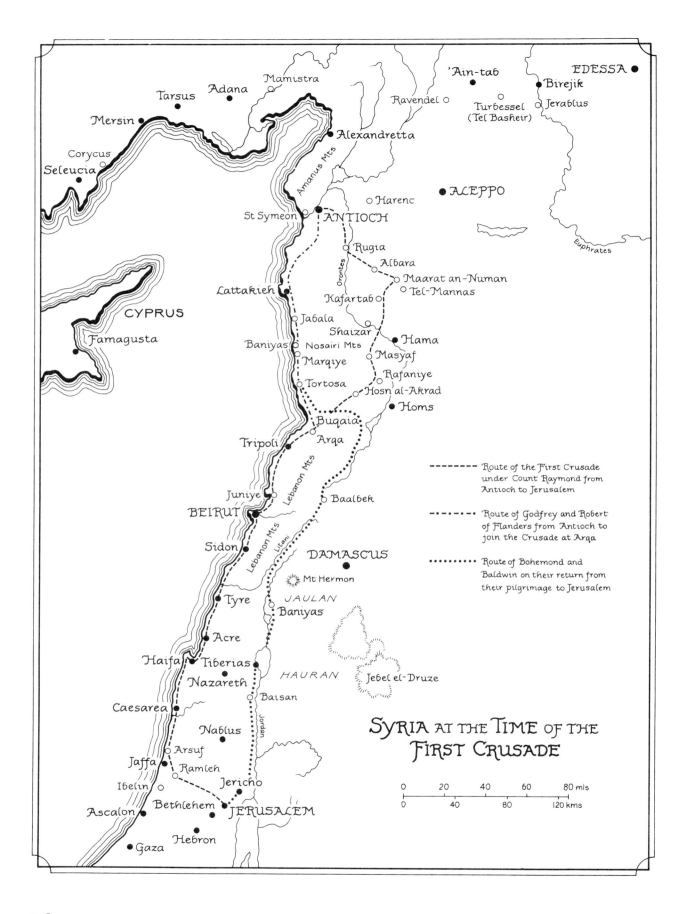

'Ain-tab

EDESSA

Birejik

Tarsus   Adana   Mamistra   Ravendel   Turbessel   Jerablus
                                            (Tel Basheir)

Mersin

Corycus
Seleucia

Alexandretta

Amanus Mts

Harenc   ALEPPO

St Symeon   ANTIOCH

Rugia

Euphrates

Albara

Orontes   Maarat an-Numan
            Tel-Mannas

Lattakieh   Kafartab

Jabala   Shaizar   Hama

CYPRUS   Baniyas   Nosairi Mts   Masyaf

Famagusta   Marqiye   Rafaniye

Tortosa   Hosn al-Akrad

Homs

Buqaia

Arqa

Tripoli

Lebanon Mts

Juniye   Baalbek

BEIRUT

Lebanon Mts

Sidon   Litani

DAMASCUS

Mt Hermon

Tyre   JAULAN
        Baniyas

Acre

Haifa   Tiberias   HAURAN

Nazareth   Jebel el-Druze

Caesarea   Baisan

Jordan

Nablus

Arsuf

Jaffa   Ramleh

Ibelin   Jericho

Ascalon   Bethlehem

JERUSALEM

Hebron

Gaza

- - - - - - - Route of the First Crusade
             under Count Raymond from
             Antioch to Jerusalem

-·-·-·-·-·- Route of Godfrey and Robert
             of Flanders from Antioch to
             join the Crusade at Arqa

··········   Route of Bohemond and
             Baldwin on their return from
             their pilgrimage to Jerusalem

SYRIA AT THE TIME OF THE
FIRST CRUSADE

0   20   40   60   80 mls
0   40   80   120 kms

The conquest and establishment of Antioch between c.1098 and c.1119 is another exercise and demonstration of *Normanitas*, with southern Italy and Sicily as the particular analogy. It was above all a characteristic example of aristocratic colonization, the new Frankish nobility, almost exclusively Normans from Italy,[96] displacing or subduing their Moslem predecessors and very heavily outnumbered by the indigenous population. As in Italy, they were able to take advantage of pre-existing divisions, here between Moslems and resident Christians, each also divided amongst themselves.[97] Nevertheless, by comparison with the county of Edessa which was an almost peaceful take-over by Baldwin of Boulogne and his few followers,[98] in the establishment of the principality of Antioch there was hard fighting to be done, against entrenched Moslem lords and against a resurgent Byzantium which, alone among crusading rulers, the princes of Antioch had to face. By the end of the Hauteville period they ruled over a compact territory, not too large for management, comprising to the west, on the north shores of the Mediterranean, part of Byzantine Cilicia; extending north to Marash; marching on the east with the county of Edessa, though in this direction the Moslem centre of Aleppo was never taken with fatal results for the future; and marching to the south, where Roger of Salerno founded the great castle of Margat,[99] with the newly established crusading state of Tripoli.[100] Within, there was the great and rich city of Antioch,[101] with its industry and commerce and its inhabitants almost entirely Christian. There was also the vital and prosperous east-west trade of northern Syria, and, as lifelines to the Latin west, there were the three ports of Alexandretta, St Symeon and Lattakieh,[102] the last and most important finally taken from Byzantium by Tancred in 1108. In the history of the principality there were set-backs and disasters, and echoes across the ages of romance and tragedy, to remind us both of the Normans in Italy and Sicily and of those contemporary *romans* and *chansons de gestes* they loved.[103] Thus there was Bohemond's capture and imprisonment by the Danishmend Emir Malik Ghazi between 1110 and 1103; the same prince's despairing journey west the next year to raise his doomed crusade against Byzantium;[104] or the slaughter of Roger of Salerno in 1119 at the Field of Blood (*Ager Sanguinis*) with most of his chivalry about him;[105] or the careless death of the young Bohemond II, son of the Great Warrior and last of the Hauteville princes, in Cilicia in 1130, his embalmed head sent to the caliph as a gift.[106] 'These', wrote Orderic Vitalis at St Evroul in Normandy, 'are the things that I have learned about the fortunes of the Christians who live in exile in the east for the sake of Christ Jesus'.[107]

Like the Normans in Italy from amongst whom they came, the Normans in Antioch, and those other Franks who joined them there, were absurdly outnumbered. The total number of knights in Antioch has been estimated at about five hundred,[108] a statistic which is, of course, both military and social. In war, when in any case the knights could be supported by horsed sergeants (of whose social status one would like to know more), 'Turcopoles' (native levies some of whom were mounted and served as light cavalry, and some of whom may have been horsed archers), and infantry,[109]

Knights of the Temple riding out of the castle of Crac des Chevaliers to the battle of la Bouquée in 1163—from a twelfth-century fresco on the north wall of the Templar church at Cressac (Charente).

such small numbers obviously and characteristically did not prevent victories against amazing odds, but they were equally obviously a severe disadvantage in terms of settlement and the imposition of lordship. The result was a thinly dispersed military aristocracy, essentially alien in spite of fraternization and occasional social contacts or the adoption of native dress and habits, held together by a sense of identity and by kinship, by the bonds of feudal loyalties, service and obligation, and by the over-riding motivation of Christian versus Pagan, however much this last might from time to time be bent by the practical realities of immediate politics and diplomacy.[110] This aristocracy was, of course, not only military but mounted, an aristocracy of knights and heavy cavalry, whose horsemanship, equipment and specialist techniques, above all the couched lance and the charge, more than all other factors enabled the crusade improbably to succeed and the crusaders to remain as lords of Antioch and Outremer. Amongst the Franks, wrote the Arab observer and commentator Ousâma, 'all pre-eminence belongs to the horsemen. They are in truth the only men who count'.[111]

This alien military and mounted aristocracy, who could never become integrated with native society as the Normans in England or southern Italy were eventually to do, and whose rent collection from the surrounding peasantry often proved to be a military expedition,[112] lived of course in castles, which dominated the countryside and were the active centres of their lordships. It is appropriate that the best-known fact or recollection of crusading history remains the 'crusader castles', for nowhere else perhaps do castles show more dramatically their fundamental value, which is to control an area with the maximum economy of manpower, and nowhere else perhaps did the political régime of a feudal society so obviously depend upon them. As for the lords and their ladies within, we are afforded glimpses of them in the pages of Ousâma

140

and a more sustained view in the pages of one of our most distinguished modern historians of the crusades, Sir Steven Runciman. Both, friend and foe, alike, insist upon their courage. Runciman continues:

'Their lives were precarious and they knew it. They were trying their best to fit themselves into a country which would never quite accept them, and to make themselves acceptable in a part of the world where their intrusion was resented in the vain hope that thus their establishments might endure . . . The Orient remained strange and hostile. Unfamiliar diseases abounded. No one could be trusted. There was never security or peace for long. In any alley-way an assassin might be lurking, sent down from the Old Man of the Mountain.[113] At any moment the lord might have to rise from his couch to ride out against enemy raiders. At any moment his lady might find herself in charge of the defence of her castle. At any moment the festivities might be interrupted by the sound of the infidel mangonels pounding against the walls.[114] Life was merry, but it was short; and when the crisis came there was no lack of gallantry among the lords and ladies of Outremer. They had tasted with relish the gracious things of life; and they faced their doom with pride and resolution.'[115]

Crac des Chevaliers from the south-west.

Courage, military prowess, a knowledge of how to live and die according to the noble standards of the age (*noblesse oblige*), these characteristics were not, of course, in Outremer confined to the Normans of Antioch, and nor was feudalism. Nevertheless they are, as we have seen, part of the essence of *Normanitas*, and we should not be surprised to find that feudal customs and feudal institutions, brought with them by the Normans more particularly from Norman Italy,[116] did most to hold together their society and thus their principality. Indeed in the circumstances of Norman Antioch feudalism showed its true nature as politically and socially a positive not a negative force, cohesive not divisive, centripetal not centrifugal, too clearly for even the most determined anti-feudalist amongst French or even English-speaking historians to deny. There were, after all, only two 'baronial revolts', that is, serious movements of political opposition, in the whole history of the principality, and those in most exceptional circumstances.[117] In Antioch, to a characteristically Norman degree, feudalism added mightily to the power of the prince, and was indeed its base. The Hautevilles, with true Norman eclecticism, may have adopted from their Byzantine and Arab predecessors certain governmental and administrative offices, titles and institutions, like the provincial judges and 'dukes', and the 'secrète' or 'diwan'; but their principal officers and agents were their constables and marshals, seneschals and chamberlains, *vicomtes*, bailiffs and *châtelains*. They themselves remained, like their kinsmen in the Norman Sicilian kingdom,[118] in spite of oriental trappings, fundamentally feudal suzerains and princes, their power derived primarily from their comparatively vast demesne (exceeding that of all lesser lords), their feudal patronage, their feudal military and other services, and even their feudal revenues to be added to others more mundane—the profits of justice, the monopoly of the coinage, and taxes on both commerce and lands not enfeoffed and therefore exempt from feudal exactions.[119]

The trouble with analyses of this kind is that personalities are left out. If we put them in again, not least the extraordinary capacities of the first Hauteville princes,[120] and not least those of Tancred, never officially 'prince' but, as regent in his twenties in Bohemond's absences, showing abilities at least equal to those of his slowly ageing uncle, then we have indeed a potent mixture, *Normanitas contra mundum*. To it we add next the ingredient of the Church. Here prestige was paramount, for the see of Antioch was a foundation of Saint Peter and as such chronologically superior even to Rome. A close association of 'Church and state' was the rule in Norman Antioch, especially in the early period to the end of the patriarchate of Bernard of Valence in 1135,[121] the association all the closer as Franks and Latins found themselves a tiny minority seeking to impose their authority upon an alien population wherein Moslems were far outnumbered by the more divisive members of other Christian churches. 'We have got rid of the Turks and pagans', runs an early letter after the capture of Antioch, 'but the heretics, Greeks and Armenians, Syrians and Jacobites, we have not yet been able to expel'.[122] In the event, they never would nor wholly try to: the analogy is with Norman Italy, and a non-Latin lower clergy had to remain to look after the indigenous Christians of whatever denomination, left in occupation of their own less important churches.[123] Yet, though at first the Greek patriarch John was restored to the cathedral church of St Peter at Antioch, it was inevitable that a substantial Latinization of the church should take place in its upper reaches if only for social reasons, and it was politically essential that a Latin hierarchy be established, owing obedience to Rome on the one hand and exacting obedience from the local Greek Orthodox churches especially on the other. The Latinization of the church in Antioch, moreover, especially *vis à vis* the Greeks, became more urgent as political relations with Byzantium declined. Thus Latin bishops were appointed as opportunity offered, and the proud Patriarchate of Antioch, some of its sees (*e.g.* Tartous and Edessa) conveniently outside the principality, reconstructed and reformed on Latin lines. So, too, monasticism, given a fertile field by the ancient prestige of Antioch, played a fundamental role alike in the Latinization of the church and the establishment of Norman and Frankish lordship, with the foundation or refoundation of great Benedictine abbeys especially—St Paul, St George, St Simeon—western monks replacing or placed beside their Greek and other brothers.[124] The advent of the Military Orders, most notably the Templars and Hospitallers, and their rise from the mid-twelfth century onwards to dominate religious, military and political affairs in Antioch as in the rest of Outremer, must lie, in any detail, beyond the confines of this book.[125] Nevertheless their unique combination of chivalry and monasticism may be thought to consummate the ideals of *Normanitas* which themselves had contributed so much to the concept of Holy War and its activation in crusade.

Beneath the glittering, expensive and efficient superstructure of lords and knights and castles, of prelates, monks and churches, lay, as it had to, wealth—derived in Antioch from land, of course, but also from industry and commerce.[126] It is unlikely that the Normans from southern Italy especially would be unappreciative of the value of trade, however beneath the knightly role of their leaders its actual practices might lie, and it is thought that the lower orders of Normans and Franks made up to half the population of the great cities, Antioch at the head.[127] The products of Antioch included wine and oil, textiles, especially silk, war-horses and an abundance of building stone, including marble; but its principal commercial wealth was derived from the east-west trade. Though in this the principality of Antioch, even with its great port of Lattakieh, could not compete with Palestine and the port of Acre—which was also the principal centre of the lucrative pilgrim trade—yet, even so, important trade routes lay across it, and its polyglot merchants acted as middlemen therein. As elsewhere in Outremer this commerce was principally concentrated in the hands of north Italian merchant cities,[128] in Antioch especially Genoa and Pisa, Venice tending to be the ally of Byzantium in Italy, and the south Italian Norman ports of Bari and Amalfi playing only a surprisingly minor role. The Italian communes of Genoese and Pisans were highly—probably too highly—privileged in return for their services and so, in Antioch as elsewhere, weakened the power of central government; but their services were essential, not least for trade and communications with the West. The princes of Antioch, moreover, like other crusading rulers, were able to tap the commercial wealth engendered, and distributed it through their patronage of all kinds, in architecture and art as well as warfare, and in the granting of money-fiefs (*fiefs-rentes*)[129] whose number is always held to be amongst the peculiarities of feudal society in Outremer.

Wherever the Normans went they left behind them great buildings expressing their lordship and their faith, their concept of their honour and the honour of God. In the principality of Antioch all the great churches have now gone beyond recognition, including the patriarchal cathedral of St Peter and the city in which it stood. Of the cathedral and abbey churches only St Paul at Tarsus in Cilicia remains, though now a mosque. Here in 1101 Hugh of Vermandois was buried when he died of wounds received at the Battle of Heraclea on his second and disastrous crusade. This cathedral,

Cathedral of our Lady of Tartous in the county of Tripoli, west front (thirteenth century).

however, is small and undistinguished, perhaps because it was the earliest of the crusader churches in Outremer and was certainly near the exposed border of the principality.[130] Possibly one may get closer to the vanished ecclesiastical splendours of Antioch in the cathedral of Our Lady at Tartous[131] (Tortosa), a major church still

Tartous, cathedral, interior; nave
north aisle and shrine of Our Lady.

surviving, though now a partly ruined museum, in the neighbouring county of Tripoli to the south. Though it pertained to the
patriarchate of Antioch it cannot be regarded as Norman for it was
not in the principality, and in fact it has some architectural affinities
with Provence whence came its lords and patrons. It may neverthe-

less be suggestive that in plan it is rectangular and basilican, like St Paul at Tarsus and most of the Norman churches in Italy and Sicily.[132] Built between the second quarter of the twelfth century (in its eastern parts) and the second half of the thirteenth (in the western), it is a combination of both Romanesque and Gothic in general style. At Tartous St Peter had stayed, preaching and converting, *en route* from Jerusalem to Antioch, and had raised there a small chapel, the first church ever to be dedicated to the Virgin Mary. That chapel was incorporated in the great church which became a pilgrimage centre, and as such was visited by, amongst so many others, Joinville the biographer of the French King St Louis (IX) in 1253.[133]

If the principal monuments of Norman spirituality in Antioch have gone, secular monuments of feudal and military power remain, including, for example, the castles of Baghras, Bourzey, Margat (Marquab), Saone (Sahyun), and the twin castles (*château-jumelé*) of Bakas-Shoghr.[134] Though by common consent Crac des Chevaliers is the most magnificent of the crusader castles, Margat may be thought almost to rival it. Once seen never forgotten, its immense size seeming to fill the whole horizon, it towers on its spur

Ruins of the castle of Baghras.

high above the narrow coastal route near Banyas, between Tartous and Lattakieh (Laodicea). It thus locks Antioch against the south, and also guards against the Assassins to the east. In its great strength, crowned by its massive cylindrical donjon, Margat was not surprisingly one of the last Latin strongholds in Outremer to fall to the Moslems in the thirteenth century (1285). This splendid castle, however, had been made over to the Hospitallers by its lord, Reynald II of Mazoir, in 1186, to become, like Crac des Chevaliers, one of the Order's principal fortresses, so that what we see now is (as at Crac) mainly their work of the late twelfth and earlier thirteenth centuries. Saone, on the other hand, is as its Norman Frankish lords left it when they were obliged to yield it to Saladin in 1188. The first of those lords, responsible, it is thought, for the building of the castle in *c*.1120, were Robert son of Fulk and Robert's son William. Nothing is known of their origins in the West, but of their wealth and power in Antioch there can be no doubt; and so it is to be noted that the crucial castles both of Margat and Saone were held not by the prince direct but by his vassals. The *seigneurs* of Saone, perhaps *nouveaux riches*, constructed with immense skill and labour what in the twelfth century, before the later

Margat, the chapel of the Hospitallers (1186–1285) at the heart of the great crusader castle.

development of Margat and Crac des Chevaliers, may have been the most impressive of the castles of Outremer. Here certainly something of the spirit of *Normanitas* is to be found; in the prodigious scale of the place, its strength, the sophistication of the masonry tailored to the scarped rock from which it rises, the colossal rectangular tower keep or donjon, the amazing rock-cut fosses, and the no less amazing needle of rock left standing from the base of *le grand fossé* to bear the bridge which crossed it. Still almost inaccessible, still bearing the signs of its last siege, Saone is held now from within, if one is fortunate or alone, by a potent silence broken only by the drip of water into its great cisterns.

In the absence of the great churches, the castle of Saone might seem a suitable monument to the Normans of Antioch with which to end this chapter, yet I prefer to end with a very different one far away in Apulia in Norman Italy. The mausoleum of Bohemond, to which his mother Aubrey's tomb at Venosa now directs the traveller ('If you seek [our] son, he lies at Canosa'),[135] stands half hidden and neglected by the south side of the small cathedral church of St Sabinus at Canosa di Puglia. It is significantly remarkable in being oriental and Moslem, fit for an Eastern prince, in architectural form and style,[136] while the reputation of the man it majestically commemorates seems to me in need of some amendment. Bohemond was, of course, the founder of the Norman principality of Antioch in Outremer—though in this he was worthily assisted by his nephew, Tancred, who was a highly competent regent during his uncle's absence, first as a captive in Turkish hands in 1100–1103 and then in the West raising his ill-fated expedition against Byzantium after 1105. Bohemond also, it is generally agreed, showed himself the outstanding soldier on the First Crusade, so that he became effectively its military leader. Beyond that, however, and because of his seizure of Antioch, he is invariably presented as the archetype of the materialistic crusader, exploiting a religious movement for his own advantage.[137] This, however, is likely to be as unfair as it is simplistic. The probability of mixed motives among Crusaders as among other men, and the improbability of their being neatly divisible into sheep and goats, has previously been urged above. In that age we have usually only the actions of men by which to judge them. Bohemond's recorded actions point at least as clearly to contemporary piety as they do to self-advancement: the two motives have never been incompatible and were certainly not so in his age of conscience-stricken warriors, for whom pilgrimage and the new concepts of armed pilgrimage and Holy War—in short, crusade—themselves afforded the best means of the expiation of sin. We may think it inevitable that Bohemond would win a principality through his crusade—he was an Hauteville in every inch of his great frame, and a disinherited eldest son to boot—though we do not know in fact at what stage he determined on the seizure of Antioch for himself. By his retention of it he undoubtedly broke his oath to the despised Emperor Alexius, but it is difficult to show that he broke any crusading vow. He more than any other man was responsible for the miraculous military success of the crusade, and those taking part believed that St George had ridden with him and them at the Great Battle.[138] He, too, was more responsible than anyone for the freeing of the Petrine Church of Antioch, and many others beside, and, while Jerusalem was by no means certainly amongst the explicit objectives at Clermont,[139] he nevertheless duly made his pilgrimage there—as, indeed, he had sent on Tancred and others of his small and precious force with the main crusading armies to Jerusalem from Antioch in January 1099. In November of that same year, according to Fulcher of Chartres who went with them,[140] he set off with that other alleged arch-materialist, Baldwin of Edessa, and a great company of horse and foot, on an armed pilgrimage evidently in no way differing from that of his predecessors some months before, its perils certainly no less. On arrival at Jerusalem they visited the Holy Sepulchre and all the Holy Places, and on the fourth day went to Bethlehem where they passed the whole night of Christmas Eve in vigil and in prayer. We know, too, that Bohemond fulfilled another vow, taken during his captivity at Niksar in the hands of the Danishmend Emir Malik Ghazi, to visit the shrine near Limoges of St Leonard de Noblat, the patron saint of prisoners. This he accomplished on his journey to the West in 1105, during which he also visited the new shrine of St Nicholas at Bari, in his own lordship of Taranto, to which he had sent, amongst other gifts, Kerbogha's pavilion taken at the Great Battle at Antioch.[141]

Certainly to contemporaries in the West Bohemond prince of Antioch was the crusading hero *par excellence*. When, according to Orderic Vitalis, the news came of his capture by the Turks in 1100, 'the whole Church prayed for him, beseeching God graciously to deliver him from the hands of his enemies'.[142] A year later the Lombard crusading expedition to the Holy Land brought disaster on itself by the rank-and-file's insistence on a mad diversion towards Niksar to liberate Bohemond,[143] and when he himself came back to the West to visit the shrine of St Leonard and raise forces and support for his war against Byzantium he was everywhere acclaimed. In Italy people flocked to look at him 'as if they were going to see Christ himself'.[144] In France the king, Philip I, gave him his daughter, Constance, in marriage (and another, Cecilia, for Tancred), and the high-point came at his nuptials in the cathedral at Chartres in the spring of 1106, when Bohemond preached his crusade to an immense and distinguished throng and was royally feasted afterwards with his bride by the countess Adela, daughter of William the Conqueror and by now the widow of the unfortunate Stephen of Blois.[145]

At the close of 1104, recently released from Turkish captivity by a huge ransome, and finding himself with inadequate resources hemmed in at Antioch by Byzantium reoccupying his Cilician provinces to the west and the Turks of Aleppo pressing hard upon his principality from the east, Bohemond had determined to return to Europe, for aid and to fulfil his vow to St Leonard. The aid, however, and the expedition he planned with it, was to be turned against Byzantium, for him as prince of Antioch a worse enemy than the Turks. In his outright hostility to Constantinople Bohemond gave only particular expression to the common prejudice of most of his fellow crusaders, of public opinion in the West, and, by now, of the Papacy which, in the person of Paschal II, gave blessing and a banner to the enterprise and thus made it a crusade. It thus became 'a turning point in the history of the crusades', a foreshadowing of the Fourth Crusade of 1204 which was turned against the city of Constantinople itself, and historians in general have shown little sympathy toward it.[146] In the event, unlike 1204, it was to be a military disaster, and for Bohemond himself a personal tragedy. In October 1107 he sailed with his forces from Brindisi for the Albanian coast and proceeded to lay siege to the great fortress of Durazzo which he and his father, Robert Guiscard, had taken a quarter of a century before.[147] This time, however, he was himself surrounded by the cool strategy of Alexius ('For the moment let us have luncheon. We will attend to Bohemond's affairs later')[148] who occupied all the passes about the city in the spring and also had command of the sea. A winter of discomfort was therefore followed by a summer of increasing famine and disease, plummetting morale depressed further by propaganda and poison-pen letters sent by Alexius.[149] In September 1108 Bohemond, 'the most renowned warrior in Christendom',[150] surrendered. The terms imposed do

The mausoleum of Bohemond, prince of Antioch (d. 1111), by the south side and east end of the cathedral of Canosa di Puglia.

The entrance to Bohemond's mausoleum.

Bohemond's mausoleum, bronze doors, detail; a lion's mask, (left-centre roundel).

not seem to us unduly harsh—a reduced principality to be held under the acknowledged suzerainty of the Eastern Emperor, the Church of Antioch to be put back under a Greek Orthodox patriarch, the whole confirmed by the most solemn oaths imaginable, taken upon the True Cross, the Crown of Thorns, the Nails and the Lance which had wounded Christ—and they were never accepted by Tancred at Antioch; but for Bohemond they were evidently an humiliation and a stain upon his honour hard to endure. He never returned to Outremer but died preparing to do so in his Apulian lordship in 1111.[151] He begat two sons by his royal wife Constance, John, who died in infancy, and another Bohemond who succeeded his father in Antioch as Bohemond II. The great bronze doors of Bohemond's tomb at Canosa, which now open into nothing, themselves cast in Byzantine fashion at Melfi in 1120, depict in beautiful niello work, his family and himself and his achievements. They are also inscribed with verses which end, 'Look on these doors; read what is written; pray for Bohemond that he may have his place in the Kingdom of Heaven'. In this world, it seems, Bohemond never attained, or kept, a place commensurate with his boundless ambition, which may have envisaged the conquest of Byzantium and a Mediterranean empire stretching from Bari and Taranto to Antioch and Aleppo.[152] According to Romuald archbishop of Salerno he was 'always seeking the impossible';[153] but a man's reach should exceed his grasp, and perhaps we may counter-quote from Shakespeare, 'Were it farther off, I'll pluck it down'. Perhaps, too, he is the noblest Norman of them all, and the bravest of the brave. His modern biographer places him amongst the three great Norman conquerors, and with that there can be no disagreement, save perhaps to extend the list to five, by adding to William the Conqueror, Robert Guiscard and Bohemond, Roger the Great Count of Sicily and Bohemond's nephew Tancred. Of these five, four were Hautevilles.

Chapter 7 Epilogue

In this book I have sought to describe, analyse and illustrate Norman achievement in the Norman age of the eleventh century, and also to explain it in so far as that may be done. To undertake this in the confines of a relatively short volume has not been easy, but it is still more difficult to end; for to assess the results of the Norman impact upon their world would require at least another volume,[1] dealing with much of the subsequent history of Europe and beyond. So, for example, the Normans first established Normandy itself, and though the duchy was improbably taken by the French king Philip II 'Augustus' in 1204, whereupon its proper history ends, it is a commonplace among historians that thereafter the influence of the conquered province, not least of its governmental institutions, upon the French kingdom was very great indeed. Again, in one direction the loss of Normandy by king John, and his subsequent efforts to regain it, lead straight to Magna Carta, while, in others, these events should remind us that as the direct result of 1066 the political history of England was so entwined with that of France that for centuries neither can be understood without the other. Here, indeed, the line of cause and effect leads far into the modern period and almost to our own time. Queen Mary Tudor in the sixteenth century died with Calais written on her heart, and England, for long after 1066 in fact French, continued to fight France until 1815 at Waterloo, and expected to fight her again for much of the remainder of the nineteenth century. In an hundred-and-one ways also the Norman kingdom of England, which in misplaced national sentiment we call 'Anglo-Norman', is still with us, for in the continuity of English history the Norman Conquest is the last real break as it is the Last Invasion. The Normans in Britain also arguably began the conquest of Wales, from the Marches of Wales which they characteristically and militantly established, and they penetrated deep into southern Scotland as also (in the twelfth century) into Ireland. The impact of the Normans upon Italy is scarcely less than upon Britain though perhaps even less well remembered. They brought unity to the south of that divided land, and they wrested Sicily from Islam back to Christendom. The fundamentally Norman kingdom of the Two Sicilies thus established by Roger II's coronation at Palermo in 1130 lasted thereafter until the Italian unification in the nineteenth century. Antioch, of course, has long since gone with the rest of Outremer, but the Norman principality there established stood for the better part of two centuries as the strongest of the crusading states, and the double and disproportionate Norman contribution to the First Crusade itself has to be listed separately as an addition to any summary of Norman achievements. The lasting effects of the crusading movement upon the West may sometimes now seem elusive to historians, yet that movement can still be described as 'a central fact in medieval history',[2] and amongst the most profound must be placed the final breach between the two halves of Christendom which it brought about, between East and West, Greek and Latin, Rome and Constantinople. In that development also the role of the Normans was crucial, from Robert Guiscard to Bohemond and his successors.

In these last considerations we have begun to move from the immediate political and military achievements of the Normans to their often leading and dominant part in the general developments of their age—in the Reform Movement of the Church and the Reform Papacy as the allies of the Holy See and the champions of Holy War; in religion and in monasticism; in architecture and in art (not excluding sculpture); in learning and in education; and in government and in warfare. In all this, and more, their role was all the more important because of their eclecticism, bringing together, fusing, integrating and developing the best that they could find in the whole wide arc of their experience and domination from the Irish Sea to the Middle East. The eleventh century was, by common consent, a decisive and formative period, and the Normans perhaps more than any other people made it so.

Elites and Supermen are nowadays out of fashion among the avant-garde of historians, who themselves may seem to be diminished figures as they eschew the dramatic—to say nothing of the romantic—yet stand upon the shoulders of the giants, their predecessors. In England, furthermore, there has long been a powerful lobby of Norman detractors, consisting for the most part of those Anglo-Saxon scholars who in their justified admiration for Old English society were and are unjustifiably reluctant to admit any Norman superiority, or even victory.[3] The short answer to that thesis has nearly always been that it was based upon insularity, and could not stand if pre-Conquest Normandy were studied with the same close sympathy as pre-Conquest England, or if the Norman Conquest of England, were placed in the full context of Norman achievement. Of late, further and new dimensions have been added to the denigration of the Normans, first by a savage demotion, both in military and social status, of the knights who were responsible for much of their achievement,[4] and, most recently, in the only modern, full-length study of pre-Conquest Normandy available in

English. There, by the application of demographic techniques and the following of fashionable and Continental trends, the conclusions are reached, amongst others, that the Normans had no 'special and exceptional aptitude for war', that their conquest and settlement of southern Italy was simply 'part of a wider demographic movement', and that they were in general no different from anybody else, unless inferior.[5] This makes a change from insularity, but if these are the results of demography then we should do well to beware the current enthusiasm for it, and rest instead upon the erudition, scholarship, and, above all, perception, of such old historians as C. H. Haskins, Marc Bloch and P. Guilhiermoz.[6] From France Georges Duby has instructed us that as new historians we must count 'everything capable of being counted in a continuous documentation',[7] but the truth is that the medieval period is most reluctant to supply statistics and was in any case emphatically not the age of the Common Man. One may add that the more generally one seeks to apply alleged demographic trends across the expanse of Latin Christendom the less they are likely to explain the particular and unusual. What may be thought the most outstanding features of eleventh-century Normandy are its differences (not least its foundation as late as 911 and after) and, in many respects, its superiorities. Its achievements are not likely satisfactorily to be explained by denying both, but, rather, by seeking to discover those differences and superiorities which enabled the Normans to do what others did not do, or did not do so well. Further, in that endeavour an appreciation and acceptance of what the Normans thought of themselves, and what others thought of them, are likely to be more constructively helpful than misleading allusions to a 'Norman Myth'.[8] Of course the Normans did not live *in vacuo* but in northern France in a dynamic period, and shared to the full in the spirit and the developments of the age. One may add, too, that their achievements and territorial expansion might have been inconceivable at any other time but this, with its crumbling past, and expanding horizons, when almost anything seemed possible to a small élite holding all power, recently acquired. But the Normans seized and even created their opportunities, and they were adapters as well as adopters. It is the unique amalgam which they made of their eclectic borrowings, and the resultant *Normanitas*, which we must discover and appreciate if we are to understand them or comprehend their virtual supremacy.

Select Bibliography

This bibliography is not intended to be comprehensive but to consist of the principal works consulted in the writing of this volume and of those most useful for further reading. The editions given are generally those cited in the text and notes.

Abbreviations

Battle, Proceedings of the Battle Conference in Anglo-Norman Studies, now *Anglo-Norman Studies*.

B.I.H.R., Bulletin of the Institute of Historical Research.

Château-Gaillard, Etudes de Castellologie médiévale, Centre de Recherches Archéologiques Médiévales, Caen.

E.H.R., English Historical Review.

H.M.S.O., Her Majesty's Stationery Office.

M.G.H., SS, Monumenta Germaniae Historica, Scriptores, Hanover 1826– in progress.

Pat.Lat., Patrologia Latina in cursus completus. . . , ed. J. P. Migne, Paris, 1839–64.

R.H.S., Royal Historical Society.

T.R.H.S., Transactions of the Royal Historical Society.

i Primary Sources

Adémar de Chabannes, *Chronicon*, ed. J. Chavanon, Paris, 1897.

The Alexiad of Anna Comnena, ed. and trans. E. R. A. Sewter, Harmondsworth, 1969.

Amatus (Aimé), *Storia de' Normanni di Amato di Montecassino*, ed. V. Bartholomaeis, Rome, 1935.

Anglo-Saxon Chronicle: a revised translation, ed. D. Whitelock with D. C. Douglas and S. I. Tucker, London, 1965.

The Bayeux Tapestry, ed. F. M. Stenton, London, 1965.

Calendar of Documents preserved in France. . . , i, *A.D. 918–1216*, ed. J. H. Round, 1899.

Carmen de Hastingae Proelio, ed. C. Morton and H. Munz, Oxford Medieval Texts, 1972.

Chronicle of Battle Abbey, ed. E. Searle, Oxford Medieval Texts, 1980.

Gilbert Crispin, *Vita domini Herluini abbatis Beccensis*, in J. Armitage Robinson, *Gilbert Crispin, abbot of Westminster*, Cambridge, 1911.

Gesta Francorum, ed. R. Hill, Nelson Medieval Texts, London, 1962.

Documents de l'histoire de la Normandie, ed. M. de Boüard, Toulouse, 1972.

Dudo of St Quentin, *De moribus et actis primorum Normanniae ducum auctore Dudone sancti Quintini decano*, ed. J. Lair, Caen, 1865.

Encomium Emmae Reginae, ed. A. Campbell, R. H. S. Camden 3rd, ser. lxxii, London, 1949.

Fauroux, M., *Recueil des actes des ducs de Normandie (911–1066)*, Mémoires de la Société des Antiquaires de Normandie, xxxvi, Caen, 1961.

Flodoard, *Les annales de Flodoard*, ed. Ph. Lauer, Paris, 1906.

—, *Historia Rememsis Ecclesiae*, ed. J. Heller and G. Waitz, *M.G.H., SS,* xiii, 1881.

Florence of Worcester, *Chronicon ex Chronicis*, ed. B. Thorpe, London, 1848–9.

Fulcher of Chartres, *Fulcherii Carnotensis Historia Hierosolymitane*, in *Pat. Lat.*, clv.

Geoffrey Malaterra, *Historia Sicula (De rebus gestis Rogerii Calabriae et Siciliae comitis et Roberti Guiscardi ducis fratris eius)*, in *Pat. Lat.*, cxlix. Also ed. E. Pontieri, in *Rerum Italicarum Scriptores*, new edn, v, 1928.

Gesta Tancredi, in *Pat. Lat.*, clv.

Historia Belli Sacri, in *Recueil des Historiens des Croisades, Historiens Occidentaux*, iii.

Hugo Falcandus, *La Historia o Liber de Regno Sicilie de Ugo Falcando*, ed. G. B. Siragusa, Fonti per la Storia d'Italia, xxii, Rome, 1896.

Leo of Ostia, *Chronicon monasterii Casinensis*, ed. H. Hoffman, *M.G.H., SS*, xxiv, 1980.

Liber Eliensis, ed. E. O. Blake, R. H. S., Camden 3rd. ser. xcii, London, 1962.

Musset, L., *Les actes de Guillaume le Conquérant et de la reine Mathilde pour les abbayes Caennaises*, Mémoires de la Société des Antiquaires de Normandie, xxxvii, 1967.

Orderic Vitalis, *The Ecclesiastical History of Orderic Vitalis*, ed. M. Chibnall, Oxford Medieval Texts, 6 vols 1969–80.

Plummer, C., *Two of the Saxon Chronicles Parallel*, Oxford, 1892, repr. 1952.

Raoul Glaber, *Les cinq livres de ses histoires*, ed. M. Prou, Paris, 1886.

Raymond d'Aguilers, *Historia Francorum qui ceperunt Jerusalem*, in *Pat. Lat.*, clv.

Recueil des actes de Charles III le Simple, roi de France, ed. P. Lauer, Chartes et Diplomes relatifs à l'histoire de France, Paris, 1940.

Recueil des actes des ducs de Normandie, see Fauroux.

Regesta regum Anglo-Normannorum, i, ed. H. W. C. Davis, Oxford, 1913.

Richer of Rheims, *Histoire de France (888–995)*, ed. R. Latouche, Paris, 1930–7.

Roberti Monachi S. Remigii . . . Historia Hierosolymitana, in *Pat. Lat.*, clv.

The Song of Roland, ed. and trans. Dorothy Sayers, Harmondsworth, 1957.

Romuald of Salerno, *Romualdi II archiepiscopi Salernitani Annales c. 893–1178*, ed. W. Arndt, *M.G.H., SS*, xix.

Vita Ædwardi Regis, The Life of King Edward, ed. and trans, F. Barlow, Nelson Medieval Texts, London, 1962.

Wace, *Le Roman de Rou*, ed. A. J. Holden, Paris, 1970–3.

Walter the Chancellor, *De bello Antiocheno*, in *Pat. Lat.*, clv.

William of Apulia, Guillaume de Pouille, *La geste de Robert Guiscard*, ed. M. Mathieu, Palermo, 1961.

William of Jumièges, *Gesta Normannorum Ducum*, ed. J. Marx, Société de l'histoire de Normandie, Rouen, Paris, 1914.

William of Malmesbury, *Gesta Regum Anglorum*, ed. W. Stubbs, Rolls Series, London, 1887–9.

—, *De Gestis Pontificum Anglorum*, ed. N. E. S. A. Hamilton, Rolls Series, London, 1870.

William of Poitiers, *Gesta Guillelmi ducis Normannorum et regis Anglorum*, ed. R. Foreville, Paris, 1952.

ii *Secondary Sources*

Abulafia, D. S. H., 'The Norman kingdom of Africa and the Norman expeditions to Majorca and the Muslim Mediterranean', *Battle*, vii, 1984.

Anderson, William, and Swaan, William, *Castles of Europe*, London, 1970.

Armitage, E. S., *Early Norman Castles of the British Isles*, London, 1912.

Armitage Robinson, J., *Gilbert Crispin, Abbot of Westminister*, Cambridge, 1912.

Bachrach, B. S., 'Charles Martel, mounted shock combat, the stirrup, and feudalism', *Studies in Medieval and Renaissance History*, vii, 1970.

Baring, F. H., *Domesday Tables for the counties of Surrey, Berkshire, Middlesex, Hertford, Buckingham and Bedford and for the New Forest*, London, 1909.

Barlow, F., *The English Church 1000–1066: a constitutional history*, London, 1963.

—, *Edward the Confessor*, London, 1970.

—, *The English Church 1066–1154: a history of the Anglo-Norman Church*, London, 1979.

Bates, D., *Normandy before 1066*, London, 1982.

Beeler, J., *Warfare in England 1066–1189*, New York, 1966.

—, *Warfare in Feudal Europe 730–1200*, Ithaca and London, 1971.

Bertaux, E., *L'Art dans l'Italie Méridionale*, t. i, Paris, 1904.

Bloch, Marc, *Feudal Society*, trans. L. A. Manyon, London, 1961.

Boase, T. S. R., *Castles and Churches of the Crusading Kingdom*, London, 1967.

Boüard, Michel de, *Guillaume le Conquérant*, Paris, 1958.

—, *Le Château de Caen*, Archéologie Médiévale numéro spécial, Caen, 1979.

—, ed. *Histoire de la Normandie: Documents de l'histoire de la Normandie*, Toulouse, 1970, 1972.

—, 'De la Neustrie carolingienne à la Normandie féodale: continuité ou discontinuité?' *B.I.H.R.*, xxviii, 1955.

—, 'Le duché de Normandie', in F. Lot and R. Fawtier, *Histoire des institutions francaises, i, Institutions seigneuriales*, Paris, 1957.

Brackmann, Albert, 'The beginnings of the national state in medieval Germany and the Norman monarchies', in *Medieval Germany 911–1250*, ed. G. Barraclough, Oxford, 1948.

Brett, M., 'John of Worcester and his contemporaries', in *The Writing of History in the Middle Ages: essays presented to R. W. Southern*, ed. R. H. C. Davis and J. M. Wallace-Hadrill, Oxford, 1981.

Brooks, N. P. and Walker, H. E., 'The authority and interpretation of the Bayeux Tapestry', *Battle*, i, 1978.

Brown, R. Allen, *The Normans and the Norman Conquest*, London, 1969.

—, *The Origins of English Feudalism*, London, 1973.

—, *English Castles*, London, 1976.

—, *Dover Castle*, H.M.S.O., 1983.

—, *The Tower of London*, H.M.S.O., 1984.

—, 'The Norman Conquest and the genesis of English castles', *Château-Gaillard*, iii, 1966.

—, 'The Battle of Hastings', *Battle*, iii, 1980.

—, 'The status of the Norman knight', in *War and Government in the Middle Ages: Essays presented to J. O. Prestwich*, Woodbridge, 1984.

Bur, M., *La formation du comté de Champagne*, Nancy, 1977.

Cahen, C., *La Syrie du Nord à l'époque des Croisades et la principalité franque d'Antioche*, Paris, 1940.

—, *Le régime féodal de l'Italie normande*, Paris, 1940.

Campbell, J., ed. *The Anglo-Saxons*, Oxford, Phaidon, 1982.

Chalandon, F., *Histoire de la domination normande en Italie et en Sicile*, Paris, 1907.

Chibnall, M., 'Military service in Normandy before 1066', *Battle*, v, 1982.

Clapham, A. W., *English Romanesque Architecture*, i, *Before the Conquest*; ii. *After the Conquest*, Oxford, 1930, 1934 (repr. 1964).

Conant, K. J., *Carolingian and Romanesque Architecture 800–1200*, Harmondsworth, 1973.

Cowdrey, H. E. J., *The Age of Abbot Desiderius: Montecassino, the Papacy and the Normans in the Eleventh and Early Twelfth Centuries*, Oxford, 1983.

—, 'Pope Urban II's preaching of the First Crusade', *History*, lv, 1970.

David, C. W., *Robert Curthose*, Harvard, 1920.

Davis, R. H. C., *The Normans and their Myth*, London, 1976.

—, 'The *Carmen de Hastingae Proelio*', *E.H.R.*, xciii, 1978.

—, 'William of Jumièges, Robert Curthose and the Norman succession', *E.H.R.*, xcv, 1980.

—, 'William of Poitiers and his *History of William the Conqueror*', in *The Writing of History in the Middle Ages: Essays presented to R. W. Southern*, ed. R. H. C. Davis and J. M. Wallace-Hadrill, Oxford, 1981.

Decaens, J., 'La datation de l'abbatiale de Bernay: quelques observations architecturales et résultats des fouilles récentes', *Battle*, v, 1982.

Décarreaux, J., *Normands, Papes et Moines en Italie méridionale et en Sicile, xie–xiie siècle*, Paris, 1974.

Deschamps, Paul, *Terre Sainte Romane*, Zodiaque, 1964.

Dodwell, C. R., 'The Bayeux Tapestry and the French secular epic', *Burlington Magazine*, civ, 1966.

Douglas, D. C., *William the Conqueror*, London, 1964.

—, *The Norman Achievement*, London, 1969.

—, *The Norman Fate, 1100–1154*, London, 1974.

—, 'The Norman episcopate before the Norman Conquest', *Cambridge Historical Journal*, xiii, 1957.

Engels, L. J., and others, 'The Carmen de Hastingae Proelio: a discussion,' *Battle*, ii, 1979.

Enlart, C., *Les monuments des croisés dans le royaume de Jérusalem: architecture religieuse et civile'*, Paris, 1928.

Fécamp, *L'abbaye benedictine de Fécamp*, Fécamp, 1959–60.

Fedden, R., and Thomas, J., *Crusader Castles*, London, 1957.

Fixot, M., 'Les fortifications de terre et la naissance de la féodalité dans le Cinglais', *Château-Gaillard*, iii, 1966.

Foreville, R., 'Aux origines de la renaissance juridique', *Le Moyen Age*, lviii, 1952.

Freeman, E. A., *The Norman Conquest* (6 vols.), Oxford, 1867–79.

Galbraith, V. H., *Studies in the Public Records*, London, 1948.

—, *Domesday Book: its place in administrative history*, Oxford, 1974.

Galasso, G., 'Social and political developments in the eleventh and twelfth centuries', in *The Normans in Sicily and Southern Italy*, Linei Lectures, Oxford, 1977.

Gallo, A., *Aversa Normanna*, Naples, 1938.

Ganshof, F. L., *Feudalism*, trans. P. Grierson, London, 1952.

Gem, R., 'The Romanesque rebuilding of Westminster Abbey (with a reconstruction by W. T. Ball)', *Battle*, iii, 1980.

Gibson, M., *Lanfranc of Bec*, Oxford, 1978.

Glover, R., 'English Warfare in 1066', *E.H.R.*, lxvii, 1952.

Godfrey, John., 'The defeated Anglo-Saxons take service with the Eastern Emperor', *Battle*, i, 1978.

Grousset, R., *Histoire des Croisades*, Paris, 1934–6.

Hamilton, B., *The Latin Church in the Crusader States: the Secular Church*, London, 1980.

Harper-Bill, C., 'The piety of the Anglo-Norman knightly class', *Battle*, ii, 1979.

Harvey, S., 'The knight and the knight's fee in England', *Past and Present*, 49, 1970.

Haskins, C. H., *The Normans in European History*, New York, 1915.

—, *Norman Institutions*, New York, 1918.

Hill, R., 'Crusading Warfare: a camp-follower's view, 1097–1120', *Battle*, i, 1978.

Hockey, S. F., 'William fitz Osbern and the endowment of his abbey of Lyre', *Battle*, iii, 1980.

Hyde, J. K., *Society and Politics in Medieval Italy: The Evolution of Civil Life, 1000–1350*, London.

James, E., *The Origins of France: From Clovis to the Capetians, 500–1000*, London, 1982.

Jamison, E., 'The Norman administration of Apulia and Capua, more especially under Roger II and William I', *Papers of the British School at Rome*, vi, 1913.

—, 'Some notes on the Anonymi Gesta Francorum with special reference to the Norman contingent from south Italy and Sicily in the First Crusade', in *Studies . . . presented to . . . M. K. Pope*, Manchester, 1939.

John, E., 'Edward the Confessor and the Norman succession', *E.H.R.*, xciv, 1979.

Joranson, E., 'The inception of the career of the Normans in Italy—legend and history', *Speculum*, xxiii, 1948.

Kapelle, W. A., *The Norman Conquest of the North*, London, 1979.

Knowles, D., *The Monastic Order in England*, Cambridge, 1963.

Lemarignier, J. F., *Recherches sur l'hommage en marche et les frontières féodales*, Lille, 1945.

Lennard, R., *Rural England, 1086–1135*, Oxford, 1959.

Le Patourel, J., *The Norman Empire*, Oxford, 1976.

—, 'The Norman Succession 996–1135', *E.H.R.*, lxxxvi, 1971.

Loud, G. A., 'How "Norman" was the Norman conquest of southern Italy?', *Nottingham Medieval Studies*, xxv, 1981.

—, 'The *Gens Normannorum* -myth or reality?', *Battle*, iv, 1981.

McGurk, P., and R. R. Darlington, 'The *Chronicon ex Chronicis* of "Florence" of Worcester and its use of sources for English history before 1066', *Battle*, v, 1962.

MacKay, A., *Spain in the Middle Ages: From Frontier to Empire, 1000–1500*, London, 1977.

Mason, J. F. A., *William I and the Sussex Rapes*, Historical Association, 1972.

Mayer, H. E., *The Crusades*, trans. J. Gillingham, Oxford, 1972.

Ménager, L. R., 'L'institution monarchique dans les états normands d'Italie', *Cahiers de Civilisation Mediévale*, ii, 1959.

—, 'La "Byzantisation" religieuse de l'Italie meridionale (ix–xii siècles) et la politique monastique des Normands d'Italie', *Revue d'Histoire Ecclesiastique*, liv, 1959.

Müller-Wiener, W., *Castles of the Crusaders*, London, 1966.

Munro, D. C., 'The speech of Pope Urban at Clermont', *American Historical Review*, xi, 1906.

Musset, L., *Les invasions: le second assaut contre l'Europe chrétienne (viie–xie siècles)*, Paris, 1965.

—, *Normandie Romane*, i. *La Basse Normandie*; ii. *La Haute Normandie*, Zodiaque, 1967, 1974.

—, 'A-t-il existé en Normandie au xie siècle une aristocratie d'argent?', *Annales de Normandie*, ix, 1959.

—, 'L'aristocratie normande au xie siècle', in *La Noblesse au Moyen Age xie–xve: Essais à . . . Robert Boutruche*, ed. P. Contamine, Paris, 1976.

Navel, H., 'L'enquête de 1133 sur les fiefs de l'eveché de Bayeux', *Bulletin de la Société des Antiquaires de Normandie*, xlii, 1934.

—, 'Recherches sur les institutions féodales en Normandie (région de Caen)', *Bulletin de la Société des Antiquaires de Normandie*, li, 1952.

Norwich, J. J., *The Normans in the South*, London, 1966.

—, *The Kingdom in the Sun*, London, 1970.

Noyé, G., 'Le château de Scribla et les fortifications normandes du bessin de Crati', *Società potere e populo nell'età de Ruggero II* (III Giornate normanno-suevi, Bari, 1977), Rome, 1979.

—, 'Féodalité et habitat fortifié en Calabre dans la deuxième moitié du xie siècle et la premier tiers du xiie siècle', in *Structures féodales et féodalisme dans l'Occident Mediterranéan, x^e–xii s., Rome*, 44, Rome, 1980.

Oleson, T. J., *The Witenagemot in the reign of Edward the Confessor*, London, 1955.

—, 'Edward the Confessor's promise of the throne to Duke William of Normandy', *E.H.R.*, lxxii, 1957.

Porée, A. A., *Histoire de l'abbaye du Bec*, Evreux, 1901, repr. Brussels, 1980.

Prentout, H., *Etude critique sur Dudon de Saint-Quentin et son histoire des premiers ducs Normands*, Paris, 1916.

—, *Histoire de Guillaume le Conquérant*, Caen, 1936.

Pryor, J. H., 'Transportation of horses by sea during the era of the Crusades, eighth century to 1285 A.D.', *Mariner's Mirror*, 1982.

Renoux, A., 'Fouilles sur le site du château ducal de Fécamp (x^e–xiie siècle)', *Battle*, iv, 1981.

Rey, G., *Etude sur les monuments de l'architecture militaire des croisés en Syrie et dans l'Ile de Chypre*, Paris, 1871.

Riley-Smith, J., 'The title of Godfrey de Bouillon', *B.I.H.R.*, lii, 1979.

—, 'The motives of the earliest crusaders and the settlement of Latin Palestine. 1095–1100', *E.H.R.*, xcviii, 1983.

Ritchie, R. L. G., *The Normans in England before the Norman Conquest*, Inaugural Lecture, Edinburgh, 1948.

Robinson, I. S., 'Gregory VII and the soldiers of Christ', *History*, lviii, 1973.

Ross, D. J. A., 'L'originalité de "Turoldus": le maniement de lance', *Cahiers de civilisation médiévale*, vi, 1963.

Runciman, S., *History of the Crusades*, Cambridge, 1953–4.

—, *The families of Outremer*, Creighton Lecture, London, 1960.

Salvini, R., 'Monuments of Norman art in Sicily and Southern Italy', in *The Normans in Sicily and Southern Italy*, Lincei Lectures, Oxford, 1977.

Sawyer, P. H., 'The density of the Danish settlement in England', *University of Birmingham Historical Journal*, vi, 1957.

Searle, E., 'The abbey of the conquerors: defensive enfeoffment and economic development in Anglo-Norman England', *Battle*, ii, 1979.

—, 'Women and the legitimization of succession at the Norman Conquest', *Battle*, iii, 1980.

—, 'Fact and pattern in heroic poetry: Dudo of St Quentin', *Viator*, 15, 1984.

Smail, R. C., *Crusading Warfare*, Cambridge, 1956.

Southern, R. W., *The Making of the Middle Ages*, London, 1953.

—, *St Anselm and his Biographer*, Cambridge, 1963.

—, *Western Society and the Church in the Middle Ages*, Harmondsworth, 1970.

—, 'The place of England in the twelfth-century renaissance', *History*, xlv, 1960 and in *Medieval Humanism and other studies*, Oxford, 1970.

Stenton, F. M., *First Century of English Feudalism*, Oxford, 1932.

—, *Anglo-Saxon England*, Oxford, 1947.

—, 'The Danes in England', *Proceedings of the British Academy*, xiii, 1927.

Stubbs, W., *Select Charters and other illustrations of English Constitutional History . . .* , 9th edn, ed. H. W. C. Davis, Oxford, 1946.

Sumption, Jonathan, *Pilgrimage: an image of medieval religion*, London, 1975.

Taylor, A. J., 'Evidence for a pre-Conquest origin for the chapels in Hastings and Pevensey castles', *Château-Gaillard*, iii, 1969.

—, 'Three early castle sites in Sicily: Motta Camastra, Sperlinga and Petralia Soprana', *Château-Gaillard*, vii, 1974.

Touring Club Italiano, *Guide d'Italia*.

Van Houts, E. M. C., 'The *Gesta Normannorum Ducum*: a history without an end', *Battle*, iii, 1980.

Verbruggen, J. F., 'La tactique militaire des armées de chevaliers', *Revue du Nord*, xxix, 1947.

Vogüé, M. de, *Eglises de Terre Sainte*, Paris, 1860.

Waley, Daniel, '"Combined operations" in Sicily, A.D. 1060–1078', *Papers of the British School at Rome*, xxii, 1954.

Wallace-Hadrill, J. M., 'War and peace in the earlier Middle Ages', *T.R.H.S.*, (5) xxv, 1975.

White, L. T., *Latin Monasticism in Norman Sicily*, Cambridge, Mass., 1938.

White, Lynn, *Medieval Technology and Social Change*, Oxford, 1962.

Wickham, C., *Early Medieval Italy: Central Power and Local Society, 400–1000*, London, 1981.

Williams, A., 'Problems connected with the English royal succession, 860–1066', *Battle*, i, 1978.

—, 'Land and power in the eleventh century: the estates of Harold', *Battle*, iii, 1980.

Yewdale, R. B., *Bohemond I, Prince of Antioch*, Princeton, 1924.

Yver, J., 'Les premières institutions du duché de Normandie', *I Normanni e la loro espansione in Europa nell'alto medioevo*, Centro Italiano di Studi sull' Alto Medioevo. Settimano xvi, Spoleto, 1969.

Notes

Chapter I

1. See J. Le Patourel, *The Norman Empire*, Oxford, 1976, p. 352.

Chapter II

1. See especially Lucien Musset, *Les invasions: le second assaut contre l'Europe chrétienne (viie–xie siecles)*, Paris, 1965, to which work, together with Le Patourel's *Norman Empire*, this chapter is indebted. For a magisterial discussion of early Norman institutional history before the mid-eleventh century (in so far as the sparse evidence will allow), see Jean Yver, 'Les premières institutions du duché de Normandie', *I Normanni e la loro espansione in Europa nell'alto medioevo*, Centro Italiano di Studi sull'Alto Medioevo, Settimana xvi, Spoleto, 1969, 299–366.
2. Cf. F. M. Stenton, 'The Danes in England', *Proceedings of the British Academy*, xiii, 1927; P. H. Sawyer, 'The Density of the Danish Settlement in England', *University of Birmingham Historical Journal*, vi, 1957.
3. F. M. Stenton, *Anglo-Saxon England*, 2nd ed., Oxford, 1947, pp. 370–1.
4. Below p. 50.
5. William of Jumièges, *Gesta Normannorum Ducum*, ed. J. Marx, Société de l'histoire de Normandie, Rouen and Paris, 1914, pp. 76–7.
6. *Ibid.*, pp. 109–11 and below p. 52.
7. Below pp. 49ff.
8. Thus Brown, *The Normans and the Norman Conquest*, pp. 20ff., derived especially from the seminal work of J. F. Lemarignier, *Recherches sur l'hommage en marche et les frontières féodales*, Lille, 1945.
9. *Norman Empire*, especially Chapter I.
10. Dudo of St Quentin, *De moribus et actis primorum Normannorum ducum auctore Dudone Sancti Quintini decano*, ed. J. Lair, Caen, 1865, pp. 168–9; Flodoard, 'Historia Remensis Ecclesiae', *Mon. Germ. Hist.*, Scriptores, xiii, 1881, p. 577, and *Annales*, ed. Ph. Lauer, Paris, 1906, pp. 24, 55. For Dudo, see also p. 20 below. Flodoard says that the 924

grant was of the Bessin and Maine, and describes that of 933 as 'the land of the Bretons by the sea coast'. For 911, Flodoard speaks of 'certain maritime *pagi*, with the city of Rouen which they had almost destroyed and others dependent upon it'; Dudo speaks vaguely of the land between the Epte and the sea, which might stand for Upper Normandy. Cf. Le Patourel pp. 6, 8. For Maine and Brittany, see p. 50 below.

11. Le Patourel, p. 12.
12. Eleanor Searle, 'Fact and pattern in heroic poetry: Dudo of St Quentin', *Viator*, 15, 1984 (forthcoming).
13. Le Patourel, p. 283.
14. See D. C. Douglas, *William the Conqueror*, London, 1964, pp. 58–60.
15. Below, p. 42.
16. Le Patourel, pp. 4, 281–3.
17. Dudo, ed. Lair, p. 221; William of Jumièges, p. 40.
18. *Histoire de France*, ed. and trans. Robert Latouche, Paris, 1930–64, ii, 329.
19. *Op. cit.*, p. 256.

Chapter III

1. Above, p. 16.
2. Above, p. 16.
3. Above, p. 17.
4. Below, p. 44.
5. Ed. F. M. Stenton and others, 2nd ed., London, 1965, Pls. 42–5. The building of the ships is shown in Pls. 38–9.
6. Musset, *Les invasions*, p. 255; Yver, 'Les premiers institutions', pp. 319–23.
7. Cf. Musset, *ibid.*, p. 254: 'Les traditions nordiques, jusqu'à la fin du xe siècle, etaient peu favorables à l'autorité du prince tandis que l'Etat carolingien, tel qu'il fonctionnait encore en 911, pouvait offrir à une souverain bien des éléments utilisables'. Cf. below, p. 41.
8. The point is worth emphasising because so often denied at least by implication by English historians putting the doubtful case for Old English superiority both of quantity and quality in this respect. For details of editions, usually with introduction and notes, see Bibliography. For Dudo of St Quentin and William of Jumièges, see also especially Elizabeth Van Houts in *Proceedings of the Battle Conference on Anglo-Norman Studies* (now *Anglo-Norman Studies* but hereafter, *Battle*), iii, 1980, and R. H. C. Davis, *The Normans and their Myth*, London, 1976, pp. 50ff. For Dudo alone, see Eleanor Searle in *Viator*, 15, 1984, and Gerda C. Huisman in *Battle*, vi, 1983. For William of Poitiers, see R. H. C. Davis in *The Writing of History in the Middle Ages, Essays presented to R. W. Southern*, ed. R. H. C. Davis, J. M. Wallace-Hadrill, Oxford, 1981. For the pre-Conquest Norman charters, see Marie Fauroux, *Recueil des Actes des ducs de Normandie*, Mémoires de la société des Antiquaires de Normandie, xxxvi, Caen, 1961.
9. One knows that history is usually written by the victors and the ruling class and of course allowance must be made for the bias of Norman writers, though emphatically not to the point of denigration.
10. For the Norman contribution to the idea of Holy War, see below, p. 121.
11. Cf. p. 7 above.

12. Raoul Glaber, *Les cinq livres de ses histoires*, ed. M. Prou, Paris, 1886, p. 62. 'One would have thought the world was shaking itself to cast off its old age and was clothing itself in a white robe of churches'.

13. For Mont-St-Michel, Cerisy and Lessay, see also p. 42 below.

14. Dated by L. Musset to *c.*990 (*Normandie Romane*, ii, Zodiaque, 1974, p. 63).

15. David Knowles, *The Monastic Order in England*, Cambridge, 1963, p. 84.

16. Cf. René Herval in *L'Abbaye Benedictine de Fécamp*, Fécamp, 1959–60, i, 34.

17. H. Prentout, *Etude critique sur Dudon*, Paris, 1916, p. 326. For Fécamp, see also Annie Renoux in *Battle*, iv, 1981.

18. *The Ecclesiastical History of Orderic Vitalis*, ed. and trans. M. Chibnall, 6 vols, Oxford Medieval Texts, 1969–80, ii, 10. Cf. the similar, and in some ways better, passage in Orderic's 'edition' of William of Jumièges, ed. Marx, p. 173: *In diebus illis maxima pacis tranquillitas fovebat habitantes in Normannia et servi Dei a cunctis habebantur in summa reverentia. Unusquisque optimatum certabat in predio suo ecclesias fabricare et monachos, qui pro se Deum rogarent, rebus suis locupletare.*

19. For Richer's castigation of the Normans see p. 16 n. above. Most of the following paragraph is taken from Brown *The Normans and the Norman Conquest*, pp. 28–30.

20. *Ecclesiastical History*, ed. Chibnall, ii, 50. 'Strive constantly to avoid sloth as deadly poison, for as our holy father Benedict says: "Idleness is the enemy of the soul"'.

21. J. Armitage Robinson, *Gilbert Crispin, Abbot of Westminster*, Cambridge, 1911.

22. Knowles, *Monastic Order*, p. 86.

23. *Ibid.*, p. 96.

24. *Ecclesiastical History*, ii, 250, 296.

25. *Ibid.*, iii, 120–2.

26. Michel de Boüard, *Guillaume le Conquérant*, Paris, 1958, p. 67.

27. *Op. cit.*, p. 134. In this connection see the useful genealogical table by Raymonde Foreville at p. 137.

28. See especially D. C. Douglas, 'The Norman Episcopate before the Norman Conquest', *Cambridge Historical Journal*, xiii, 1957.

29. For a recent survey and analysis of the Norman aristocracy of the eleventh century, confirming D. C. Douglas' earlier conclusions (*William the Conqueror*, London, 1964, pp. 83ff), see L. Musset, 'L'aristocratie normande au xie siècle', in *La Noblesse au Moyen Age* xie–xv^{e}s: *Essais à le memoire de Robert Boutruche*, ed. P. Contamine, Paris, 1976, pp. 71–96. For Tosny, see Musset in *Docs. de l'histoire de la Normandie*, ed. M. de Boüard, pp. 90ff. It is instructive that Dudo does not write, as often asserted, of a deserted region taken over by Rollo and his followers, but of a region deserted by its lords— *pauperes homines inopesque mercatores . . . sed armigeris militibusque est vacus* (ed. Lair, 152–3; cf. Searle, *Viator*, 15, n. 5).

30. For the comital title and others, see below, p. 41.

31. *Ecclesiastical History*, vi, 16.

32. Ed. Foreville, p. 240.

33. Cf. Le Patourel, *Norman Empire*, pp. 335–6 and n.

34. Much misconception has evidently followed Stenton's remarks on the lack of social distinction attaching to the eleventh-century knight. Thus 'although knighthood . . . implied military proficiency, it carried no social distinction', *First Century of English Feudalism*, Oxford, 1932 edn, p. 142. Cf. *Anglo-Saxon England*, 2nd edn, Ox-

ford, 1947, p. 628; and Sally Harvey, 'The Knight and the Knight's Fee in England', *Past and Present*, No. 49, November 1970. For the whole subject and the controversy now surrounding it, see R. A. Brown, 'The status of the Norman knight', in *War and Government in the Middle Ages*, ed. J. C. Holt and others (forthcoming).

35. Ed. Foreville, p. 12.
36. *Ecclesiastical History*, ii, 90.
37. Fauroux, *Recueil des Actes*, No. 2, p. 70, *S [ignum] Teofridi militis*. See Brown, 'Status of the Norman knight'.
38. E.g. *Ecclesiastical History*, ii, 40, 126; iii, 110–12.
39. Pl. 27.
40. Below.
41. Thus the four knights before they murdered Thomas Becket are said to have put on their hauberks, which they cannot have needed for their own defence, presumably to give their action some kind of official standing (David Knowles, *Thomas Becket*, London, 1970, p. 144, from William of Canterbury).
42. Quoted by Marc Bloch, *Feudal Society*, trans. Manyon, London, 1961, pp. 152, 293–4.
43. *Ecclesiastical History*, ii, 40.
44. See further C. Harper-Bill, 'The Piety of the Anglo-Norman Knightly Class', *Battle*, ii, 1979.
45. Bertran von Born, ed. C. Appel, Hallé, 1931, no. 40.
46. William of Poitiers, pp. 38–40.
47. For a useful summary of the controversy and debate surrounding the date and provenance of the *Chanson de Roland* see D. C. Douglas, *The Norman Achievement*, pp. 97–8 with the notes and references there given. See also D. J. A. Ross, 'L'originalité de "Turoldus": le maniement de lance', *Cahiers de civilisation médiévale*, vi, 1963.
48. See especially D. J. A. Ross, *art. cit.*
49. This remains true whatever the date of the introduction of the stirrup in the West. For that question, see Lynn White, *Medieval Technology and Social Change*, Oxford, 1962, Chapter I. Cf. David Bullough, *The Age of Charlemagne*, London, 1980, p. 36, and *E.H.R.*, lxxxv, 19; R. H. Hilton and P. H. Sawyer in *Past and Present*, No. 24, 1963.
50. Ed. Stenton, Pls. 53, 59–62, 65. See further, Brown, 'Battle of Hastings', *Battle*, iii, 1980, pp. 12–14. For Richard Glover's unacceptable presentation of Norman cavalry at Hastings as mere 'mounted javelineers' and their tactics as 'infantile' (together with much else), see *E.H.R.*, lxvii, 1952. The comparatively few instances of the couched lance on the Tapestry are presumably to be explained by the early date and the fact that the technique was first developed for the unhorsing of horsed opponents, of whom there were none at Hastings.
51.   *e.g.* 'Gerin the Count bestrides his steel Sorel,
                Gerier his comrade on Passëcerf is set;
                Eagerly both loose rein and spur ahead
                And go to strike a Paynim, Timozel,
                One on the shield, the other on the chest.
                Both spears at once are broken in his breast'.
Examples could be many times multiplied. For the breaking of the lance cf. Oliver who, 'goes riding through the press;
                His spear is broken, only the shaft is left',
and compare Duke William who at the end of the battle of Hastings in William of Poitiers (p. 202) has only the stump of a broken lance in his hand. (The above extracts from the Roland are taken from

Dorothy Sayers edition and translation, Harmondsworth, 1957, pp. 104–5. The word 'spear', of course, is her translation).

52. *The Alexiad of Anna Comnena*, ed. and trans. E.R.A. Sewter, Harmondsworth, 1969, p. 416.

53. See the classically stupid statement of Sir Charles Oman in the first and worst edition of his *History of the Art of War in the Middle Ages*, reissued by the Cornell University Press (Ithaca, New York, 1953) ed. John H. Beeler, p. 58—which is better not quoted here in the hope that it may one day be forgotten.

54. For the difficult estimation of the numbers engaged at Hastings, see Brown, *Normans*, pp. 150–1, n. 47.

55. Below.

56. See especially Len Deighton, *Fighter*, London, 1977. During World War II, and doubtless on both sides, the comparison of fighter pilots with knights was often made, and the comparison contains more than a romantic truth.

57. For the *conroi*, which like most subjects to do with medieval warfare deserves further study, see J. F. Verbruggen, 'La tactique militaire des armées de chevaliers', *Revue du Nord*, xxix, 1947.

58. See Brown, *Normans*, pp. 48–9. NB the Norman earl of Chester, Hugh d'Avranches, in England, of whom Orderic Vitalis declared that his retinue was more like an army than a household—*non familiam secum sed exercitum semper ducebat*—(and of the same earl that 'his hunting was a daily devastation of his lands'), *Ecclesiastical History*, ii, 260–2. Under Norman influence in England after 1066 even the Old English bishop, Wulfstan of Worcester, went about *pompam militum secum ducens*, which perhaps might be translated as 'followed by a pride of knights' (*De Gestis Pontificum Anglorum*, ed. N. S. A. Hamilton, Rolls Series, 1870, p. 281).

59. *Vita Herluini*, ed. Armitage Robinson, pp. 87–90.

60. Thus Oman, ed. Beeler, *ut supra*, p. 63.

61. For both and what follows see Brown, *English Castles*, London, 1976, Chapters I and VII; Sir John Hackett's Foreward to William Anderson, *Castles of Europe*, London, 1970.

62. For both points elaborated, and for what follows concerning commendation and the fief, see Brown, *Origins of English Feudalism*, pp. 21ff. For commendation see especially F. L. Ganshof, *Feudalism* (trans. P. Grierson), London, 1952.

63. Ed. J. Lair, pp. 168–9. For other early instances from Dudo see Yver, 'Les premières institutions', p. 313, n. 4.

64. Ed. Foreville, p. 104. See also p. 58 below.

65. *Ibid.*, pp. 78–80, *sibi manus perdomitas daret, fidelitatem quam satelles domine debet, jurans.*

66. *Ibid.*, p. 88, *manibus ei sese dedit, cuncta sua ab eo, ut miles a domino, recepit.*

67. The fundamental work on early Norman feudalism is that by H. Navel, *viz* 'l'enquête de 1133 sur les fiefs de l'evêché de Bayeux' in *Bulletin de la société des antiquaires de Normandie*, xlii, 1934, and 'Recherches sur les institutions féodales en Normandie (région de Caen)', *ibid.*, li, 1952. See also C. H. Haskins, *Norman Institutions*, New York, 1918, Chapter I; Marjorie Chibnall, 'Military Service in Normandy before 1066,' *Battle*, v, 1982.

68. Haskins, *op. cit.*, p. 6.

69. *Ibid.*, p. 5. The statement, since confirmed in almost the same words by Michel de Boüard (*Guillaume le Conquérant*, Paris, 1958, p. 61), is not less true because Norman feudalism in the mid-eleventh century

was less developed and less defined than it will be in the twelfth century, nor because precise quotas of knight-service may not have been fixed for the duke's tenants-in-chief. Much of the history of feudal custom and law is of a continuing definition, and thus limitation, of services and obligations which were open in the beginning; and thus the absence of fixed quotas in pre-Conquest Normandy is not pre-feudal but proto-feudal and very feudal indeed.

70. Pl. 29. For the Host see N. B. Brooks in *Battle*, i, 5.

71. For the emergent feudal 'incidents' and their value, see Brown, *Normans*, pp. 242ff.

72. R. H. C. Davis, *History of Medieval Europe*, London, 1957, p. 295.

73. Above, p. 28.

74. In Normandy only the older houses founded before about 1050 owed military service (Haskins, *Norman Institutions*, pp. 9–10); Chibnall, *Battle*, v, 65.

75. Orderic Vitalis, *Ecclesiastical History*, ii, 90–2. For Robert see also p. 35 above and p. 118 below.

76. For the banishment of Lanfranc, afterwards rescinded, see *Vita Herluini*, ed. Armitage Robinson, pp. 97–8.

77. William of Poitiers, pp. 124–5.

78. The only prince to succeed without such prior recognition was Robert the Magnificent in the unexpected circumstances of 1028. He, however, was careful to have his infant son, the future Conqueror, accepted as his successor before departing on his fateful pilgrimage (William of Jumièges, p. 111).

79. Above, p. 20.

80. Fauroux, *Recueil des actes*, pp. 49–50.

81. One is reminded of R. W. Southern's splendid epitaph on the new comital families of the period—'War made them conspicuous, grants of land established their position, marriage consolidated it, and the acquisition of ancient titles of honour cloaked their usurpations' (*Making of the Middle Ages*, London, 1953, p. 82).

82. Fauroux, *loc. cit.*

83. Musset, *Les invasions*, p. 162.

84. *Recueil des actes de Charles III*, ed. Lauer, Paris, 1940, no. 92, p. 209; Yver, 'Les premières institutions', pp. 314–15.

85. For the frontiers see above, p. 15 and for exceptions both to their definition and coincidence with the archbishopric, see Le Patourel, *Norman Empire*, pp. 8–10.

86. For the problem of Lower Normandy, see Michel de Bouard, *Guillaume le Conquérant*, pp. 23ff; Le Patourel, *Norman Empire*, pp. 305–6 and below, p. 45.

87. For Bayeux, see Musset in *Documents de l'histoire de la Normandie*, pp. 87–9; for Caen, M. de Bouard, *Le château de Caen* (Archéologie Médiévale, numero speciale), C.R.A.M., Caen, 1979.

88. For details of Norman government and administration see Yver, 'Les premières institutions'; Haskins, *Norman Institutions*, Chapter I; de Bouard, 'Le duché de Normandie' in Lot and Fawtier, *Histoire des institutions françaises*, i.

89. The point is worth emphasis in view of the marked tendency amongst English historians to denigrate the purely Norman contribution to government and administration. Thus Stenton, 'In comparison with England, Normandy in the mid-eleventh century was still a state in the making' (*Anglo-Saxon England*, 2nd ed., p. 546). By contrast, see Albert Brackmann, 'The beginnings of the national state in medieval Germany and the Norman monarchies', in

Medieval Germany 911–1250, ed. and trans. G. Barraclough, Oxford, 1948, ii, 281ff.

90. For a glimpse of Duke Richard II holding a *placitum generale* in the great tower at Rouen, see the interpolation in William of Jumièges, ed. Marx, p. 89.

91. *Les invasions*, p. 239. Cf. Yver 'Les premières institutions', pp. 344ff.

92. See de Bouard, 'Le duché de Normandie', p. 16 and Lemarignier, *L'hommage en marche*, pp. 19ff.

93. L. Musset, 'A-t-il existé en Normandie au xie siècle une aristocratie d'argent?', *Annales de Normandie*, ix, 1959; also in *Revue d'histoire du droit français et étranger*, 1960, pp. 433–4.

94. *Dialogus de Scaccario*, ed. Charles Johnson, Medieval Classics, London, 1950, p. 14; cf. de Bouard, 'Le duché de Normandie', pp. 10, 18; Haskins, *op. cit.*, pp. 39–45.

95. Cf. V. H. Galbraith, citing W. H. Stevenson, 'William . . . as Duke of Normandy had neither seal nor chancery' (*Studies in the Public Records*, London, 1948, p. 38). and Stenton, *Anglo-Saxon England*, 2nd ed., p. 547, 'as evidence of a central authority in government, the scanty records of the Conqueror's Norman reign are in no way comparable to the long succession of writs and solemn charters produced by the clerks of Edward the Confessor'. Marie Fauroux's edition of the Norman ducal charters down to 1066, published after both the quoted extracts were written, has scarcely been absorbed yet on this side on the Channel. For ducal seals before 1066, see Fauroux, pp. 45–7; Yver, 'Les premières institutions', p. 333.

96. Below, p. 60.

97. Cf. above, p. 31.

98. The story was told of Tancred of Hauteville. See H. Prentout, *Histoire de Guillaume le Conquérant*, t. i, Caen, 1936, p. 87, n. 1.

99. *Ecclesiastical History*, ii, 58, 98. See also below, p. 86.

100. Interpolations in William of Jumièges, p. 163.

101. *Ibid.*, p. 169.

102. *Ecclesiastical History*, ii, 20.

103. The fullest and most recent account of William's minority will be found in Chapter 2 of D. C. Douglas, *William the Conqueror*.

104. *Ecclesiastical History*, iv, 82. Duke Robert died on his pilgrimage to Jerusalem in 1035. For the date and circumstances of William's birth, see Douglas, *op. cit.*, Appdx. A.

105. The religious houses which Orderic had in mind when writing this passage are identified by Dr Chibnall as probably Jumièges, Fécamp, Mont St-Michel, St-Ouen (Rouen), St-Wandrille, Bernay, Cerisy-la-Fôret, possibly Bec and La Trinité-du-Mont (Rouen), and perhaps St-Taurin (Evreux). The nunnery was Montivilliers.

106. Identified (as above) by Dr Chibnall as probably St Stephen's (Caen), Montebourg, Grestain, St-Pierre-de-Préaux, St-Pierre-sur-Dives, Lire, St-Sauveur-le-Vicomte, St Evroul, Séez, Conches, Troarn, Lessay, Le Tréport, Cormeilles, St-Sever, St Victor-en-Caux and Fontenay. The nunneries were Holy Trinity (Caen), St-Léger-de-Préaux, Almenèches, St-Sauveur-d'Evreux, St-Amand (Rouen) and Notre-Dame-du-Pré (Lisieux).

107. *Ecclesiastical History*, iv, 90–2 and notes.

108. *Ibid.*, p. 80.

109. Douglas, *op. cit.*, pp. 67–72.

110. See p. 42 above.

111. See p. 16 above.

112. See p. 50 below.

113. An examination of the remains of Mathilda in 1961 is said to have shown that she was little above 4 ft in height (Douglas, *op. cit.*, p. 370).

114. Ed. Foreville, pp. 246–54.

115. Le Patourel, *op. cit.*, p. 289.

116. For the Norman conquest of the county of Maine, see below, p. 00.

117. Cf. Le Patourel, p. 300, who writes of Norman monks having 'a feeling of distinction and a sense of mission that associated easily with the ambitions of the duke and the aristocracy'.

118. *Ecclesiastical History*, ii, 102.

119. *Chronicles of the Reigns of Stephen, Henry II and Richard I*, ed. R. Howlett, iii, Rolls Series, 1886, pp. 185–6, cited by Le Patourel, p. 353.

120. Cf. Le Patourel, pp. 297–8: S. F. Hockey, 'William fitz Osbern and the endowment of his abbey of Lyre', *Battle*, iii, 1980, pp. 96ff.

121. For the particular enthusiasm of the Normans for pilgrimage in its great age, see Jonathan Sumption, *Pilgrimage: an Image of Medieval Religion*, London, 1975, pp. 117–18. See also p. 83 below.

Chapter IV

1. Above, p. 12.

2. *Norman Empire*, p. 12. There follows a useful summary and, more important, interpretation of Norman expansion from the beginning. Cf. p. 15 above.

3. Cf. p. 37 above.

4. Below, p. 53.

5. Above, p. 14.

6. *Norman Conquest*, i (1870), 302.

7. Both dealt with below.

8. For the Norman sources, see p. 20 above.

9. At Bayeux on the Tapestry (Pl. 29); at Bonneville-sur-Touques in Poitiers (p. 102). Orderic Vitalis placed it at Rouen (*Ecclesiastical History*, ii, 134–6).

10. Florence or Worcester for this period, though close to the 'D' version of the Anglo-Saxon Chronicle, has other information of unknown derivation and must therefore be regarded as partly an additional literary source. The much needed modern critical edition of 'Florence' by the late R. R. Darlington is currently being prepared for the press by, P. M. McGurk. See also the same scholar's 'The *Chronicon ex Chronicis* of "Florence" of Worcester and its sources for the Anglo-Saxon period', in *Battle*, v. 1982.

11. Ed. Foreville, pp. 172, 206–8.

12. Pl. 33.

13. Above, p. 49.

14. See R. L. G. Ritchie, *The Normans in England before the Norman Conquest* (Inaugural Lecture, Exeter, 1948), pp. 14–15; Brown, *Normans*, pp. 111, 114–16, and below.

15. For Emma, see especially A. Campbell's Introduction to the *Encomium Emmae Reginae*. Married first to Ethelred and then to Cnut, Edward the Confessor was her son by the former and Harthacnut by the latter. She was in exile in Flanders during the brief reign of Harold 'Harefoot' (1037–40), Cnut's son by his former marriage and his immediate successor. Cf. p. 14 above.

16. F. Barlow, *Edward the Confessor*, p. 29.

17. *A-S C*, 'C(D, E)', ed. Whitelock, p. 93. Cf. p. 14 above.

18. *A-S C* p. 106 and n. 4.

19. Below, p. 53.

20. *Pace* Barlow, *Edward the Confessor*, p. 41. A possible visit to his mother at Bruges in 1038 is scarcely to the point. The Norman court was more than sufficiently cosmopolitan, and Norman society sufficiently 'open', to account for the Confessor's wide range of friends and acquaintance as a royal prince.

21. Above, p. 16.

22. Florence, ed. Thorpe, pp. 196–7; *A-SC*, 'C', p. 108. Cf. pp. 54–5 below.

23. Above, p. 14.

24. Jumièges, p. 109.

25. *Gesta Regum*, i, 218; ii, 300.

26. Jumièges, pp. 111–12. In view of Cnut's earlier sharing of the kingdom with Edmund Ironside, Harthacnut's later sharing of it with Edward in 1041, and the confused and disputed succession on Cnut's death in 1035, there seems nothing inherently improbable in this proposal.

27. *Recueil des actes des ducs de Normandie*, no. 76, pp. 216–18. For a charter of Edward dated 25 December 1016 at Ghent whereby he promises to restore its English possessions to the abbey of St Peter there if he should become king, see A. Van Lokeren, *Chartes et documents de l'abbaye de Saint-Pierre au Mont-Blandin à Gand*, i (Ghent, 1869), no. 96, pp. 72–3; J. H. Round, *Calendar of Documents preserved in France*, no. 1374.

28. Fauroux, *Recueil des actes*, no. 85, pp. 223–6.

29. Barlow, *Edward the Confessor*, p. 44.

30. Ed. Marx, pp. 120–2.

31. Ed. Foreville, pp. 4–12.

32. The fullest discussion of Alfred's expedition and murder is that of Campbell in *Encomium Emmae Reginae*, pp. lxiv–vii. The author of the *Vita Edwardi* has the sore opened again in Edward's mind in 1051 (p. 20).

33. *A-S C,* 'C (D)', p. 106. Cf. Jumièges, p. 122.

34. See Douglas, *William the Conqueror*, pp. 15, 379–82.

35. Ed. Foreville, pp. 28–32.

36. Above, p. 51.

37. For details, see Brown, *Normans*, pp. 114–19. Not all were strictly Norman, though much too much may be made of the point.

38. Ed. Barlow, p. 17.

39. Brown, *Normans*, pp. 116–17; 'The Norman Conquest and the Genesis of English castles', *Château-Gaillard*, iii, 1966.

40. *Ibid.*; Round, V.C.H. *Essex*, i, 345.

41. Ed. Barlow, pp. 17ff.

42. Cf. p. 19 above.

43. For what follows, see Brown, *Normans*, pp. 119ff.

44. Jumièges, p. 132; Poitiers, pp. 30, 100, 109, 174–6.

45. Enigmatically as ever, we are merely told that Eustace 'went to the king and told him what he wished, and then went homewards' ('E', ed. Whitelock, p. 117).

46. Brown, *Château-Gaillard*, iii, pp. 10–11.

47. *A-S C*, pp. 120–1.

48. Florence, ed. Thorpe, i, 207.

49. For this and what follows, see Brown, *Normans*, pp. 125ff.

50. Ed. Thorpe, i, 212, 215.

51. Ed. Whitelock, p. 133.

52. *Anglo-Saxon England*, 2nd. ed., p. 563.

53. See especially Richard Gem, 'The Romanesque rebuilding of West-minster Abbey', *Battle*, iii, 1980. William of Malmesbury's percipient remark, written in the earlier twelfth century and the great age of Norman building and rebuilding in England, that at Westminster Edward was the first to build 'in that style which all now emulate at vast expense', should certainly be quoted here (*Gesta Regum*, i, 280).

54. For a recent study of the lands of the house of Godwin, see Ann Williams in *Battle*, iii, 1980.

55. Jumièges, pp. 132–3; Poitiers, pp. 100ff; *Bayeux Tapestry*, ed. Stenton, Pls. 1 et seq. It may seem like straining the evidence to take the *Vita Edwardi*'s remark about Harold's being 'rather too generous with oaths' as an oblique reference to the event, as is some-times done. Cf. however the same source's reference to Harold's having visited the princes of Gaul on his way to Rome (pp. 33, 53).

56. Orderic Vitalis later placed it at Rouen (*Ecclesiastical History*, ii, 134 and n. 5). The fact that leading Norman sources can disagree on such a matter does not accord with theories of 'an official Norman version of events' (cf. p. 50 above).

57. In his account of Harold's visit William of Poitiers makes no mention of the betrothal of one of the duke's daughters to him, though he refers to it later (p. 230).

58. Ed. Stenton, Pl. 27. Cf. Brown, *Normans*, pp. 96–7. Above, p. 33.

59. Literally—whether we follow the conventional interpretation of the Tapestry or that of C. R. Dodwell ('The Bayeux Tapestry and the French secular epic', *Burlington Magazine*, civ, 1966) its artistic arrangement is of the fate which overtakes a man who breaks his oath, and the oath-taking is thus the central scene.

60. See Brown, *Normans*, pp. 129–30.

61. Above, p. 50. Le Patourel, *Norman Empire*, p. 18. That homage was certainly accompanied by a marriage treaty.

62. Cf. Brown, *Normans*, pp. 131–2, 134.

63. Thus Poitiers (p. 146) and the Tapestry (Pl. 34), with Orderic Vitalis (*Ecclesiastical History*, ii, 138; vi, 320). The significant silence of the Anglo-Saxon Chronicle is broken by Florence of Worcester who, writing in the twelfth century, asserts that archbishop Ealdred of York performed the ceremony, as does the York chronicle (Florence, ed. Thorpe, i, 224; *Historians of the Church of York* ed. J. Raine, R.S., ii, 348). See Barlow, *English Church 1000–1066*, n. 4, p. 60.

64. Pls 34–5; *A-S C*, p. 140.

65. Ed. Foreville, pp. 174–8.

66. For what follows, see Brown, *Normans*, pp. 132ff, and the important paper of Ann Williams, 'Problems connected with the English royal succession, 860–1066', in *Battle*, i, 1978. See also R. Foreville, 'Aux origines de la renaissance juridique', *Le Moyen Age*, lviii, 1952.

67. *Vita Edwardi*, pp. 79–80.

68. Above, p. 58.

69. Ed. Foreville, p. 172–4; cf. 206–8. The Bayeux Tapestry seems also to accept it in Pl. 33 which is almost an illustration of the death-bed scene as described in the *Vita Edwardi*.

70. Pls 36–42.

71. See Wace, *Le Roman de Rou*, ed. A. J. Holden, Paris, 1970–3, *ll* 6423–5. Cf. p. 19 above. The transport of horses by sea is not the least impressive feature of the Norman Conquest, and for that, cf. p. 98 and n. 79 below.

72. Poitiers, p. 150.

73. Cf. Harper-Bill, 'The piety of the Anglo-Norman knightly class', *Battle* ii, 1979, and p. 35 above.

74. Brown, *Normans*, p. 150 and n. 47.

75. Cf. p. 37 above.

76. Ed. Whitelock, 'C' and 'D', p. 141.

77. William of Poitiers, while praising the admirable discipline maintained by the duke (p. 152), admits to some desertions (p. 160). William of Malmesbury, writing in *c*.1125 and perhaps enlarging on this, speaks of mutterings in the ranks that it would all come to nothing like Duke Robert's abortive expedition some 33 years before (*Gesta Regum*, ii, 300. Cf. p. 52 above). For these events, see Brown, *Normans*, pp. 151–3.

78. For the prayers and a solemn procession from the abbey with the relics of St Valery, see William of Poitiers, p. 160.

79. See Brown, 'The Battle of Hastings', *Battle*, iii, p. 10 and n. 49.

80. *A-S C*, 'C', p. 142.

81. William of Poitiers, p. 154. William of Malmesbury later opined that Harold made no counter-move 'either because he was proud by nature, or because he feared that his envoys would be obstructed by William and his supporters who beset every port' (*Gesta Regum*, ii, 299). Catherine Morton has sought to cast doubt upon the papal banner and blessing sent by Pope Alexander II on the ground that among contemporary writers we have only the word of William of Poitiers who is never to be believed. See *Latomus*, xxxiv, 362ff. See also the later letter of Gregory VII evidently referring to his own role in the matter, there cited (printed P. Jaffé, *Monumenta Gregoriana*, Bibliotheca Rerum Germanicorum, ii, Berlin, 1865, pp. 414–16).

82. Fauroux, *Receuil des actes*, no. 231; H. W. C. Davis, *Regesta Regum*, i, no. 1. For other grants by other lords, see Brown, *Normans*, pp. 146–7.

83. Cf. above, p. 48.

84. Above, p. 45; Brown, *Normans*, pp. 152ff.

85. Above p. 17.

86. For pre-Conquest England, see Brown, *Normans*, Chapter III. For a recent full-scale study of the north and ancient Northumbria, see W. A. Kapelle, *The Norman Conquest of the North*, London, 1979.

87. Above and Brown, 'Battle of Hastings', p. 10. For the ravaging, see also Poitiers, p. 180 and the Tapestry, Pl. 52.

88. A full and recent account of the battle of Hastings and the campaigns preceding it, from which the present account is largely drawn, will be found in Brown, 'The Battle of Hastings', *Battle*, iii, 1980.

89. For the strong probability that both Pevensey and Hastings were burghs in 1086, see A. J. Taylor, 'Evidence for a pre-Conquest origin for the chapels in Hastings and Pevensey castles', *Château-Gaillard*, iii, 1969.

90. *A-S C*, 'D' (which is contemporary), p. 143.

91. *Bayeux Tapestry*, Pls 57–8.

92. The English sources are explicit that Harold engaged William with less men than he might have had, Florence adding that many others deserted because of the confined space (*A-S C*, 'E', p. 141; Florence of Worcester, i, 227).

93. Above, p. 60.

94. Only one English archer appears upon the Tapestry (Pl. 63).

95. Ed. Foreville, pp. 192, 194.

96. Pl. 68.

97. Pp. 190–2.

98. Because the manoeuvre of the feigned flight at Hastings has so often been doubted or denied by *soi-disant* military historians for no other reason than the exemplary discipline it requires, it must be emphasized not only that it is well attested by the sources for the battle but is also known to have been used by Norman knights on other, and earlier, occasions in this period, and, indeed, to have been a long established tactic by both horse and foot in the west. See Brown, *Battle*, iii, p. 16.

99. Ed. Foreville, p. 200.

100. Brown, *Battle*, iii, pp. 18–21.

101. Poitiers, p. 204.

102. For Dover cf. p. 54 above, and for the castle see also Brown, *Dover Castle*, H.M.S.O., pp. 6–8.

103. For the identification as Little, rather than Great, Berkhamsted, see Baring, *Domesday Tables*, pp. 210, 212, 213.

104. Thus Poitiers, p. 236. The Anglo-Saxon Chronicle has them submit at Berkhamsted ('D', p. 144. Cf. Brown, *Normans*, p. 180 n. 189).

105. Poitiers, p. 216.

106. For the identification of Poitiers' *Gwenta* (p. 238) as Norwich, with which not all agree and in which the argument is finely balanced against Winchester, see Brown, *Normans*, n. 221, p. 185.

107. The fullest account is by Poitiers, pp. 242–62, with a long and ingenious diversion comparing in William's favour his conquest of England with that of Julius Caesar (for which see also p. 45 above).

108. Poitiers, p. 254, glossed by Orderic, *Ecclesiastical History*, ii, 196.

109. For the latter, see especially William of Jumièges, p. 137.

110. For these events and what follows, see Brown, *Normans*, pp. 190ff.

111. Above, p. 60.

112. *A-S C*, 'D', p. 148.

113. M. de Bouard, *Guillaume le Conquérant*, Paris, 1958, p. 103.

114. *A-S C*, 'D', p. 150.

115. Orderic Vitalis, ii, 232, whose well-known condemnation of this devastation of the north should be tempered by the qualification that he was himself no friend to the Normans.

116. Orderic, ii, 256–8; iv, 96. For the affair of Ely and Hereward the Wake, which soon faded into legend, see Freeman, *Norman Conquest*, iv, 454ff; V.C.H. *Cambridgeshire and the Isle of Ely*, ii, 381–5; E. O. Blake, *Liber Eliensis*, pp. liv–lvii.

117. For the Scottish campaign of 1072, its interest and importance, see Douglas, *William the Conqueror*, pp. 226–7.

118. Above, p. 51.

119. Stenton, *Anglo-Saxon England*, 2nd. ed., p. 618.

120. For the presence of large numbers of exiles from England in the Varangian Guard of the eastern Emperors at Constantinople, see the late John Godfrey in *Battle*, i, 63ff—though the significance of their presence is less the tradition of loyalty in pre-Conquest English society than the degree of its Scandinavianization which made its members welcome in that essentially Viking force.

121. Stenton, *op. cit.*, p. 671. Giso of Wells, though a surviving pre-Conquest bishop, was himself a Lotharingian.

122. See Brown, *English Castles*, pp. 49ff.

123. For Battle, see especially Eleanor Searle, 'The abbey of the conquerors . . .', *Battle*, ii, 1979; for the rapes, J. F. A. Mason, 'The Rapes of Sussex and the Norman Conquest, *Sussex Arch. Collections*, 1964; for the revival of monasticism in the north, Knowles, *Monastic Order*, pp. 164ff; for the Cinglais, M. Fixot, 'Les fortifications de

terre et la naissance de la feodalité dans le Cinglais', *Château-Gaillard*, iii, 1966.

124. Brown, *Normans*, pp. 208–10.

125. Brown, *Normans*, pp. 211–12.

126. For this large subject, see especially Brown, *Origins of English Feudalism*.

127. Cf. above, p. 41.

128. For a survey of the subject, see Brown, *Normans*, pp. 66ff, 245ff.

129. A very full and up-to-date discussion of these matters will be found in Barlow, *The English Church 1000–1066*, London, 1963, and *The English Church 1066–1154*, London, 1979.

130. Thus as an instance R. W. Southern writes of the new books introduced into the library of Christchurch, Canterbury, by archbishop Lanfranc that 'they are the best testimony to the intellectual revolution effected by the Conquest' (*St Anselm and his Biographer*, pp. 267–8). See also the same author's, 'The place of England in the Twelfth-century Renaissance', *History*, xlv, 1960; reprinted in *Medieval Humanism*, Oxford, 1970.

131. A. W. Clapham, *English Romanesque Architecture*, ii, *After the Conquest*, Oxford, 1934, 1964, p. 1.

132. Above, p. 53.

133. Above, p. 55. Waltham we must assume to have been left alone because its close association with Harold inhibited any new patron until Henry II's rebuilding of it in the late twelfth century.

134. Above, p. 22; *Gesta Regum*, p. 484; Ps. xxvi, 8.

Chapter V

1. The love interest, which in a book like this must be relegated to a footnote, could easily be supplied—in Robert Guiscard's divorce, perhaps, of his first wife Albereda or Aubrey to marry the extraordinary and Amazonian Lombard princess Sichelgaita; or Roger of Hauteville's joyful marriage to his first wife and first love, Judith, who had left the shelter of the cloister at St Evroul (where they had first met) with her brother the abbot to join him in Italy, and whose side he left soon after the wedding at Mileto in Calabria to return to his war in Sicily in spite of her tears. The lady had her way in the end, however: for the couple's adventures at the siege of Troina in 1062–3, with which the film might well continue, see J. J. Norwich, *The Normans in the South*, London, 1967, pp. 151–4. For Judith and her wedding see also Orderic Vitalis, *Ecclesiastical History*, ii, 102–4, who is most unfair to her.

2. Amatus of Montecassino, *Storia de' Normanni*, ed. V. de Bartholomaeis, Rome, 1935, pp. 78–9. Trans. Norwich, *op. cit.*, p. 57.

3. *Ibid.*

4. Gaufridus Malaterra, *Historia Sicula*, ed. Migne, *Patrologia Latina*, t. 149, cols. 1103–4.

5. Cf. pp. 139ff. below.

6. Cf. above, pp. 42, 49.

7. Cf. above, p. 71.

8. Above, p. 51.

9. below, p. 81.

10. Cf. G. A. Loud, 'How "Norman" was the Norman Conquest of Southern Italy?' *Nottingham University Studies*, xxv, 1981. I wish to acknowledge also much personal help and kindness from Dr Loud in the preparation of this chapter.

11. Cf. p. 50 above.

12. *Storia de' Normanni di Amato di Montecassino. . .* , ed. V. de Bartholo-maeis, Rome, 1935. Also as *Ystoire de li Normant*, ed. O. Delarc, Rouen, 1892. The former is used here. Much of the original Latin text survives in the second redaction of Leo of Ostia's *Chronicle of the Monastery of Montecassino* into which it was inserted by Peter the Deacon. See E. Joranson, *Speculum*, xxiii, 1948, p. 356, and n. 15 below.

13. Guillaume de Pouille, *La Geste de Robert Guiscard* (with French translation), ed. and trans. Marguerite Mathieu, Palermo, 1961. Also in *Mon. Germ. Hist.* SS., ix, and *Patrologia Latina*, t. 149.

14. The edition of J. P. Migne, *Patrologia Latina*, t. 149 (1853) is used here. Modern edition by E. Pontieri in Muratori, *Rerum Italicarum Scriptores*, new edition, v, 1928.

15. For the last two see below, p. 83. For Leo of Ostia see *Chronica monasterii Casinensis* (*Die Chronik von Montecassino*), ed. H. Hoffman, MGH, SS, xxiv, 1980. For Montecassino see H. E. J. Cowdrey, *The Age of Abbot Desiderius*, Oxford, 1983.

16. D. C. Douglas, *The Norman Achievement*, London, 1969, p. 19; C. Wickham, *Early Medieval Italy . . . 400–1000*, London, 1981, p. 147. For its importance and use, see G. A. Loud, *op. cit.*, and 'A calendar of the diplomas of the Norman princes of Capua', *Papers of the British School at Rome*, xlix, 1981.

17. The great and best compendium is Emile Bertaux, *L'Art dans l'Italie Méridionale*, t. 1, Paris, 1904. For the traveller and field archaeologist the splendid guide books (*Guida d'Italia*) of the Touring Club Italiano are simply invaluable.

18. For an exhaustively thorough discussion of the origins of Norman involvement in Italy, the legends surrounding it, the sources dealing with it, and all previous commentary upon it, see E. Joranson, 'The inception of the career of the Normans in Italy—legend and history', *Speculum*, xxiii, 1948. Invaluable though it is, this seems to me by expecting too much to accept too little, and rejects entirely both the Salerno tradition of Amatus and the Monte Gargano tradition of William of Apulia (below) in favour of the different stories in Leo of Ostia, Adémar of Chabannes and Raoul Glaber (below).

19. For the date, see H. Hoffman, 'Die Anfange der Normannorum in Süd-italien', *Quellen und Forschungen aus Italienischen Archiven und Bibliotheken*, xlvii, 1969, pp. 95–144. Cf. G. A. Loud, *op cit.*, p. 15.

20. Amatus, pp. 21–4; Joranson, *op. cit.*, pp. 356–8.

21. Note the horses, three times insisted upon by the narrative.

22. For Melo, see below.

23. Ed. Mathieu, pp. 98–102; Joranson, pp. 359–60.

24. Below, p. 85.

25. Leo of Ostia Bk. II, chap. 37, Redaction 1, *Mon. Germ. Hist.* SS., vii, p. 652, note a; Raoul Glaber, *Les cinq livres de ses histoires*, ed. M. Prou, Paris, 1887, pp. 52–3; Adémar de Chabannes, *Chronicon*, ed. J. Chavanon, Paris, 1897, p. 178. Cf. Joranson, pp. 371–2.

26. See D. C. Douglas, *Norman Achievement*, p. 38.

27. Cf. Joranson, *op. cit.*, p. 370, who writes imperceptively of 'invented legends . . . furnishing the Norman emigrations to Italy with a non-existent background of pilgrim piety'. As for an alleged legend of participation by invitation, all mercenaries by definition serve by invitation.

28. Loud, *Nottingham University Studies*, xxv, pp. 18–19; cf. p. 48 above.

29. Loud, *op. cit.*, p. 20.

30. Loud, *op. cit.*, p. 19.

31. See J. Décarreaux, *Normands Papes et Moines en Italie méridionale et en Sicile, xie–xiie siècle*, Paris, 1974, p. 24 n. 1, Cf. p. 23 above.

32. Above and cf. Loud, p. 17.

33. Ed. Mathieu, pp. 102–3.

34. 'Rome elle-même fait parfois petite figure auprès de la Sainte Colline', Décarreaux, *op. cit.*, p. 44. Cf. Cowdrey, *Abbot Desiderius*, p. xiv.

35. Décarreaux, p. 44.

36. Loud, *op. cit.*, p. 15.

37. Ed. Bartholomaeis, pp. 27–30.

38. William of Apulia, p. 107; pp. 82, 85 above. See also A. Gallo, *Aversa Normanna*, Naples, 1938, pp. 1ff: genealogical table in Chalendon, i, opp. p. 112, and Loud, 'Calendar of Diplomas', p. 117.

39. Ed. Bartholomaeis, p. 53.

40. Chalandon (i, 82 and n. 2) thought that Humphrey came a little later.

41. It is sometimes said that he held a fief of ten knights (which scarcely warrants the phrase 'petty lord' often applied to him. See Chalendon, i, 81), but that is not the language of the time, and what Malaterra actually says is that he served in the ducal household with ten knights—*in curia comitis decem milites sub se habens servivit*—which sounds like one of Round's *constabularie*. For Hauteville-le-Guichard (Manche), see R. H. C. Davis, *The Normans and their Myth*, p. 92 and n. 13.

42. *Cum jam adolescentiam unus post alium attigissent, coeperunt militaribus disciplinis adhaerere, equorum et armorum studia frequentare, discentes seipsos tueri et hostem impugnare*—Malaterra, I, iv, *Pat. Lat.* 149, col. 1103.

43. *Primo patria digressi, per diversa loca militariter lucrum quaerentes, tandem apud Apuliam Italiae provinciam, Deo se ducente, pervenerunt*—ibid., I, v. Cf. above, pp. 79–80.

44. Above, p. 85.

45. Ed. Bartholomaeis, p. 86.

46. Above, p. 86.

47. Amatus, p. 94; Chalandon, i, 105.

48. Amatus, pp. 95–6. For Rainulf as duke of Gaeta (before December 1041), see *ibid.*, p. 97 and n. 1. The names of the Norman lords and their new fiefs are listed with commentary by Chalandon (i, 105–6) who suggested that the absence of Humphrey of Hauteville is evidence of his later arrival in Italy (1043 x 1045). Cf. p. 86 n. 40

49. Amatus, p. 110; trans. J. J. Norwich, *op. cit.*, p. 69.

50. *The Alexiad of Anna Comnena*, (I, x) ed. and trans. E. R. A. Sewter, Penguin Classics, Harmondsworth, 1969, p. 54.

51. For Scribla, see G. Noyé, 'Le château de Scribla et les fortifications normandes du bassin du Crati,' *Società, potere e popolo nell'età di Ruggero II* (III Giornate normanno-suevi, Bari, 1977), Rome, 1979.

52. Amatus has no doubt of it—'Et puiz vint en Calabre et acquesta villes et chasteaux; et devora la terre. Ceste choze [*i.e.* the marriage alliance and the knights which he has just described] fut lo comencement de tout bien à Robert Viscart' (III, 11, ed. Bartholomaeis, p. 126).

53. See Mathieu, p. 342; Bertaux, i, 320–1 says the inscription is 'modern' and harshly calls it *ridicule*. For the foundation of Holy Trinity see p. 95 below.

54. *Op. cit.*, p. 123.
55. Cf. p. 83 above.
56. Chalandon, i, 124; Migne, *Pat. Lat.*, t. 143, p. 798.
57. See p. 90 above.
58. J. J. Norwich, *op. cit.*, p. 90.
59. The site of Civitate lies a mile or two north-west of the modern village of San Paolo di Civitate. Destroyed in the early fifteenth century, little now remains beyond the ruins of the cathedral and the line of the ramparts.
60. Ed. Mathieu, p. 144.
61. J. J. Norwich, *op. cit.*, p. 96; but cf. p. 71 above.
62. Ed. Mathieu, p. 147. Cf. the penances imposed in 1067 after Hastings. Cf. also H. E. J. Cowdrey, 'The Anglo-Norman *Laudes Regiae*', Viator, 12 (1981), pp. 59–60.
63. Chalandon, i, 141–2; Norwich, pp. 94–6.
64. Amatus, pp. 191–2; cf. Décarreaux, *op. cit.*, pp. 55–6; Cowdrey, *op. cit.*, p. 50, n. 47.
65. Chalandon, i, 170; Norwich, p. 128.
66. Décarreaux, *op. cit.*, pp. 89–90.
67. See below, p. 110.
68. Orderic, ed. Chibnall, pp. 100–2. Berengar, who had come to Italy with the exiled abbot Robert of Grandmesnil (and Judith: see n. 1 above) 'excelled in reading and chanting and above all in calligraphy'.
69. Cf. pp. 108–9 below.
70. Cf. p. 80 above.
71. Above, p. 85.
72. Above, p. 85.
73. The cathedral of Salerno is now heavily Baroque (1768), and the tomb of Gregory VII was 'restored' in 1578.
74. He was formally and properly acclaimed by the assembled Norman barons at a great council at Melfi. Norman Apulia was no place at this stage for minors and minorities.
75. Of the eight Hauteville brothers, four, William, Drogo, Humphrey and Robert, became counts of Apulia and more; the career of Roger as count of Sicily will rival or excel them all. The other three, Geoffrey, Mauger and another William ('of the principate'), did less well only by Hauteville standards, becoming, of course, great lords in Norman Italy.
76. I, xix, *Pat. Lat.* 149, col. 1113.
77. *Ibid.*
78. For an early breach, and for the extraordinary story of the brothers' quarrel over Judith's 'morning-gift', see Norwich, pp. 113–15, 147–51.
79. Cf. pp. 59–60 above. For the sea-transport of horses in the Mediterranean in the eleventh century, see Daniel Waley, '"Combined Operations" in Sicily, A.D. 1060–1078', *Papers of the British School at Rome*, xxii, 1954; and John H. Pryor, 'Transportation of horses by sea during the era of the Crusades: eighth century to 1285 A.D.', *Mariner's Mirror*, 1982. It's being unlikely that Normans from Italy played any significant part in the Norman Conquest of England (the only source to mention their participation is the highly suspect source of the *Carmen de Hastingae Proelio*), some separate Norman initiative and/or north-European tradition seems necessary to explain the transportation of horses across the Channel in 1066. For a reference to Viking shipping of horses to England from Boulogne in 892, see *A-SC*, p. 54.

80. See Chalandon, i, 195; Norwich, pp. 138–141; Amatus, ed. Bartholomaeis, pp. 235–8; Malaterra, II x–xii, *Pat. Lat.* 149, cols. 1126–7.
81. Norwich, p. 142.
82. Castrogiovanni, *Castrum Joannis*, in the sources. See Amatus, pp. 240–43; Malaterra, II, xvii.
83. Cf. Norwich, p. 144.
84. Largely destroyed by an earthquake in 1783, and now sadly undistinguished.
85. Malaterra, II, xviii, *Pat. Lat.* 149, col. 1129.
86. *Ibid.*, xix–xx.
87. *Ibid.*, II, xxxiii, *Pat. Lat,* 149, cols. 1139–42.
88. Norwich, *op. cit.*, p. 167.
89. Above p. 20 and Malaterra, II, xxxiii. For St George, *apparuit quidem eques splendidus in armis, equo albo insidens, album vexillum in summitate hastilis alligatum ferens, et desuper splendidam crucem* (col. 1141). St George also appeared before the Crusaders at Antioch, p. 133 below.
90. For a convenient summary of the policies and conquests of Roger II in North Africa, see Douglas, *The Norman Achievement*, pp. 55–60, 74–8. See also D. S. H. Abulafia in *Anglo-Norman Studies*, vii, 1984.
91. For defeated and exiled Old English or Anglo-Scandinavian lords in the Verangian Guard of the Eastern Emperors, see Norwich, *op. cit.*, p. 231 and John Godfrey in *Battle*, i, 1978, Cf. p. 71 above.
92. For a detailed account of Guiscard's Illyrian campaigns and death, see R. B. Yewdale. *Bohemond I. Prince of Antioch*, Princeton, 1924, pp. 9–24.
93. *Ibid.*, p. 247. Cf. p. 90 above and William of Malmesbury, *Gesta Regum*, ii, 322.
94. See L. R. Ménager, 'L'institution monarchique dans les états normands d'Italie', *Cahiers de Civilisation Mediévale*, ii, 1959, especially pp. 466–7. The same author points out (*ibid.*, p. 306 and n. 27), *à propos* the famous mosaics of the Martorana and Monreale showing respectively kings Roger II and William II crowned by Christ, into which so much is always read, that a Limousin mosaic at Bari shows Roger II crowned by St Nicholas without raising any comparable interest in historians. Cf. G. Galasso, 'Social and political developments in the eleventh and twelfth centuries', in *The Normans in Sicily and Southern Italy*, Lincei Lectures 1974 Oxford, 1977, pp. 59–60.
95. Cf. p. 46 above.
96. Cf. G. Galasso, *op. cit.*, p. 56.
97. See above p. 92. For the subject of marriage in Norman colonization, see also Eleanor Searle in *Battle*, iii, 1980.
98. For the Norman introduction of feudalism into Italy and Sicily see Claude Cahen, *Le régime féodal de l'Italie Normande* (Paris, 1940) and for the present point especially p. 91—'sous la haute noblesse des conquérants se maintient une petite noblesse indigène et, plus généralement, une masse de populations dont les institutions ni la vie n'ont été modifiées par le changement de maître'.
99. See Evelyn Jamison, 'The Norman administration of Apulia and Capua, more especially under Roger II and William I', *Papers of the British School at Rome*, vi, 1913.
100. Galasso, *op. cit.*, pp. 59–60.
101. Above p. 93.
102. Décarreaux, pp. 40ff, 66–7, 67ff.
103. Above, p. 95; L. R. Ménager, 'La "Byzantinisation" religieuse de

l'Italie méridionale (ix–xii siècles) et la politique monastique des Normands d'Italie', *Revue d'Histoire Ecclesiastique*, liv, 1959, pp. 32–3.

104. *Ibid.*, pp. 15, 18.

105. *Ibid.*, p. 17.

106. Cf. above, p. 80.

107. Above, p. 96; Décarreaux, *op. cit.*, pp. 89–90; L. T. White, *Latin Monasticism in Norman Sicily*, Cambridge Mass., 1938, p. 48.

108. Décarreaux, pp. 91–3; White, pp. 47–8.

109. Décarreaux, pp. 94–5; White, p. 48.

110. Décarreaux, p. 105.

111. *Ibid.*, pp. 87–9; Ménager, *loc. cit.*, pp. 28–9. The few foundations or restorations of Greek monasteries in Sicily by Roger I at the end of the eleventh century have been exaggerated in number and were for special reasons as the reverse of the policy of suppression in Calabria (*ibid.*, pp. 23–4).

112. Cf. Ménager, *loc. cit.*, pp. 35–6 and n. 1.

113. See now G. Noyé, 'Feodalité et habitat fortifié en Calabre dans la deuxième moitié du xie siècle et le premier tiers du xiie siècle', in *Structures féodales et féodalisme dans l'Occident Méditerranéen (x^e–xiiie s.): Bilan et perspectives de recherches.* (Collection de l'Ecole Française de Rome, 44), Rome, 1980. Cf. A. J. Taylor in *Château-Gaillard*, vii, 1974, pp. 209–11; p. 71 above. See also e.g. Malaterra, I, xx and II, xx, *Pat. Lat.* 149, cols. 1113, 1129 (the latter reference concerning Petralia Soprana discussed by A. J. Taylor).

114. The master work remains Emile Bertaux, *L'art dans l'Italie Méridionale*, t. i, 1904.

115. With reference to Baroque and what it has done to Norman churches in the south, to quote the angry Lord Norwich is irresistible—'those simpering cherubs and marzipan madonnas that mark the real dark ages of European religious art' (*Kingdom in the Sun*, p. 96).

116. The original abbey church of the Hautevilles at Venosa is the present old church, modest in scale and basilican in plan with a single apse, still containing the tomb of Alberada or Aubrey on the north side (cf. p. 92 above), and consecrated by Pope Nicholas II in 1059. Recently restored, it is no longer *sordide et déjetée* as Bertaux found it. Behind it, axially, lie the splendid ruins of the new church, begun in 1135, built in two stages, but never completed, entirely 'French' in style and plan with aisled nave, transepts, transeptual chapels, ambulatory and chevet. See Bertaux, *op. cit.*, i, 318ff; cf. R. H. C. Davis, *The Normans and their Myth*, London, 1976, pp. 97–100. The latest discussion of Bernay, giving the dates of *c.*1015 for its commencement and *c.*1050 for its completion, is by Joseph Decaens, 'La datation de l'abbatiale de Bernay: quelques observations architecturales et résultats des fouilles récentes', *Battle*, v, 1982.

117. Bertaux, p. 335.

118. Roberto Salvini, 'Monuments of Norman Art in Sicily and Southern Italy', in *The Normans in Sicily and Southern Italy*, Lincei Lectures 1974, p. 83.

119. *Ibid.*, p. 80.

120. *Ibid.*, pp. 74–5.

121. *Ibid.*, 75–7, 85–6.

122. *Ibid.*, pp. 82–3.

123. *Op. cit.*, p. 107.

124. Hugo Falcandus, *La Historia o Liber de Regno Sicilie de Ugo Falcando*, ed. G. B. Siragusa (Fonti per la Storia d'Italia, xxii, Rome, 1896),

p. 6; See G. A. Loud, *Nottingham Medieval Studies*, xxv, p. 24 (n. 125 below).

125. On this matter, see especially G. A. Loud, 'How "Norman" was the Norman Conquest of Southern Italy?', *Nottingham Medieval Studies*, xxv, 1981, and 'The *Gens Normannorum*—Myth or Reality?', *Battle*, iv, 1981. Cf. R. H. C. Davis, *The Normans and their Myth*.
126. Above p. 44.
127. Above p. 44.
128. Above p. 79.
129. Above p. 86.
130. Above p. 11.

Chapter VI

1. See S. Runciman, *History of the Crusades*, Cambridge, 1953–4, i, 106–8.
2. For Urban's speech, see especially D. C. Munro, 'The Speech of Pope Urban II at Clermont', *American Historical Review*, xi, 1906; H. E. J. Cowdrey, 'Pope Urban II's Preaching of the First Crusade', *History*, lv, 1970. See also H. E. Mayer, *The Crusades* (trans. J. Gillingham), Oxford, 1972, pp. 9ff.
3. For the 'People's Crusade' and the 'German Crusade', see Runciman, *op. cit.*, pp. 121–41.
4. See Runciman, i, 337. From Runciman's Appdx. II, 'The numerical strength of the crusaders', all the estimates given here are taken.
5. *Ibid.*, p. 339.
6. *Ibid.*, pp. 338–9. Runciman reckons the proportion of infantry to cavalry at the outset of the First Crusade as 7 to 1 though not all of good quality (*ibid.*, p. 337).
7. The names of all those known or thought to have been in the contingent of Robert Curthose on the First Crusade are listed and annotated in C. W. David, *Robert Curthose*, Harvard. U.P., 1920, Appdx. D, pp. 221ff.
8. Cf. p. 102 above. During that winter Odo, bishop of Bayeux, made a visit to Palermo and died there to be buried in the new cathedral (where, at least to my enquiry, his tomb seems now to be unknown).
9. For Bohemond's contingent see especially E. Jamison 'Some notes on the *Anonymi Gesta Francorum*, with special reference to the Norman contingent from south Italy and Sicily in the First Crusade', in *Studies . . . to M. K. Pope*, Manchester, 1939.
10. Above, p. 83. Mayer, Crusades, p. 15.
11. Conveniently summarized in Runciman, i, 59ff.
12. Runciman, i, 103–5; Mayer, *Crusades*, p. 8.
13. See especially Runciman 33ff; Douglas, *Norman Achievement*, pp. 89ff; Mayer, *Crusades*, chap. 2; Robinson, 'Gregory VII and the soldiers of Christ', History, lviii, 1973. Cf. p. 101 above.
14. For the subtleties of indulgence, its theological meaning and its popular interpretation, see Mayer, *Crusades*, pp. 25ff.
15. Above, p. 79.
16. R. W. Southern, *The Making of the Middle Ages*, London, 1953, p. 54.
17. *Gesta Francorum*, ed. Rosalind Hill, Nelson Medieval Texts, London, 1962, pp. 19–20. See p. 127 below.
17a For a recent discussion of early crusading motivation, published after the above words were written, see Jonathan Riley-Smith in *E.H.R.*, xcviii. 1983. For Bohemond, see also pp. 148–52 below.
18. Above, p. 102.

19. *Studies . . . M. K. Pope*, p. 208.

20. These immortal labels were, of course, first attached to Cavaliers and Roundheads respectively by W. C. Sellar and R. J. Yeatman in their immortal history book, *1066 and All That*, London, 1930, C. W. David's *Robert Curthose*, though very useful, belongs to that old-fashioned but still flourishing genre of medieval history wherein the main interests of a 'good' king or prince must be administration and the repression of his own vassals—thus destroying the society of which he is the head.

21. The best discussion and interpretation of that occasion will be found in J. Le Patourel's 'The Norman Succession, 996–1135', *E.H.R.*, lxxxvi, 1971, but cf. the same author's *Norman Empire*, especially p. 183, n. 1.

22. His tomb which slightly makes amends is in Gloucester cathedral. See p. 123 above.

23. *Gesta Regum*, ii, 460, 'nunquam a Christiano vel pagano potuerit ex equite pedes effeci'. The same writer evidently began the erroneous story that the crown of Jerusalem was offered to Robert and refused by him (*ibid.*, p. 461). See David, *Robert Curthose*, pp. 190ff.

24. R. B. Yewdale, *Bohemond I, Prince of Antioch*, Princeton, 1924, is a rather short work, largely consisting of a very well documented narrative or outline of Bohemond's remarkable career, and is in fact the posthumous publication of the doctoral thesis of the author who was prevented by a tragically early death (1921, aged 29) from revising or enlarging it for the press.

25. Above, p. 90.

26. *Alexiad*, I, xiv, ed. and trans. E. R. A. Sewter, p. 66.

27. *Ibid.*, XIII, x, pp. 422–3.

28. Ed. Rosalind Hill, Nelson's Medieval Texts, p. 7; cf. E. Jamison, *Studies . . . M. K. Pope*, pp. 188–9. For a discussion of this and other versions of Bohemond's taking of the cross, see Yewdale, 34–6.

29. *Roberti Monachi S. Remigii . . . Historia Hierosolymitana*, II, ii; Migne, *Pat. Lat.*, clv, cols. 678–9.

30. *Gesta Francorum*, p. 7.

31. Above, p. 102.

32. Tancred, Bohemond's nephew, avoided the oath at Constantinople but took it at Nicea (Runciman, i, 181–2). Count Raymond of St-Gilles took it only in a modified form, but his reluctance seems of little practical consequence since at Antioch and after he placed himself firmly in favour of the Emperor's rights.

33. Above, p. 120.

34. Runciman, i, 145.

35. *Alexiad*, X, xi; ed. Sewter, p. 329.

36. Ed. Hill, p. 12.

37. See especially Jamison, *Studies . . . M. K. Pope*, pp. 193–5.

38. For the march of the crusaders across Asia Minor, see Runciman, i, 175ff.

39. *Gesta Francorum*, p. 16.

40. 'Turci undique iam erant circumcingentes nos, dimicando et iaculando ac spiculando, et mirabiliter longe lateque sagittando', *Gesta Francorum*, p. 19.

41. Migne, *Pat. Lat.*, clv, col. 836, 'trecenta et sexaginta millia pugnatorum, scilicet sagittariorum . . . Equites erant omnes . . . cunctis nobis tale bellum erat incognitum'.

42. *Gesta Francorum*, p. 19.

43. For other accounts of the battle of Dorylaeum, see Runciman, i,

185–6; R. C. Smail, *Crusading Warfare*, Cambridge, 1956, pp. 117–20, 168–9.

44. *Gesta Francorum*, p. 21.
45. *Alexiad*, XI, iii; ed. Sewter, p. 342.
46. Claude Cahen, *La Syrie du nord à l'époque des croisades . . .* , Paris, 1940, pp. 205–11. The historian Fulcher of Chartres joined Baldwin's party at Marash.
47. Above, p. 124.
48. Cahen, *Syrie du nord*, pp. 127ff.
49. Runciman, i, 228.
50. *Ibid.*, p. 227; above, p. 67.
51. A common phrase, not quite a metaphor, referring to the four points of the Cross.
52. *Gesta Francorum*, p. 37.
53. See Smail, *Crusading Warfare*, p. 171; Runciman, i, 225–6.
54. *Gesta Francorum*, p. 33. William had evidently deserted once before, on an expedition against the Moors in Spain, an incident of which he was now forcefully reminded by the outraged Bohemond.
55. Above, p. 128.
56. Runciman, i, 224.
57. Thus the *Gesta Francorum*, pp. 63–5, which also tells of the passionate but unavailing lament of Guy, Bohemond's half-brother and then on the Emperor's staff.
58. Runciman, i, 240.
59. Thus Runciman, i, 165 ('She wished him to go, and he went'), 240–1; ii, 78 (of his death at Ramleh—'The Countess Adela could sleep content'). Cf. Orderic Vitalis, *Ecclesiastical History*, iv, 324 (the countess urging Stephen back to Palestine 'between conjugal caresses'). But for the most recent discussion of Stephen-Henry's reputation and that of his family, which may owe something both to the propaganda of the family's enemies and to the absence of any official history of their house, see Michel Bur, *La formation du comté de Champagne*, Nancy, 1977, pp. 479ff.
60. Above, p. 124.
61. Runciman, i, 225, 231 and the sources there cited.
62. *Ibid.*, pp. 225–35.
63. For what follows, see especially Runciman, i, 236ff.
64. 'There he married Robert Guiscard's daughter, Mabel, called Courte Louve, and received fifteen *castella* with her', Orderic Vitalis, iv, 338. See also *Gesta Francorum*, pp. 56–7; Jamison, 'Some notes on the *Anonymi Gesta Francorum . . .*', pp. 199–200.
65. The full story is given by Raymond d'Agiles who was present when the relic was found, *Historia Francorum qui ceperunt Jerusalem*, cc. xiv–xv, Migne, *Pat. Lat.*, clv, cols. 610–14.
66. Smail, *Crusading Warfare*, pp. 172–4; Runciman, i, 247–9. Good contemporary accounts by the author of the *Gesta Francorum* (pp. 67–70) and Raymond d'Agiles, *op. cit.*, c. xvii, *Pat. Lat.* clv, cols. 646–9, both of whom were eye-witnesses and participants.
67. See Rosalind Hill, *Gesta Francorum*, p. 68, n. 1.
68. For the half-starved Frankish horses which could scarcely be led to the battlefield, pitted only by God's help against the well-fed and faster Turkish mounts, see Raymond d'Agiles, *loc. cit.*, col. 648, *Operabatur ibi mirabiliter Dominus tam in viris quam in equis nostris . . .*
69. 'Vidi ego haec quae loquor, et Dominicam lanceam ibi ferabam', *Pat. Lat.*, clv, col. 648.
70. 'Multiplicavit insuper adeo Dominus exercitum nostrum ut qui ante

pugnam pauciores eramus quam hostes, in bello plures eis fuimus', *ibid.* Cf. the vision of St George at Cerami in Sicily in 1063, p. 101 above.

71. *Gesta Francorum*, p. 69.
72. *Ibid.*, p. 70.
73. *Ibid.*, pp. 70–1.
74. For Tatikios' withdrawal see above, p. 131; an embassy under Hugh de Vermandois was in fact sent to Alexius to explain the situation (Runciman, i, 250; *Gesta Francorum*, p. 72).
75. Runciman, i, 251.
76. For a percipient study of the attitudes of ordinary and average crusaders who bore the heat and burden of the day, see Rosalind Hill, 'Crusading Warfare; a Camp-follower's view 1097–1120', *Battle*, i, 1978.
77. Above, p. 129.
78. Above, p. 120.
79. This action by the 'Anonymous', who was evidently a knight and vassal of Bohemond, does not, I think, necessarily imply disapproval of his lord's decision. Cf. Rosalind Hill, *Gesta Francorum*, pp. xii–xiii; *Battle*, i, 75.
80. Runciman, i, 268.
81. Fulcher of Chartres, I, xviii, *Pat. Lat.* clv, col. 851.
82. Runciman, i, 278; *Gesta Francorum*, p. 87 and n. 3.
83. Runciman, i, 265, 279.
84. Psalm xlvii, 1–2, quoted appropriately by Runciman, i, 279.
85. *Gesta Francorum*, pp. 95–6. The fact that here as elsewhere after Antioch Tancred appears with a contingent of his own indicates that he did not leave alone but with a contingent of Italian Normans. According to Ralph of Caen there were 80 *Wicardides* at Jerusalem after Ascalon (*Gesta Tancredi*, c. 139, *Pat. Lat.*, clv, col. 578).
86. For Duke Robert's feat of arms in personally slaying the emir see David, *Robert Curthose*, p. 251; and p. 118 above which evidently depicts it.
87. On his election in 1099 Godfrey had refused to be crowned as king on the grounds that none should wear a crown in the city where Christ had worn a crown of thorns. There is, however, no good evidence that he ever took the title 'Advocate of the Holy Sepulchre' usually given him by modern writers. See J. Riley-Smith, *Bulletin of the Institute of Historical Research*, lii, 1979, pp. 83–6.
88. Douglas, *The Norman Fate 1100–1154*, London, 1976, pp. 181–2.
89. The kingdom of Jerusalem fell at Hattin in 1087, the resulting Third Crusade recreating no more than the kingdom of Acre. The city of Antioch fell to Baibars in 1268, and, of the rest of the principality, the great castle of Margat (Marqab) fell in 1285 and Lattakieh in 1287. Acre, the last Latin stronghold in Outremer, fell in 1291.
90. For the monuments, both vanished and surviving, see the remarkable *tour de force* of Claude Cahen's second chapter, 'Topographie historique et archéologique', *La Syrie du nord* . . . , Paris, 1940, pp. 109ff. See also below.
91. For an exhaustive *catalogue raisoné* and discussion of the sources for the history of both Antioch and Edessa, see Cahen, *op. cit.*, pp. 1–104. For Walter the Chancellor's *De Bello Antiocheno*, see *ibid.*, p. 16. The edition of Migne, *Pat. Lat.*, clv, cols. 994–1038 is used here.
92. *Op. cit.* The degree to which the following pages are dependent upon Cahen's work will be evident from the references.
93. See Cahen, *Syrie du nord*, pp. v, 225–6, 435.
94. *Ibid.*, p. 438.

95. *Ibid.*, pp. 224–5, 439.

96. *Ibid.*, pp. 535–6. A great exception is the family of Mazoir, with others probably deriving, via the contingent of Raymond of St-Gilles, from the Massif Central or the Midi. The original Italian Norman predominance in Antioch was later diluted by new arrivals from the west, not least with the succession of Raymond of Poitiers in 1136, and doubtless by the terrible defeat at the Field of Blood (*Ager Sanguinis*) in 1119 (*ibid.*, p. 289 and below).

97. See *e.g. Syrie du nord*, pp. 187ff. The resident Christians comprised not only the Greek Orthodox churches, not yet officially regarded as in schism from Rome, but also the separated churches of the Armenians, Maronites, Jacobites and Copts.

98. See p. 129 above.

99. Below, p. 146.

100. For the country of Tripoli eventually established by Raymond of St-Gilles and his successors, see Runciman, ii, 56ff.

101. For Antioch, see Cahen, *Syrie du nord*, pp. 127ff.

102. For Lattakieh (Laodicia), see *ibid.*, pp. 165–7.

103. One of which, the Chanson des Chétifs, was produced in Antioch for the court of Raymond of Poitiers, *ibid.*, pp. 569–70.

104. Below, p. 150.

105. Runciman, *Crusades*, ii, 150.

106. *Ibid.*, 182–3.

107. *Ecclesiastical History*, ed. Chibnall, vi, 137.

108. Cahen, *Syrie du nord*, p. 328.

109. *Ibid.*, and for the Turcopoles see Smail, *Crusading Warfare*, p. 112.

110. R. Grousset (*Histoire des Croisades*, 3 vols., Paris, 1934–6) with his thesis of *esprit politique* versus *esprit croisade* as a fundamental division in crusader politics and history, rightly emphasizes the paradox that the Holy land, once won or liberated, could only be held by something other than bellicose religious enthusiasm—a fact of life generally appreciated by the resident lords and old hands but not by new arrivals from the West.

111. H. Derenbourg, *Ousâma Ibn Mounkidh*, i (Paris, 1886, Publications Ecole Langues Orientales, 2nd. s., t. xii, 1) p. 476. For Ousâma, see Cahen, *op. cit.*, p. 45.

112. Cahen, p. 327.

113. For the sect of the Assassins (whose name, from their practice, is still very much with us), see *ibid.*, pp. 189, 344.

114. The reference is to the siege of the castle of Kerak of Moab (Petra Deserti) in 1183 while a wedding feast was held inside. It is said that Saladin ordered his engines not to assault the tower containing the bridal chamber. See Runciman, ii, 440–2.

115. Runciman, *The Families of Outremer* (Creighton Lecture, Athlone Press, London, 1960).

116. Cahen, *op. cit.*, p. 527. 'La noblesse franque a apporté en Syrie les principes de l'organisation féodale qui la régissaient en Occident, et la noblesse italo-normande, en particulier ceux qu'elle avait connu dans les premiers temps de l'état normand d'Italie'. Here, for once, there can surely be no argument about the origins of feudalism.

117. Cahen, pp. 534–5.

118. Cf. p. 103 above.

119. Cahen, pp. 452–68. For Norman feudalism in Antioch, see *ibid.*, pp. 527ff.

120. For the names and dates of the early princes of Antioch, see p. 137 above.

121. 'Toutefois l'association avec le clergé parait avoir été partout la politique systématique des premiers Normands, et, pour autant que nos textes nous permettent de la savoir, nulle part elle ne paraît avoir été aussi étroite qu'à Antioche'. (Cahen, p. 313). For the church in Antioch, see also Bernard Hamilton, *The Latin Church in the Crusader States: The Secular Church*, London, 1980. Bernard of Valence was himself a Provençal and formerly the chaplain of Ademar bishop of Le Puy.

122. Cited by Cahen, p. 333. Cf. Hamilton, *op. cit.*, p. 9. The inclusion of the Greeks among the 'heretics' is noteworthy, and not at all what Pope Urban had intended.

123. For the problem of the Greeks in Calabria especially, see p. 107 above. See also Cahen, pp. 308ff., 331ff.

124. Cahen, pp. 323–6.

125. For the Military Orders in Antioch, see Cahen, pp. 510ff.

126. See especially Cahen, pp. 472ff.

127. *Ibid.*, pp. 527, 547ff.

128. *Ibid.*, pp. 487ff.

129. The money-fief (*fief rente*) is a fief not of land but of money, in the form of a regular, usually annual sum, held of a lord in return for feudal services including knight-service. In this sense we still use the word 'fee' *i.e.* fief.

130. See T. S. R. Boase, *Castles and Churches of the Crusading Kingdom*, London, 1967, p. 100. For Hugh of Vermandois, see Runciman, ii, 29. The principal works on the churches of the Holy Land are M. de Vogüé, *Eglises de Terre Sainte*, Paris, 1860; C. Enlart, *Les Monuments des Croisés dans le Royaume de Jerusalem: Architecture religieuse et civile*, 2 vols, 2 albums of plates, Paris, 1928. See also P. Deschamps, *Terre Sainte Romane*, Zodiaque, 1964.

131. History and description, with splended photographs, conveniently in Deschamps, pp. 231ff.

132. Cf. p. 111 above.

133. 'I asked the king to let me go on pilgrimage to Our Lady of Tortosa. Her shrine was greatly resorted to by pilgrims, because it was there that the first altar was erected in honour of the Mother of Our Lord. Our Lady performed many great miracles there . . .'—*Joinville and Villehardouin: Chronicles of the Crusades*, ed. and trans. M. R. B. Shaw, Harmondsworth, 1963.

134. For the castles, see generally G. Rey, *Etude sur les Monuments de l'architecture militaire des croisés en Syrie et dans l'Ile de Chypre*, Paris, 1871; R. Fedden and J. Thomson, *Crusader Castles*, London, 1957; W. Müller-Wiener, *Castles of the Crusaders*, London, 1966; Boase, *Castles and Churches of the Crusading Kingdom*; R. C. Smail, *Crusading Warfare*; P. Deschamps, *Terre Sainte Romane*.

135. Above, p. 92.

136. Bertaux, *L'art dans l'Italie meridionale*, i, 316.

137. Thus even Yewdale, e.g. p. 135.

138. Of Antioch. See p. 133 above.

139. Above, p. 117. Mayer, *Crusades*, pp. 10–11 and pp. 290–1. n. 5.

140. *Fulcherii Carnotensis, Historia Hierosolymitane*, I, xxi; Migne, *Pat. Lat.*, clv, cols. 858–60.

141. Yewdale, pp. 102, 106, 109.

142. Ed. Chibnall, v, 356.

143. Runciman, ii, 21–4.

144. *Historia Belli Sacri*, p. 228, in *Recueil des Historiens des Croisades, Historiens Occidentaux*, Paris, 1844–95, iii.

145. Yewdale, pp. 110–11; Runciman, ii, 48–9; Orderic, vi, 70, who writes that Bohemond 'made a fine figure even among the greatest', and that 'many were kindled by his words' and followed him 'like men hastening to a feast'.

146. Runciman, ii, 48: 'It was a turning point in the history of the Crusades. The Norman policy, which aimed to break the power of the Eastern Empire, became the official Crusading policy. The interests of Christendom as a whole were to be sacrificed to the interests of Frankish adventurers'. Cf. Yewdale, p. 115.

147. Above, p. 102.

148. *Alexiad*, ed. Sewter, p. 394.

149. *Alexiad*, pp. 406ff.

150. Runciman, ii, 50. For his death, see Yewdale, p. 133, and for the uncertain date of his birth between *c.*1050 and 1058, *ibid.*, p. 5.

152. Yewdale, p. 135.

153. *Romualdi archiepiscopi Salernitani, Annales* (ed. Arndt), *MGH*, SS, xix, 415.

Epilogue

1. So, presumably, D. C. Douglas felt constrained to add a second volume, *The Norman Fate, 1100–1154*, London, 1976, to his *Norman Achievement*.

2. Runciman, *Crusades*, i, xi (Preface).

3. Thus, for Freeman, long ago, the agony of the English defeat at Hastings could only be explained away by the foreign use of Dirty Tricks like horses. More recently Catherine Morton and Hope Munz have come close to making Hastings a famous English victory in their edition of *The Song of the Battle of Hastings* (*Carmen de Hastingae Proelio*, Oxford, 1972, especially Appendix B).

4. R. A. Brown, 'The status of the Norman knight', in *War and Government in the Middle Ages* (forthcoming).

5. David Bates, *Normandy before 1066*, Harlow, 1982, pp. 244–5 and *passim*.

6. Respectively *Norman Institutions, Feudal Society*, and *Essai sur l'origine de la noblesse en France au moyen âge*, Paris, 1902. The first two are dismissed by Dr Bates and the third is not mentioned.

7. *The Chivalrous Society*, trans. Cynthia Postan, London, 1977, p. 82.

8. The phrase originates with R. H. C. Davis' *The Normans and their Myth*, but has since been taken up by others less perceptive.

Sources of illustrations

Black and white plates
Numbers refer to pages
Aerofilms Ltd: 67, 69, 72, 74
Alinari: 94, 95, 151 (top)
Archives nationales photographiques, Paris: 27, 42, 108, 113 (top), 140
W. T. Ball (from *Proceedings of the Battle Conference III*): 56
Bibliothèque municipale, Rouen: 18
Bibliothèque nationale: 118, 119, 126, 127, 128, 132, 133, 136, 137
Bodleian Library, Oxford: 29 (left), 46 (bottom)
British Library: 51, 71
British Museum: 33, 130
J. Allan Cash: 101
Combier: 26
Italian State Tourist Office: 2, 88, 109, 151 (bottom)
A. F. Kersting: 8, 21 (top), 63, 70, 74, 77, 110, 111, 112, 123, 141, 144, 145, 146, 147, 148
Leiden, Rijksbibliothek: Half-title
Mansell Collection: 78, 84, 102, 103, 107
Foto Marburg: 10, 21 (bottom), 24 (bottom), 116
H. Roger-Viollet: 9, 46 (top)
Edwin Smith: 99
Stuttgart, Landesbibliothek: 135
Zodiaque: 22 (left), 23, 24 (top), 46, 57 (bottom), 62, 70, 76, 97, 113 (bottom), 114, 115
All pictures of the Bayeux tapestry are by Michael Holford: the publishers and author are most grateful to him for his help in this connection.
Colour pictures (other than the Bayeux tapestry) are acknowledged in the captions.
All photographs not acknowledged are by the author.
The publishers and author are grateful to Diana Souhami for her assistance with picture research.